GW00602738

# Praise for *Management Design*

"After phrasing the theory in his book *Performance Triangle,* Lukas Michel now introduces a fresh workbook called *Management Design*, which gives a pragmatic overview about organizational performance and the diagnostic mentoring methodology. This book truly enables the reader to work through the logic, gain new insights and provides a flavour of the potential power. Leaders and managers can easily gain new insights on improvement options. This book reflects Lukas' personality and unlocks the full potential of people in 'enabled organizations' during turbulent times."

**Michael Eckert**, Senior Project Manager, Merck Group, Germany

"To be most effective, management needs design. The book makes a strong case for managers to take creative action and design a management system tailored to the needs of their strategy, organization, culture and environment – with the ultimate goal of letting people thrive and be at their best every day. In true 'Druckerish' tradition, the book is not only rich with insights but also very practical – almost guaranteed to elevate the practicing manager's game to the next level and lead to superior performance. Highly recommended reading!

**Raymond Hofmann**, management consultant, Founder of Hofmann Management and former COO of Avaloq

"Rarely do we find this much clarity of purpose and clarity of approach in management literature. In his new book, Lukas brings his highly analytical and personal approach to the art of management to the next level. Very accessible, readable and – most importantly – applicable."

**Hans Martin Graf**, Head of Online/Mobile Banking & Retail Solutions, Credit-Suisse, Switzerland

"As companies increasingly face challenges that seem to come out of nowhere and are a real mess to address, having the kind of tools and methods as the ones Lukas Michel provides is extraordinarily important."

**Dr. Patricia Seemann**, former member of the Group Management Board of Zurich Financial Services and CEO of The 3am Group

"Readers will be inspired to refine their facilitative leadership skills and to develop more effective people-oriented managerial approaches. The author shares his deep understanding of the determinants of individual and group performance to highlight the importance of genuine personal interactions and engagement for organizational readiness. Higher education professionals could gain new perspectives by exploring their thoughts on the issues raised by the insightful questions posed in this book."

**Rana Zeine**, MD, PhD, MBA, Professor and Research Director, St. Martinus University, Curacao

# MANAGEMENT
# DESIGN

MANAGING PEOPLE AND ORGANIZATIONS IN TURBULENT TIMES

Published by
LID Publishing Ltd
Garden Studios
71-75 Shelton Street
Covent Garden
London WWC2H 9JQ
United Kingdom
info@lidpublishing.com
www.lidpublishing.com

www.businesspublishersroundtable.com

Printed in Great Britain by TJ International Ltd.
ISBN: 978-1-907794-66-7

Page design: Thomas Kupferschmeid
Cover design: Laura Hawkins

# MANAGEMENT
# DESIGN

## MANAGING PEOPLE AND ORGANIZATIONS IN TURBULENT TIMES

## LUKAS MICHEL

LONDON      NEW YORK    SHANGHAI
MADRID      BARCELONA   BOGOTA
MEXICO CITY MONTERREY   BUENOS AIRES

*To our partners and parents*

When people experience flow, the state where they apply their full talent and perform at their peak, their mind is highly focused. They trust their own capabilities and do things out of their own will. Sports provide a playing field where people can stretch their potential and test the limits. As a result, they experience flow more often.

Climbing a mountain is one of these sports where people constantly search for their flow zone – the perfect match of challenges and skills. Imagine safely climbing a 1'000 meter altitude difference in five hours and still enjoying the effort. Experienced skiers know that in order to enjoy the day, much of the effort goes into the preparation of the tour. There are many choices like the weather, the equipment, the route, the team, the timing that influence the experience. Thoughtful tour guides know they have to create an environment where the team can experience the flow. This is relatively easy when the weather is nice, when the team is ready, and when there are no surprises. But more than not, the weather changes, equipment breaks, obstacles are in the way –all things that alter the perfect timing and experience of the tour. In such situations, teams need speed, agility and resilience to successfully master its challenges.

Work in organizations resembles much like performing a ski tour. It requires preparation and an environment where the entire team can perform and apply its talent. In a turbulent environment, it is important that teams have well-developed capabilities for a high ability to act. They make decisions fast, they anticipate change, react flexibly, implement with rigor, and learn as they go. In such organizations, management has a design that helps people cope with a turbulent environment.

Photos: Lukas Michel

# Contents

EXAMPLES **11**

FOREWORD **12**

INTRODUCTION **14**

## Management Design **17**

The Management Model Toolbox **19**

Management Matters **21**

The Purpose of the Book **23**

Management in Need of a Balanced Model **25**

Management Needs Design **27**

Six Management Designers **29**

## Framework **30**

Shared language **33**

The Management Design Framework **35**

PEOPLE **37**

ORGANIZATION **55**

STAKEHOLDERS **73**

ENVIRONMENT **87**

MANAGEMENT **101**

Operations & Design **117**

Four Archetypes **119**

Integration Framework **121**

Management Design **125**

## Insights **126**

Organizational Learning **131**

INsights Diagnostic Tools™ **133**

The Self-Assessment **134**

Potential and Interferences **139**

SUCCESS **141**

SPEED **143**

AGILITY **145**

RESILIENCE **147**

ABILITY TO ACT **149**

The Leadership Scorecard ™ **151**

Action **155**

Organizational Capabilities **157**

Management Model **159**

Environment & Challenges **163**

## Design · 166

| | |
|---|---|
| Work on the System | **171** |
| When Viruses Interfere | **173** |
| Context Frame | **175** |
| Four Management Models | **179** |
| The People-Organization Bridge | **181** |
| The Leadership Toolbox™ | **183** |
| Meaning, Coordination & Connectivity | **185** |
| The Systems-Culture Strategy | **187** |
| The Leadership-Culture Strategy | **189** |
| The Systems-Culture Strategy | **191** |
| Management Capabilities | **193** |
| The Choice of Toolbox | **199** |
| Operating Modes | **203** |
| The Design of Tools | **205** |
| The Use of Tools | **207** |

## Change · 212

| | |
|---|---|
| Intervention Points | **217** |
| Levers of Change | **219** |
| Intervention Depth | **223** |
| Change Program | **225** |
| Program Sketching | **227** |
| Transformation or Evolution? | **229** |
| Management Design as a Radical Innovation | **231** |

## Mentoring · 234

| | |
|---|---|
| Diagnostic Mentoring | **239** |
| Four Steps: Inner Game Mentoring | **241** |
| Step 1: Diagnose | **243** |
| Step 2: Interpretation | **245** |
| Step 3: Design | **249** |
| Step 4: Development & Implementation | **251** |
| Diagnostic Mentors | **253** |
| The Leadership Cycle | **257** |
| RESOURCES | **263** |
| AFTERWORD | **273** |
| BIBLIOGRAPHY | **275** |

Management Design offers Diagnostic Mentoring as a model and process for thinking about management in a turbulent environment. However, it is the reality in businesses, not the theory, that brings life to practice. To illustrate how theory translates into practice, 10 business cases highlight specific aspects of Diagnostic Mentoring.

*"The greatest danger in times of turbulence is not the turbulence; it is to act with yesterday's logic." – Peter F. Drucker (1980)*

Management Design forces leaders to think outside the box in order to match their organizations with the needs of people in the information age as a prerequisite to mastering the challenges of a turbulent world.

# Examples

51    **Leadership think tank | Switzerland** keeping race horses on track

69    **Functional department of a bank | Switzerland** from ongoing change to a superior ability to act

83    **Retail bank | Sri Lanka** the need of different structures

151   **Specialty foods | Italy** structures and tools to manage growth and transitions

159   **Farming | South Africa** the management model in an environment where control is key

175   **Professional services | UK** Moving from a market to a competency context

199   **Transportation | Switzerland** designing a toolbox to support the transformation

207   **Utilities | Switzerland** the case of over-engineered management

245   **Insurance | Switzerland** perfection with the wrong design

253   **Mining | UK** leadership think tank for 250 leaders worldwide

# Foreword

In the popular 1986 movie *Top Gun* about US Naval aviators, characters Maverick and Goose (Tom Cruise and Anthony Edwards) declare they "have a need; a need for speed" in an upcoming mission. In the life-and-death struggle of air combat, speed gives pilots a competitive advantage and faster is better. In addition to blinding supersonic speed, modern fighter pilots must be able to make necessary adjustments, then deliver a knockout blow to adversaries through a window of opportunity that may constitute seconds. Although the modern business world may not typically equate to a literal life-and-death struggle, it may feel that way to executives and managers. Threats appear and windows of business opportunity open and close at a dizzying pace. The quantity of information and data available worldwide is doubling every 13 months and is projected to double every 12 hours in the not-so-distant future (Schilling, 2013). With continued proliferation, improvement, and use of information technology, the rate of information creation will continue to increase.

Researchers and practitioners have observed that the rate of change powered by this explosion of technology, globalization, and complexity has been increasing for decades. Business leaders throughout the globe, like fighter pilots, are faced with ever-changing environments, where threats and opportunities appear rapidly; it is therefore critical to success to make necessary adjustments that will enable you to respond with a knockout blow, when it is required. Yet organizations, unlike jet fighters, are not specifically built for speed and are typically unable to make the adjustments needed to adapt quickly to change. On the contrary, typical organizational designs are essentially anti-change, burdened with rigid leadership hierarchies and organizational structures; information systems that are not aligned with current needs; and corporate cultures, characterized by an inertia, that resist new ideas or processes. The result is that identifying and implementing meaningful change in many, if not most organizations, is more like stopping a supertanker, then manoevring it in a small harbour rather than closing in for the kill at supersonic speeds in a jet fighter. Executives who recognize the critical need for speed in the form of corporate agility, when confronted with strong natural forces against agility, must find a way to overcome the inertia inherent in leadership, systems, and culture in order to prosper in the 21st century.

But, where to start? Without a proven methodology, too many executives jump on the current 'flavour of the month' idea using a 'shotgun approach' in the hope that they will hit something that produces results. Well-known and reputable consulting firms worldwide have made millions peddling their brand of change management and executives have patted themselves on the back as they report to their boards on the extensive and expensive change initiatives. Yet, we know the overwhelming majority of change initiatives fail to yield significant, permanent, results. Some studies place the failure rate at over 80%. Change initiatives where organizational culture is an element have an even lower success rate.

In his first book, *The Performance Triangle: Diagnostic Mentoring to Manage Organizations and People for Superior Performance in Turbulent Times*, Lukas Michel (2013a) offered a model, plus practical tools and methodology, that allow executives to gain insight into key aspects of the culture, systems, and leadership. The performance triangle model represents the accumulation, analysis, and synthesis of 15 years of effort from observations gathered from more than 100 organizational case studies and statistical analysis of survey data from 50 of those organizations. Diagnostic tools developed by Mr Michel provide a framework to initiate discussions on strengths and weaknesses within an organization and a baseline from which to measure progress. Think in terms of going to a doctor with certain symptoms: you know something is not right but have no idea exactly what is wrong or what the treatment should be. The doctor immediately identifies the symptoms, attempting to diagnose the root cause. Many times, the doctor determines that additional testing is needed before prescribing a treatment plan. The organizational diagnostic tools developed by Mr Michel are similar to the tests ordered by the doctor and the Diagnostic Mentoring methodology described in The Performance Triangle (Michel, 2013a) is similar to the consultation between doctor and patient. In the end, however, it is up to the patient to follow the plan of treatment. Similarly, organizational change can only be successful if senior executives and managers throughout the organization develop a plan of action and take full ownership. The Diagnostic Mentoring methodology stimulates dialogue among executives based on diagnostic data that results in internally- developed action plans with executive ownership. Without ownership, it is too easy for executives and managers to say "that is not my plan, what do those consultants know about my business?"

*Management Design: Managing People and Organizations in Turbulent Times* builds on the concepts offered in *The Performance Triangle* (Michel, 2013a) with practical insight needed to convert theory to practice. Management Design is more of a practical 'how to' book to stimulate deep thinking on the interferences that exist in their organization that inhibit the organization's ability to act quickly and decisively. More importantly, Management Design provides an easy-to-read framework leading executives down a path to greater understanding of the underlying dynamics in their organizations and practical, effective, action plans. In the end, all that matters are results and an 80% or higher failure rate is not acceptable. *The performance triangle* as a model, and *Management Design* as the practical workbook, provide tools and a methodology with the potential to yield significantly better results.

Only time will tell, but as Maverick said in Top Gun in evaluating his chances with a beautiful woman: "It's looking good at the moment."

*Dr. Herb Nold, DM, CPA*
*Professor of Business Administration,*
*Polk State College, Florida, USA*

# Introduction

There is no doubt, management in turbulent times needs change. In a volatile era, with the increasing complexity of globalization and a young generation of people that works differently from previous generations, many of our management models, capabilities, and systems are inadequate to meet the needs of 21$^{st}$ century businesses.

For the past five years, the Global Drucker Forum in Vienna has reiterated the need for change in the way we manage our businesses. The question remains, why does it not happen? Niklas Luhmann, the renowned German sociologist, puts it eloquently: "The ability to ignore is everywhere". It is part of systems theory and the way to reduce complexity. Moreover, the ability of people to suffer is well developed. However, when 'viruses' invade organizations unknown and unwanted over time, limiting their potential, it is time to act and change the way we operate our businesses.

*Management Design* has been developed for those who don't have time to wait. It translates the 'Drucker experi-ence' into an action-oriented think-tool for entrepreneurs, leaders, and managers of all kinds of organizations who want to transform their organization to cope better with a dynamic environment and to enable the talent to use its full potential. As such, the book is the tool to design management. It builds on Peter Drucker's heritage and takes it into the future.

*The Performance Triangle* (Michel, 2013a), my first book, shines through. The idea was to create a tool that translated theory into practice. The result was Diagnostic Mentoring – the approach that creates insights for leadership teams rather than offering cheap tips and 'recipes'. It builds on the recurring themes of people-centric leadership and the 'inner game' (the art of relaxing distorting thoughts) as a means of addressing the 'outer game' (The challenges organizations and people face) through speed, agility, and resilience as effective responses.

There are many ways to read and use *Management Design*. In just one hour, flipping through the concepts, executives capture the essence of the Framework with Insights; Design; Change; and Mentoring as the four steps for a successful transformation. As a comprehensive guide for professionals in organizations and management development, it facilitates change through a combination of theory, diagnostics, insights, and practical design tools.

Diagnostic Mentors use the book as a transparent, shared template to support their work with clients who want to make change happen. The book includes a straight-forward self-assessment tool to promote do-it-yourself Diagnostic Mentoring. It mirrors the comprehensive online INsights Diagnostic Tools™, which allow for a deep-dive into intangibles such as culture, leadership, and decision-making systems.

A book on design does not go without design. We felt that a somewhat complex topic required graphic design to convey the message. The task was to use what worked with clients and make it publically available in the simplest way without losing its essence. It is our contribution to facilitate transformation in dynamic times.

*Zug, November 2014*

**Lukas Michel, Owner AgilityINsights, Sphere Advisors AG, Switzerland**

**Thomas Kupferschmied, Owner, Kupferschmied: Werkstatt für gediegene Kommunikation', Switzerland**

# The design to manage organizations and people in turbulent times

Today's organizations operate in a world with increasing volatility and growing uncertainty. Organizational complexity and ambiguous market signals create an operating environment that requires fresh capabilities. Firms need to adapt with high speed and agility, strengthen their resilience to withstand the unexpected and establish a superior ability to act without being bogged down by self-initiated inertia.

Simultaneously, the nature of work has fundamentally changed in many industries. Knowledge has become more important, compared with physical work. Today's talent effectively uses readily-available technology to share knowledge and collaborate, which forces organizations to rethink the nature of work. However, traditional management models and practices are ineffective in dealing with the new environment. They are equipped with tools that are totally out of place and unsuited to support modern 'knowledge work'. To challenge the current situation, Gary Hamel (2007), the well-recognized author of many books on management and innovation, points to most critical question for today's leaders: "Are we changing as fast as the world around us?" The answer for many companies is "no".

For example, management-by-objectives, the widely-used methodology that aligns people with organizational objectives, has been proven to slow down businesses. It comes with unintended side effects, and creates a strong filter against new business opportunities. It is an inadequate tool for today's fast-moving business world. Industrial pioneers invented such tools, 100 years ago, to drive scale and efficiency. Since then, management practice has changed very little in many organizations. It is time for a fundamental

rethink of some of our assumptions, models, practices, and tools to support 'knowledge people' to perform in a dynamic environment. Management Design helps entrepreneurs, leaders, and managers think through their options to find managerial routines and practices that meet the needs of today's talent in a turbulent world.

*The Performance Triangle* (Michel, 2013a) introduced a simple, logical, and workable framework with culture, leadership, and systems at its corners and people at the centre. It forced leaders to re-examine the many assumptions underlying their leadership practice and analyze how their organization could develop agility through a people-centric approach as a means to cope with a volatile environment. Using the related INsights Diagnostic Tools™, leaders decode the essential bridge between organization and people to unlock the potential of the talent simply by removing the interferences to higher levels of performance. The book provided the scientific foundation for the triangular relationships of culture, leadership and systems and continues to serve as a guide for leaders to develop these essential capabilities.

*Management Design* builds on the performance triangle model, to explore the managerial capabilities and systems that support leaders to operate in dynamic environments.

# MANAGEMENT DESIGN

*Management Design* introduces speed, agility, resilience, and the ability to act as a comprehensive and coherent guide for management practice in a multi-faceted operating environment. People, organizations, stakeholders, environment, and management are the elements that establish a holistic *Management Design* Framework as a comprehensive guide and toolbox for Diagnostic Mentoring. The new Framework, with the extended offline and various online INsights Diagnostic Tools™, establishes the baseline for the design of the management model and capabilities. The related change approach complements Diagnostic Mentoring as a guided self-development tool for executive teams and their organizations.

Business models – how a company makes money – have been the key for the transition between the old and new economy. But, since then, distinctively new business models are hard to find and the increased speed of development resulted in businesses being hard to defend. Companies therefore search for new forms of competitive advantage that are difficult to copy and that do not 'walk away'. For many businesses, management models have become the sources of sustainable, competitive advantage. Julian Birkinshaw (2012), the pioneer of modern management models, pointed out that asking "what is your management model?" may be as important as asking "what business are you in?." Moreover, I would add that it is the distinct managerial systems and capabilities that enact the choice of management model to truly make a difference to competitive advantage. This is why *Management Design* combines a model, a set of capabilities, and a systems toolbox into one coherent approach that connects management to performance of organizations and people.

Management models result from a set of choices leaders make with respect to the sources of energy, the nature of coordination of work, the purpose of goals, the approach to change, and the art of decision-making. To support them in making these choices and to develop the related competencies and systems, *Management Design* serves as a workbook for Diagnostic Mentoring. As such, this book will turn into your personal copy, documenting your management design work.

The book consists of five parts:

**1.** five frames for reviewing, developing, and documenting the management design; **2.** a diagnostic tool, combining insights and concepts from management research; **3.** a set of options and techniques to help you decide on your management design; **4.** the strategies and steps to change towards the new model; plus **5.** a guide to help the mentoring of your team with the new model, tying together all concepts, techniques and steps for management design.

**6.** A set of practical resources supports the process. Finally, **7.** the afterword provides insights into the Diagnostic Mentoring network.

# The management model toolbox

## A concept, diagnostic toolbox, design technique, change model, and mentoring method

FRAMEWORK

INSIGHTS

DESIGN

CHANGE

MENTORING

RESOURCES

AFTERWORD

*"Management, above all, is a practice where art, science, and craft meet."* – Henry Mintzberg, renowned academic and author on business and management

Does good management make a difference? It is more than a rhetorical question. In recent years, thousands of leadership books have been published. But by comparison, only a few new management books came onto the market. It seems as if the discipline of running organization has lost interest in favor of literature that explains a multitude of features of successful leaders. Much of that literature focuses on 'one-time', singular events rather than 'integrated, encompassing, new approaches'. It is time to refocus on what truly matters: managing organizations and people in a turbulent environment. However, as Financial Times business writer Andrew Hill (2014) states: "Management is a concept that its users must constantly shape to meet new organizational challenges." The same article cites the doyen of management, Charles Handy (2013), in a recent speech at the Global Drucker Forum 2013 cautioning: "What they [managers] do about it, what the answers are, no, I don't have them. So, I'm never going to have three rules for success, or this is the answer to leadership, or anything like that. I think that's impertinent and bound to be wrong anyway most of the time because… every problem is different."

This view is shared by management scientists and business leaders from around the world who meet every year in November for the Global Drucker Forum in Vienna. The Forum publishes a list of books that relate to its annual theme (Global Drucker Forum 2013). This list represents a summary of the relevant literature that promotes a new kind of management to meet the needs of 'knowledge people' and the challenges of a dynamic environment, without crossing the line, to tips, best practice, and simple recipes. Here is my list that emerged from the forum combining the art, science, and helpful tools:

- Bouée, C. (2013), Light Footprint Management: Leadership in Times of Change. London: Bloomsbury.
- Birkinshaw, J. (2010) Reinventing Management: Smarter Choices for Getting Work Done. Chichester: Wiley.
- Brown, T. (2011). Change by Design: How Design Thinking Transforms Organizations and Inspires Innovation. New York, NY: HarperCollins.
- Denning, S. (2010). The Leader's Guide to Radical Management: Reinventing the Workplace for the 21st Century. Chichester: Wiley.
- Wartzman, R. (2011) What Would Drucker Do Now: Solutions to Today's Toughest Business Challenges from the Father of Modern Management. New York, NY: McGraw Hill.
- Gratton, L. (2012). The Shift: The Future of Work is Already Here. New York, NY: HarpersCollins.
- Martin, L. R. (2009). Design of Business: Why Design Thinking is the Next Competitive Advantage. New York, NY: McGraw Hill.
- Martin, L. R. (2011). Fixing the Game: Bubbles, Crashes, and What Capitalism Can Learn from the NFL. Boston, MA: Harvard Business Review Press.
- Hamel, G. (2012) What Matters Now: How to Win in a World of Relentless Change, Ferocious Competition, and Unstoppable Innovation. San Francisco, CA:Jossey-Bass, 2012.
- Hagel, J., Brown, J. S., and L. Davison. (2010). The Power of Pull: How Small Moves, Smartly Made, Can Set Big Things in Motion. New York, NY:Basic Books, 2010.
- Pontefract, D. (2013). Flat Army. Hoboken, NJ: Jossey-Bass.

# Management matters

## The case for a management model, a systems toolbox, and a set of capabilities

*Management Design* assumes that management matters. However, it does not ignore the ongoing fundamental debate over the underlying question: do managers make a difference?

The facts provide a clear answer. Ignoring thousands of articles linking various leadership attributes to organizational outcomes, the following summary focuses on linking the practice of management with organizational performance.

In *Realizing the Value of People Management*, the Boston Consulting Group related people management practices to a variety of organizational outcomes to find out that superior practices lead to 350% higher growth and 210% higher profit margins (Strack et al, 2012). In another study on *Maximizing your Return on People*, Bassi and McMurrer (2007) confirmed 60%-130% higher profit growth rates of well-managed business units related to a variety of human capital management practices. Research based on World Management Survey in *Does Management Really Work* related the most basic – I would argue 'outdated' – management practices to productivity, reporting that a 1% increment on a management measure resulted in 23% higher productivity, 14% higher market capitalization, and 1.4 percentage points annual sales growth.

Research at London School of Economics, relating managerial practices to organizational outcomes in turbulent times, clearly indicated a positive relationship: "Better management practices are associated with higher productivity and other organizational indicators" "… but they are also more pro-active during times of adversity" (Homkes, 2011). Towers Watson (2012), in 2012 *Global Workforce Study*, found companies with engaged employees show 280% higher profits than competitors with less engaged staff. Gallup (2013), in *State of the Global Workplace* confirms the higher productivity and higher profitability of better-managed firms. In *Google's Project Oxygen: Do Managers Matter?*, the authors (Garvin et al, 2013) provide a positive response to a question raised, with increasing regularity by a variety of writers: "Does improving management quality have an impact on profitability?" It concludes that the "smallest incremental increases in management quality were quite powerful".

The challenge with most quantitative research into these questions is that it is mostly performed on comparable tools that stem from a highly standardized, controlling mode of operations with a long history. Otherwise, tools and practices would not be comparable. Management with a focus on enabling employees uses tools and practices that are individually-designed for the specific context of every organization. Hence, they are not comparable, which makes this kind of research more difficult. Moreover, sufficient samples on the use of modern management tools are hard to find as we are just at the beginning of a fundamental transformation of work.

The answer to the initial question on whether management matters is "yes". Many organizations with superior management have made investments into modern practices. Good management relies on models, systems, and capabilities that meet the needs of people and organizations operating in a turbulent environment.

# Management models, organizational capabilities, and systems for higher challenges

Management models are immensely valuable to people in an organization as they transcend an organization's mental framework and approach a shared way of doing things. When teams share their models, they enable members to think, make decisions, behave, and act in line with the intent, without constant management action. Only when models are articulated and shared, can leaders use them to direct the decision-making in organizations. As such, shared management models save time, focus attention, and release productive energy.

Timothy W Gallwey (2000), in his renowned book on *The Inner Game of Work*, offers a simple but powerful formula that relates the potential as an organization's capabilities and interferences to performance:

**Performance = potential – interferences.**

"The greater the challenge that the organization accepts, the more important it is that there is minimum interference occurring from within." In line with this, the research documented in *The Performance Triangle* (Michel, 2013a) indicated that organizations use only 67% of their potential talent and capabilities as 'viruses' interfere and often show as a toxic culture, flawed leadership, or broken managerial systems. With the performance triangle model, we relate culture, leadership, and systems to success:

**Success = f (culture, leadership, systems, opportunities & risks, and serendipity).**

Culture, leadership, and systems, as discretionary management decisions, positively relate to success. They can be managed and therefore can make a difference. Opportunities and risks depend on endogenous factors but also require decisions. This leaves us with serendipity which is outside our control.

Organizations with a vibrant culture are clearly more successful than organizations that infected with 'viruses'; both in terms of leadership and systems positively correlated with culture. Our research concluded that organizations with high scores on culture, leadership, and systems were more agile than their counterparts. Organizations that scored high on the factors that supported 'knowledge work' were clearly faster in making changes. High scores on purpose, relationships, and collaboration made organizations better able to withstand a turbulent environment. Such organizations use the full potential of their talent and ensure there are no interferences keeping the talent from performing at its peak.

Management models, organizational capabilities, and systems tools that fit the purpose and context of an organization, reduce interferences to a minimum and unlock the potential to drive performance.

# "The purpose of this book

…is to help entrepreneurs, leaders, and managers decode, articulate, align, and promote a management design that fits the needs of the organization and people."

Here is why Management Design is an important step towards an organization that outperforms competition in a turbulent environment – freed from all organizational interferences and engaging the full potential of its people:

- **"Management is the least efficient activity in your organization."** - Gary Hamel (2011). To prevent 'viruses' from interfering with decision-making (unintentionally and unknowingly) organizations need a managerial infrastructure with the right design.
- **"The effectiveness of organizations could be doubled if managers discovered how to tap into the unrealized potential present in their workforce."** - Douglas McGregor (1969). Management design that fits the needs of people, unlocks the hidden potential of all talents to promote peak performance.
- **"94% of the problems in business are system-driven and only 6% are people-driven."** - W Edwards Deming (1994: 33). Clarity on management design is a prerequisite for managerial tools that support the people at the client rather than keeping them from doing good work.
- **"You rarely improve an organization by improving the performance of one of its parts."** - Russell Ackoff (1973). This is why Management Design takes a holistic approach to make you think of how to align the parts and maximize value creation.
- **"If you want to kill innovation, reward it."** - Alfie Kohn (unsourced). A management design that fits the needs stretches beyond traditional way of doing things. As a side effect, it removes the unintended consequences of some of our inherited, but ineffective, managerial practices.
- **"If you want truly to understand something, try to change it"** - Kurt Lewin (attributed by: Tolman, 1996). We know tips, best practices, and recipes don't work. This is why we promote experimentation as a means of learning rather than embarking on a new set of paradigms or principles.

Management Design promotes Diagnostic Mentoring as double-loop learning initiated by observation points. The related diagnostic tool focuses the attention on the things that matter most, hence it stimulates the learning and simultaneously increases performance.

- **Management**: why it matters
- **Models**: how we manage our organizations
- **Systems**: the design of the toolbox with rules, routines, and tools
- **Capabilities**: to increase an organizations ability to act

# The emergence of a more human mode of operations

The operating mode of an organization determines how work is being done. It is the result of a fundamental choice between different methods of managing organizations and people. Five assumptions help us simplify a myriad of choices to two concurrent modes of operation:

- The accepted view about human behavior and motivation has changed.
- The nature of work in the information age makes all knowledge people executives.
- Technology changes the way we work in a networked economy.
- The ability to change constantly is a competence in itself.

In a turbulent environment, with increasing 'knowledge work', the role of managers clearly shifts from 'control' to include 'enabling'. However, the distinction between control and enabling is not black or white. There are many combinations that managers find helpful for their specific operational context and situation.

It is obvious that we cannot talk about management and the need for change without a conversation about managers and employees themselves.

**What do managers do?** There is a vast amount of research and literature available that lists what managers do, way beyond the classics of 'plan, decide, act, and review cycle' approaches. However, these lists leave unanswered what managers do that nobody else does. There is little research available on the question "why do managers do what they do?" Moreover, little is known on how and why rules, routines, and tools shape managerial behavior. The research leading to *The Performance Triangle* (Michel, 2013a) has contributed to this conversation with a better understanding of the relationships between managerial systems, leadership and the culture in an organization. *Management Design* focuses on the question of how we manage organizations by offering two operating modes: the enabling mode and the controlling mode of operation.

**Is the role of managers changing?** Most discussions reveal an apparent shift from hierarchical and rules-based bureaucracies to decentralized work in networks, fundamentally altering knowledge asymmetries in organizations. The change is driven, partly, by new technologies offering new ways of working, collaboration across boundaries, and easier access to knowledge. The increasing importance of knowledge further shifted the value of expertise, problem-solving, learning, and decision-making to employees at the client front. This, in return, facilitated self-organization in small, flexible teams (Drucker, 1988; Handy, 1989). New ways of working leave middle managers in specific functions as team leaders, coordinators, and facilitators in small, decentralized business units, charged with an entrepreneurial purpose freed from traditional corporate control. This means that knowledgeable employees are charged with an entrepreneurial role and a leadership role (Kanter, 1989; Mintzberg, 1998). The manager's role shifts to coordinating diverging efforts, energizing self-organized work, providing advice, and negotiating choices. In this new setting, the manager's role clearly shifts away from command, control, and administration to an enabling role.

# Management in need of a balanced model

## Does the role of management shift?

Currently, radical new organizational forms are limited to a few celebrated business cases. Many organizations have used the new language to adopt little more than the rhetoric. Others have embarked on '2.0', 'new thinking', 'radical change', 'new paradigms', 'new codex' type-work without leaving the boundaries of bureaucratic control. As Professor Collin Hales (2001) in *Does it Matter What Managers Do* claims, "fully autonomous, self-managing work teams are restricted to a few specialized and exceptional instances…". He continues to put reality into the discussion by indicating that central ruling has only been rewritten to focus on results rather than processes. Such changes represent alterations to bureaucratic control rather than radical new forms.

Having said all of this, there is no doubt that the remnants of bureaucracy and scientific management are obstacles in a networked and knowledge-intensive era. It is obvious that managerial systems and routines that address the changed assumptions about humankind clearly make a difference to how we lead our organizations and therefore improve performance. This is why *Management Design* uses two modes of operation rather than a radical approach as an alternative choice to traditional, control-focused management. There are many reasons to believe there is a desperate need for the shift towards a more human mode of operations. But it is a shift that requires both enabling and control in the right balance.

**Enabling mode** of operation: focus on responsibility, self-organization, broad direction, flexibility, and collective wisdom.

The research leading to *Management Design* explains distinct differences among a variety of firms:

**Large corporate firms** tend to operate in a controlling mode, simultaneously experimenting with projects that de-bureaucratize work or strengthen decentralized work in 'enabling modes', when appropriate.

**Established medium-size firms** tend to make investments in managerial models, systems, and capabilities with roots in the past century that hinder their ability to act.

**Entrepreneurial growth firms** tend to be challenged by newly-installed management teams able to review their mode of operation and shift their style to enable people take risks.

**Start-up firms** tend to be free from any legacy and naturally apply management models that enable people to seize opportunities, with the entrepreneur providing direction and guidance.

**Public sector organizations** tend to install so-called 'state-of-the-art management practices' copied from the private sector, based on the fear of failure, only to find their bureaucracies hamper the talent.

**Controlling mode** of operation: focus on rules, bureaucracy, performance targets, standardization, hierarchy and power.

# Change has changed: five observations

| **Dynamic times.**<br>A trend without a return. | | **Interference**<br>limits potential and hampers performance. |
|---|---|---|
| **Knowledge is the scarce resource.** | The nature of work has fundamentally changed. In most jobs, knowledge has become more important than physical work. | Talent is widely unused. Many organizations make insufficient use of knowledge of the highly-qualified talent in their midst. |
| **Modern people work differently.** | Modern technologies provide access to information in ways that were unthinkable years ago. Collaboration across boundaries and relationships, to access knowledge in networks, enables the talent to use its creativity. | Industrial principles prevent innovation. Many organizations still work with principles that have their roots in an era that favoured efficiency over innovation. |
| **Purpose inspires!** | Talent has the choice. With this, the assumptions about what motivates people at work change. Self-responsibility[1] based on purpose is widely-recognized as the dominant principle that inspires 'knowledge people' to perform. | Tools such as goals are liable to break. Many organizations favour control over freedom with tools that fail to support people when it matters most. |
| **Change has changed!** | It is no secret that higher dynamics are the norm, self-inflicted complexity increases with size, uncertainties challenge strategy, and ambiguities demand flexibility. This new environment requires a change in the way we operate. | Normalizing people means mediocrity. Many organizations are built on standardization that normalizes people and that leads to mediocrity everywhere. |
| **Decisions need the right design.** | With knowledge that wants to be applied, access to new technologies, talent that searches for meaning, and a fast pace of change, the decision-making in organizations requires a design that uses the potential and limits inference. | Our normal reaction is to limit options. When things change, we reverse delegation, mute censors, and mistrust people: the opposite of what works in turbulent times. |

# Management needs design

## Management in the enabling mode

| | | |
|---|---|---|
| **Speed. Self-responsibility.** | In a fast-changing, dynamic environment, a fast response is an essential capability. The good news is that speed matches the needs of 'knowledge people', being about self-responsibility and the 'inner game techniques' of work. | **A high ability to act requires a new type of management.** |

Some writers call this change a true paradigm shift from control to 'the freedom of people to apply their talent in organizations that are built for that purpose'. It is obvious that this kind of change is more than a series of quick-fixes.

| | |
|---|---|
| **Agility. Self-organization.** | The ability to adapt constantly, without disruptive change, is the key feature of successful management in a turbulent environment. Self-organization uses the potential of people to get things done. |

However, the reality in many organizations may differ widely from some of these principles and capabilities. As a manager, it is important to 'work within the system', effectively applying an organization's way of working. It is the task of executive leadership to create an environment that makes people successful in what they do. Diagnostic Mentoring as 'work on the system' closes the gaps through a discussion about the model, the capabilities and the systems that meet the needs of people.

| | |
|---|---|
| **Resilience. Glue techniques.** | Resilience is an organizational capability to withstand external shocks and defend against unexpected outside influences. A strong purpose, networks, and collaboration are the defence mechanisms of successful organizations. |

| | |
|---|---|
| **Ability to act. Coherent principles.** | Speed, agility, and resilience are the features of a leadership team with a high ability to act. Such teams capture relevant opportunities by reinforcing a set of coherent principles rather than individual quick-fixes. |

Management Design supports that conversation through diagnostic mentoring with the triangle model, diagnostic tools, and a toolbox for the design.

| | |
|---|---|
| **Freedom to decide. Collective intelligence.** | In turbulent times, successful management unlocks hidden talent, establishes shared principles, and taps into collective intelligence to retain the freedom to think and decide, in ways that support the specific context. |

[1] Self-responsibility refers to the ability of humans to act on their own will and to be accountable for the consequences of their decisions and actions. Self-responsibility requires choice – the ability to say no – and represents the foundation for self-motivated behaviors.

# The chief executive.
**Global insurance, Switzerland**

Scope: Transform an organization to grow from within – change culture from cost-cutting to a growth mode.

After 10 years of successful cost-cutting in one the world's largest financial services firms, a new chief executive officer (CEO) took the helm. His gut-feeling was that something was fundamentally wrong in the way his leaders dealt with pressing daily issues. By mapping out his concerns, through several mentoring sessions, and diagnosing the management model, it became clear that managers and employees needed to change their decision-making from an emphasis on reducing risks to seizing opportunities. This meant a huge culture change, unlocking the potential of superb staff.

The leadership team successfully refined its awareness of the fine nuances of culture and developed a management model using the online diagnostic assessment tool.

# The coach.
**Sole proprietor and founder, USA**

Scope: Work with executive teams to create effective ways of tackling the managerial challenges of the 21st Century.

As an independent coach to chief executives of leading organizations, the coach used Management Design to stimulate discussion among management teams about how best to lead an organization in turbulent times. While the diagnostic tool raised the awareness for the critical leadership issues, the model discussion served as the bonding element for her executive team clients to help establishment of a shared foundation and effective way to manage the organization. These teams consistently out-performed their competition by creating strong cultures.

The management design questions guided the conversations with the executive team about how to manage their organization for turbulent times.

# The transformer.
**Public transformation, Switzerland**

Scope: Change culture from dominant administrative behaviors to enabling people to take charge

As with many public services, the managing director of the transportation system of a major city faced the challenge of transforming its organization from public administration into a competitive private company. This meant fundamentally changing the way in which things were being done: from following cumbersome procedures to fostering efficiency and effectiveness. By engaging the entire organization in creating the mission statement, a new management model emerged with a set of values that emphasized the responsibility and role of every employee in the delivery of superior performance.

Management Design served as the guide for the implementation of the transformation.

# Six management designers

## The integrator.
**Global mining firm, UK**

Scope: Align multiple organizational units to one way of doing things across a variety of businesses and geographies.

After years of managing a diverse group through a holding-type structure, the new CEO decided to build stronger bonds among businesses around the globe. She engaged an executive education firm to work with the 250 key executives to build a management model with a strong foundation in the roots of these business, but simultaneously distilled their shared principles. By facilitating the development of a new model and training people in its use, she successfully created a culture in an industry that was known for its labour-related safety issues.

Management Design served as a guide for the development and undertaking of a large scale executive development programme.

## The architect.
**Leadership think thank, Switzerland**

Scope: Establish a framework for growth beyond the founder's personal engagement and inspiration.

The task of the newly appointed chief operating officer was to ensure the smooth transition from a founder-driven leadership style to managing the organization through a small management team. The challenge was to create strong bonds among functional experts to represent the organization as a whole, rather than to promote their primary roles. By using the performance triangle model, he created a shared approach and new management model with the team that successfully replaced the founder's operational tasks with a professional team approach.

Diagnostic Mentoring created the 'common glue' to unite a diverse team of leaders.

## The board.
**Specialty nutrition firm, Italy**

Scope: Align decision-making and control between the board and the executive team.

Separating the task between the board of directors and the executive team in SME high-growth firms can be a challenge as directors often hold multiple functions. They govern the firm and simultaneously manage their business. To clarify the decision-making among the bodies and members, the administrative director used Management Design to separate the roles of the board from managing the business through the executive team. The new management team allowed them to manage multiple functions while being clear on corporate governance.

The Leadership Toolbox™ centered the conversation on the set of tools that served as the common language and work practice.

MANAGERS WITH SOPHISTICATED APPROACHES FAR OUTREACH THOSE WITHOUT THEM!

# FRAMEWORK

## What is my desired management design?

A shared language and template for decoding, designing, documenting, changing, and applying management models, systems and capabilities.

# Framework

A shared language
The Management Design Framework

People
- Organization
- Stakeholders
- Environment
- Management

Operations and design
- Four archetypes
- The integration frame
- Management design

The purpose of the *Management Design* Framework is to establish a shared language that supports people to think about what it takes to manage an organization in a turbulent environment, when knowledgeable people take the helm.

The people, organization, stakeholders, environment, and management frames outline the concepts with assumptions about the environment and choices on the design of management and organization.

The work through these frames initiates the design thinking as 'work on the system' to complement the usual 'operations mode' of management; what I call 'work in the system'. The Framework articulates the essential managerial competencies that help leaders cope with a dynamic environment.

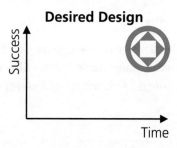

# The framework and template to create a shared language

*Management Design* establishes the logic for how leaders manage organizations and people to create value for stakeholders.

The Management Design Framework provides a shared language for leaders to help them get started with a conversation about their design. Hence:
- Frames relate to concepts and the work of leaders.
- Every organization is different and unique so management and organization require their own designs.

But be aware of the following:
"Every theory of management makes assumptions about human behaviors. The accepted view of human behavior in organizations has changed dramatically over this century." (Simons, 1995)

"All descriptive concepts, once they are used to organize reality and guide behavior become normative. As checklists or rules, they reinforce the central tendency with mediocrity as a result." (Agyris,1973)

"We cannot ignore the 'central tendency'. In the absence of management action, self-interested behaviors at the expense of organizational goals are inevitable." But: "Effective managers do not work to achieve average outcomes." We "need to reconcile self-interest with the desire to contribute." (Simons,1995)

"Many of the 'central tendencies' are caused by nonproductive forces." (Agyris et al, 1985)

# A shared language

## The blueprint for action

The *Management Design* Framework establishes the model as a shared language for every good discussion, meeting, or workshop in business on management and organization. Without a framework and shared language, people are unable to share their thoughts effectively; they make decisions in isolation, behave in their own best interests, and opti mize results in their 'silos'. As such, collaboration takes a break, interactions stall, and people are unable to reach their full potential.

Every organization needs a management model: distinct capabilities and systems to serve as a blueprint for the individual and collective thoughts, decisions, behaviors and actions of all its members. The challenge, with strong frames, is that, over time, 'viruses' interfere with their design unintentionally and unwillingly; models, capabilities, and systems become ineffective in supporting leaders and enabling employees to apply their full potential.

*Management Design* helps leaders re-install the programme code as the blueprint for the thoughts, decisions, behaviours, and actions throughout their organizations. The frames serve as facilitation tools for reviewing, developing, and documenting their approach to management. As a template, the frames captures the core ideas on a well-structured, single sheet of paper – being a flip chart poster, an aid-memoire, a toolbox, or a page of scratch notes. To facilitate an effective discussion, management design must be simple, intuitive, relevant, and unique. Once established, the framework becomes the model as the 'one way of doing things' in organizations – the shared language. As such, management models, capabilities and systems are not mobile, difficult to copy, and therefore represent a true competitive advantage.

Through research and practice with many business cases around the world, five proven frames have emerged to best describe management and organization: people, environment, stakeholders, organization, and management. They cover all areas of management and translate into a management cycle from strategy to implementation as a blueprint for action.

# Five frames, each with a symbol representing a distinct choice of concepts

**People.** Organizations comprise people who apply their knowledge, experience, and skills to perform and deliver value. They want to apply their creativity and full potential. The way in which we engage people determines much of the speed of an organization.

**Organization.** Culture, leadership, and systems frame the operating environment that enable people to apply their creativity, seize opportunities, and stimulate innovation. The way in which we organize collaboration determines so much the agility of an organization.

**Stakeholders.** Stakeholders have needs, expectations, and offer resources to an organization. The challenge is to enable collaboration, stimulate relationships, and provide purpose for growth. The way in which we set goals determines much of the resilience of an organization.

**Environment.** Environment poses a variety of external challenges to people, organization, management, and stakeholders. Creativity, innovation, and growth determine the overall performance of an organization. The way in which we deal with change determines much of the scope of management's ability to act.

**Management.** Every manager's task is to create an environment in which people make entrepreneurial decisions to provide superior value to clients. The way in which we make decisions determines much of how we get things done –our actions.

# The Management Design Framework

## Systemic links between the five frames

PEOPLE

ORGANIZATION

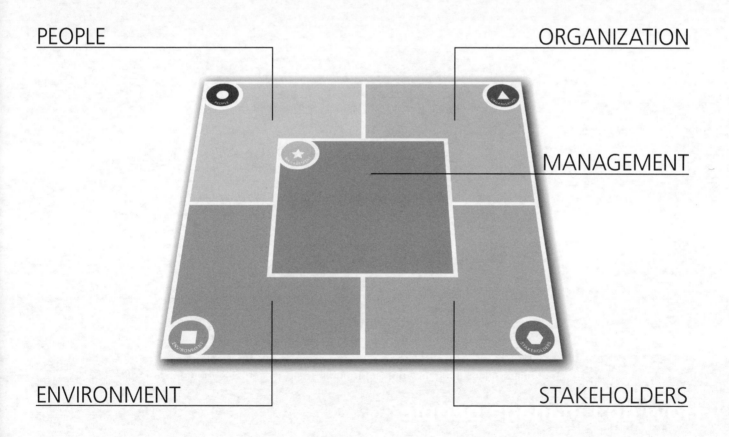

MANAGEMENT

ENVIRONMENT

STAKEHOLDERS

The triangular shape of a mountain frames the many important details that make up its unique posture.

# How do I manage people?

# PEOPLE

## The source of energy, creativity, and speed!

The 'people frame' represents the talent in an organization and their ability to apply the full potential of their creativity and create value for customers.

People represent the first frame of Management Design. Without people, there is no business, no performance, and no need for management. Hence, this frame requires identification of the right talent to meet the future needs of an organization. The assumptions we make about people determine how we lead our organizations, which is why you need a point of view – your own image of mankind. It is the creative potential of people that makes an organization innovative. The way in which we engage people unlocks much of that potential. The 'inner game' with focus, awareness, choice, and trust provides the set of tools that help people perform at their peak and represent the essence of speed in organizations. The challenge is to lead people, on a basis of self-responsibility, without losing control, in order to maximize the flow of productive energy and enhance the speed at which things are done.

- What assumptions determine my leadership style?
- What obstacles prevent my talented people from using their potential?
- From where does the motivational energy of people come?
- How do I unlock their full talent potential?
- How do I enable learning for peak performance?
- How do I engage people?

The 'people frame' determines much of the creativity and speed in your organization.  So how do I manage people?

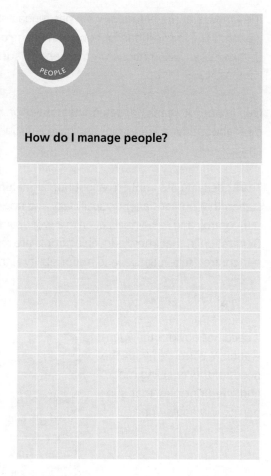

**How do I manage people?**

# What assumptions determine my leadership?

It is a new era: the nature of work has fundamentally shifted to the application of knowledge being the dominant way to working. The implications for how we manage our organizations are huge. It is important to note that "every management theory makes assumptions on the behaviors [sic] of people. The accepted view has radically changed over the years." (Simons, 1995)

Our image of mankind determines much of how things are done in organizations. This is why leaders need to be clear about their assumptions and have a distinct point of view. Two opposing positions explain the options: responsibility and control.

The underlying assumptions about human nature are drawn from the work of Douglas McGregor (1969) on Generation X, stating that humans are principally lazy and unwilling to work. The assumption was that people do not value self-direction, self-control, and self-actualization in a work context. At the other end of the continuum, McGregor (2006) suggested, with Generation Y, that knowledgeable people are responsible and want to contribute. Leaders can build on self-determination, self-control, self-initiative, and responsibility rather than 'control and command' as their method of getting things done.

It becomes obvious that Generation Y correlates with the needs of the 'enabling mode' and the principles that support 'knowledge work'.

 **Enabling mode:**
Generation Y people…

…want to contribute and have fun
…perform and are self-responsible
…control their own work
…want to develop and grow
…and are able to self-organize!

**Principles: responsibility**

 **Controlling mode:**
Generation X people …

…don't do anything for themselves, evade work
…need command and motivation
…are measured and evaluated
…are freed from weaknesses
…and need leadership!

**Principle: control**

# People first

## Choosing people-centric leadership

A primary leadership task is to manage people. In order to 'control' people, given their vital role as critical resource. 'recipes' are available everywhere on how to 'manipulate' behaviours. But it is important to note that 'human resources' cannot be purchased and owned by an employer like raw material, because the service (labour energy) and the provider (employee) are indivisible. This means that employees have considerable 'control' over how much physical and mental energy they will provide. Moreover, people are not 'controllable assets' in a legal sense as they cannot be owned by a firm.

This makes 'people are the most important assets' a well-intended but questionable statement and an opportunity to start a new conversation about motivation and control, with respect for people. 'People first' is a discrete decision and deliberate investment in people.

When leaders are asked to choose their style of people management, few of them vote for Generation X. Generation Y is the primary choice in any knowledge-driven organization. But, when we look for proof of this choice in their design of rules, routines, and tools we see the controlling mode dominating in many organisations. To gain the 'full mileage' from Generation Y, it is important that the 'video matches the audio'- meaning that leaders need to do what they say. Often, this also requires removing some of the obstacles (you could call them 'viruses') that prevent people from applying their full potential:

**Goal bargaining:** a costly process that leads to mediocrity.
**Promotion guidelines:** rules that create wrong expectations.
**Scoring lists:** ranking people contradicts hiring best talent.
**Job descriptions:** make organizations inflexible and slow.
**Time control:** creativity never follows a clock or timeline.
**Assessments:** establish pre-set filters and remove judgement.
**Incentive programmes:** have unintended consequences and may encourage the wrong behaviours.
**Employee evaluations:** assume we understand performance.
**Idea proposals:** make creativity the exception rather than the rule.
**Organization charts:** strengthen hierarchy over collaboration.

These principles, tools, and practices of the controlling mode in a knowledge-driven setting turn into 'viruses' that infect organizations unwilling and unintentionally over time. They are part of the reason why only 65% of the talent potential in organizations is used effectively.

The people-centric approach makes people successful and simultaneously reduces transaction costs. Much of the traditional control mechanism can be reduced to allow people a higher degree of freedom. People-centric leadership returns superior yields to customer, investors, and the talent in organizations.

Many of the traditional people-management practices are outdated as they were designed for the old economy. They are not suited to stimulating creativity of 'knowledge people'. They make organizations slow to react in a dynamic environment: every time there is a need for change, objectives must be renegotiated, job descriptions require an update, and incentive programs require adjustment; this stalls organizations rather than enhancing speed.

# What are the obstacles that prevent my talented people from reaching their potential?

Top performance is the result of superior thoughts, decisions, behaviors, and actions. The 'controlling mode' assumes that the thinking and decision-making remains at the top. Benefiting fully from people with knowledge and skills requires delegating decision-making to those on the periphery of the organization, and making people accountable for implementation of their decisions. Performance is the result of action not intent. People put their energy into things they care about. This means action is meaningful and it implies that people are responsible: they take the initiative and get things done. Taking action requires choices, self-control, and determination. The best people are attracted to this because they can "live their own goals".

**People want to understand.** High performance requires accurate, timely feedback about the work being done. With feedback information on performance, people can take action to address their shortcomings or meet challenges.

Too often, information is limited to the people at the top or information is not available when decisions are made. Employees often receive distorted feedback or no feedback at all.

**People want to create.** In the 'knowledge age', they make decisions. Creativity is innate to human beings; to find new ways of doing things or innovate products and solutions.

In many organizations, bureaucratic constraints, limited resources, and the lack of development opportunities are often observed as barriers to the potential.

**People want to contribute.** By nature, individuals want to achieve. This brings tangible rewards, and individuals experience learning as a reward in itself.

Managers motivate people to perform – one of the main obstacles to creativity and achievement.

**People want to do right.** Individuals have an inherent personal code of conduct that makes them act in a professional manner.

But organizations often provide opportunities that are in conflict with the explicit and implicit code of conduct.

**People want to engage.** Individuals in modern organizations are clear about the areas in which they want to engage. They set goals and priorities with attention and resources that are always limited.

Leaders often see employees as a means of executing strategy – a rather old-fashioned an ineffective perspective.

# Knowledge work

## Generation Y people want to understand, think, contribute, adhere, and engage

'Knowledge work' means making decisions based on the ability to act. Superior decision-making requires an environment in which people can apply their potential. This is in contrast to the principles of the 'controlling mode' in which interference prevents people from using their knowledge and experience to seize opportunities.

| Decide & Act | Understand | Think | Contribute | Adhere | Engage |
|---|---|---|---|---|---|
| **Employees** | Need timely feedback where the work is being done | Make decisions | Are motivated by purpose | Have degrees of freedom within clear boundaries | Have clear priorities |
| **In an ideal environment with...** | Unlimited information | Unlimited opportunities; the readiness to take risks | Increasing pressure | Higher temptations | Limited attention and limited resources |
| **Compared to the controlling mode where...** | Information is available on request | Leaders make decisions | Leaders motivate for performance | ... and control what is being done | Employees implement |
| **With interferences everywhere** | Lack of information | Lack of opportunities; fear to take risks | Lack of purpose | Lack of boundaries | Conflict of interests, lack of resources |

# Where does the energy come from?

Responsibility is motivation. In most organizations, motivation is an issue because it is not well understood. Science is unclear about what motivates people to perform. But we clearly know what demotivates us. Here are some points to explain why motivation is demotivation:

- People are motivated at their own will.
- Motivation is the responsibility of every human being.
- Most leaders demotivate.
- Group demotivation is a powerful 'virus'.
- Motivation has negative side-effects.
- The motivation of employees by leaders is always late.
- Systemic motivation always leads to its systemic undermining.

Responsibility is the number one source of motivation. It is a moral position that requires a choice. It is the accountability for the own motivation with choice for autonomous action, desire to take initiative, and responses as creative doing. Self-responsibility is the number one source of motivation. It requires a conscious choice. It gives people accountability for their own motivation, the choice to take autonomous action and gives them the desire to take the initiative, encouraging creativity.

Motivation undertaken by leaders is an action outside the control of an individual. As such, it undermines autonomy, initiative, and creativity. This is why control requires leadership attention.

# Motivation

## Who is accountable for responsibility and motivation?

Individual performance is a combination of readiness, capability, and opportunity. Self-determination is the responsibility of the individual. The institution designs the framework around outside control.

**Who is accountable for responsibility and motivation?**
Individual performance is a combination of readiness, capability, and opportunity. Self-determination is the responsibility of the individual. The institution designs the framework around outside control.

There are different roles when it comes to refueling energy in organizations: individual employee responsibilities, shared accountability, and institutional responsibility.

**Readiness**: accountability lies with the individual. Responsibility is the driving force of motivation: the intrinsic contract as a prerequisite for people getting things done. The extrinsic contract is an external-control tool that institutions use to motivate people to perform in the direction desired.

**Capability**: there is shared accountability for capability between the individual and the institution. The organization's competence management defines the talent's needs and offers development opportunities. But for this to be effective, individuals have to make choices about learning.

**Opportunity:** People need to be given scope and opportunity to perform. This is the sole accountability of institutions. Leaders represent the institution and are accountable for creating a productive working environment with adequate resources, rules, and processes. Creating such an environment saves considerable managerial time and puts the focus on opportunities rather than ineffective control.

| Energy | People<br>Self-initiative | Institution<br>Outside-control |
|---|---|---|
| **Readiness**: with the individual | Responsibility, awareness, focus, intrinsic contract | Purpose, extrinsic contract |
| **Capability**: shared accountability | Choice, skills, learning, energy | Development, competence management |
| **Opportunity**: with the Institution | Playing field | Resources, process, rules |

# How do I unlock the full talent potential?

Talent with capabilities and expertise is a critical-but-scarce resource in modern organizations. The 'war for talent' has come to an end – the talent has won. Talented people have the choice and migrate to organizations that provide meaningful work and challenging opportunities.

**What kind of talent do we need?** It is obvious that, for organizations to succeed in turbulent times, they need the right talent. Identifying talent-needs in knowledge-driven organizations means understanding competencies beyond traditional skills. This is hard work and requires a dedicated development approach. Identifying and employing talent, is not only a question of developing the right people. First, organizations must understand their future competence needs, then develop the talent to meet these needs. Professor Johanna Anzengruber's (2013) pioneering work on 'strategic competence management' explains the model and processes that help leaders match future organizational competencies with specific talent requirements, to enhance its ability to act.

**How does the talent reach its full potential?** 'Flow' is the point at which people reach peak levels of performance and use their full potential (Csikszentmihalyi, 1990). Flow requires the right balance between capabilities and challenges. People become bored when challenges are limited and they cannot apply superior capabilities. When they face challenges that are beyond their capabilities, anxiety and stress limit their performance.
It is clear it is essential to identify future competence needs and to develop people so that they attain these competencies, in order to tackle bigger challenges.

The flow concept is useful for establishing the right kind of leadership. It describes a state of high performance that can only be reached through self-initiated action, based on purpose and self-responsibility. To unlock full potential, leaders must create an environment in which people can experience flow more often.

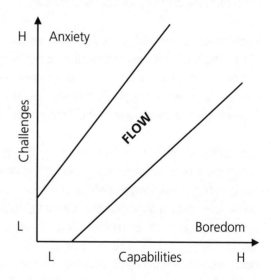

# The source of creativity

## People with a high ability to act

Talent comes with individual competencies in the form of capabilities (skills) and expertise (knowledge and experience) (Anzengruber, 2013). Creativity is one of the competencies that combines (and requires) skills, knowledge, and experience. Creativity is a prerequisite for organizations to reach higher levels of innovation and growth.

Creativity, experimentation, and the ability to surprise are needed for organizations to adapt to a fast-changing environment and creativity is the essential capability that translates knowledge into value (Kao, 2007).

Creativity requires degrees of freedom, self-responsibility, and the ability to focus. These are things that are not naturally given in organizations – even though every responsible leader would argue that "everything is under control".

**How do we know how well we use talent potential?** This is why creativity – the ability of the talent to fully apply its talents to act and create new things – is the metric to apply when judging an organization's use of its talent in the 'enabling mode'.

# How do I enable learning for peak performance?

**Learning starts with a fresh look at control.** Managing people is one of the manager's primary functions. But making 'control' work for today's organizations is a challenge. Control must balance competing demands. Individual elements of control are created to solve the tensions between freedom and constraints; between top-down direction and bottom-up creativity; between experimentation and efficiency.

Control is defined as any mechanism that managers use to direct attention, motivate, and energize organizational members to act in desired ways and meet organizational objectives. It is the attempt to influence and control others' behaviors through attention. If an individual's attention is not directed towards what needs to be done, the chances of it ever being done are very low. Hence, without attention there is no performance. This means that the structuring and management of attention is central to control processes in organizations. Moreover, control needs to resolve the conflict between self-interested behaviors and organizational goals. It needs to reconcile self-interest with the desire to contribute.

**Control with a new client.** Traditional control focuses on the choice of tools from a management perspective. This means leaders select their processes and tools according to the degree to which they understand the transformation process from input to output; they use it to observe the actions of employees, or to measure the outputs produced. Given the 'modern knowledge worker', it is time to revert control towards, what we call 'client-focused control' (the client, in this case, being the employee). The task is to structure control in a way that enables creativity and learning so that it becomes an enabling function.

# The inner game

## The foundation for faster learning and higher performance

The art of relaxing distorting thoughts is called 'the inner game'. It constitutes the technique for coping with higher challenges. Doubts, stress, fear, biased focus, limiting concepts or assumptions distort our thoughts, decisions, behaviours, and actions. This keeps us from operating at our full potential. 'The inner game', a concept initially developed by Timothy Gallwey (2000), the author of the renowned 'inner game books' on tennis, golf, and work, provides the essential insights into what is required for people to learn faster and perform at their peak.

**PEOPLE**

AWARENESS
FOCUS
CHOICE
TRUST

Awareness, choice, and trust help people focus their attention on what counts. The result is flow – the state in which learning, performance, and creativity are at their peak (Csikszent-mihalyi, 1990). It shifts control to the learner and redefines the role of the leaders as a coach.

**Awareness** is learning by translating observed data through into information without making a judgement about it. It is about having a clear understanding of the present. Non-judgmental awareness is the best way to learn. Leaders need to set their learning policy between self-confident awareness and disengagement through outside control. However, the more signals people receive, the more immune they become to the messages these signals contain (Gladwell, 2002).

**Focus** means self-initiated attention on what matters most. It is a conscious act of concentration that requires energy. The challenge for people is to maintain the focus over a period of time. Leaders need to set their policy between self-initiated focus and goal achievement.

**Choice** is the prerequisite for responsibility. It is the choice to take charge and move in the desired direction. Choice means self-determination whereas rules are determined from the outside. Leaders need to set their people policy between choice and rules.

**Trust**. Trust means speed and agility. It is the cheapest leadership concept ever invented and the foundation for every business transaction. With trust, there is no need for any re-negotiation of contracts when things change. Leaders need to determine their policy between trust and mistrust or responsibility and outside-control. But trust must be earned. The best way to earn trust is by delivering on promises (Anderson, 2004:41).

To quote R K Sprenger (2000): 'Trust is the fastest management concept."
The 'inner game' is the essential tool for speed in organizations.

# How do I engage with the talent in my business?

Managing people follows two principles that are not mutually exclusive: the choice is between responsibility and control. The challenge is to establish sufficient degrees of freedom without losing control.

Do your managers hire and support people who are responsible, who want to contribute or perform? Or, do your managers focus their work on controlling what people do, based on the belief that people need to be extrinsically motivated through attractive rewards and incentives? The choice of how we engage our talent, between control and responsibility, has implications for how we organize work.

**Responsibility**. The responsibility method assumes people are self-motivated and want to get things done. This means providing them with observation points[2] to focus their attention. Higher awareness means they sense early signs and have a significant degree of freedom to react to them. Choice is the foundation for responsibility. Once people have made their choice they will need to be trusted to maintain the right focus.

The responsibility choice follows the 'inner game' principles of work favored by Generation Y people and knowledge work.

**Control**. Goals are a way of explaining to people what to do. It is simply another word for command. Strict rules ensure people do exactly what they have been told to do and do not get distracted. Strict control ensures people maintain their performance and achieve their goals. Once there, they require new, more challenging goals to restart their cycle of plan and implementation.

The control choice follows traditional command and control principles favored by Generation X people and industrial approaches to organizing work.

**RESPONSIBILITY**

AWARENESS
FOCUS
CHOICE
TRUST

**CONTROL**

GOALS
COMMAND
RULES
CONTROL

---

[2] Observation points refer to areas of interests, measurement indicators, or leadership guidance as a means to focus attention and raise the awareness for what matters most rather than to distort the thinking.

# People engagement principles

## The choice between responsibility and control

The policy between responsibility and control is a choice of where the energy comes from. It has implications for how we motivate and engage the talent in our organizations:

**Intrinsic motivation**: Energy is the result of self-motivated people, founded on responsibility, trust and choice. This requires clarity of vision and strategy as people align their purpose with the mission of the organization.

**Social control**: Energy is the result of pressure from others. This requires a working environment in which ideas can flow, creativity can prosper and where good work is valued.

**Extrinsic motivation**: Energy is inspired by the benefits the individual gains from achieving pre-determined outcomes. The assumptions made for this to work are that there is little change in the environment and stability in goals.
In the new era, what can I do to promote responsibility without losing control?

**As an individual**
• Search for a deep sense of purpose and focus attention on important things.

**As an organization**
• Provide the means by which people can match their ambitions and competencies to future capability needs of the organization.

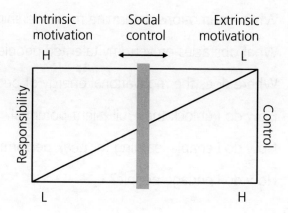

# How do I manage people?

What assumptions determine my leadership style?

What obstacles prevent my talented people from using their potential?

Where does the motivational energy of people come from?

How do I unlock their full talent potential?

How do I enable learning for peak performance?

How do I engage people?

# What is my image of mankind?

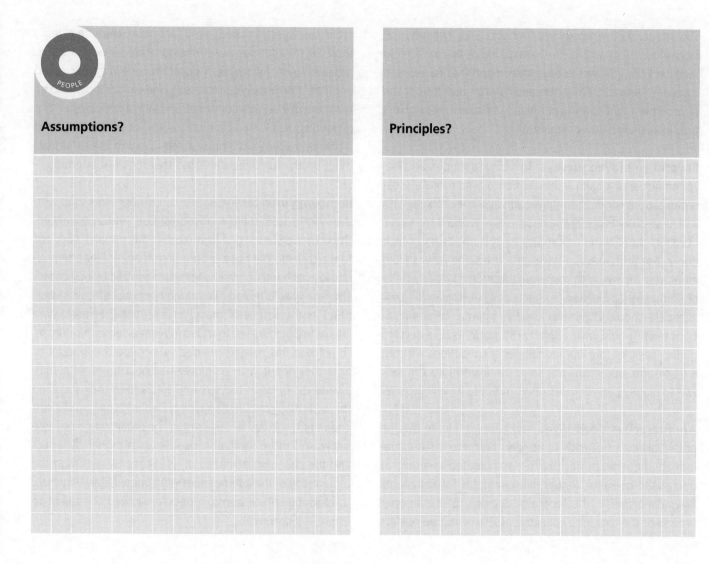

**PEOPLE**

**Assumptions?**

**Principles?**

# Keeping 'race horses' on track

The talent, skills, knowledge, thoughts and, critically, the judgement of people form the essence of any leadership think tank. People are the organization and the organization is people. Hence, it makes sense to have a closer look at the environment that enables people to use their creativity in a truly knowledge-driven organization.

**Beyond employee surveys.** To review the operating environment and to gain a sense of employee morale, most organizations conduct employee surveys. The problem with such assessments is that the responses are always the same: "Leaders don't communicate, strategy is not clear, motivation is not at its best". I have seen the same results from employee surveys with many organizations. With this, the challenge for any leadership team is: what do we do now? "Leaders should communicate; the internal communications team should write a flyer on strategy; leaders need to motive people", are traditional, generic reactions without a resolution. But it was not so in this institution. The task was to dig deeper – beyond what employee surveys achieve.

**An interactive deep-dive.** How can we release the full potential of our talent? To review the current state, the management team decided on a facilitated meeting to discuss this question. Rather than using the online INsights Diagnostic Tool™, the facilitator decided to use a paper version of the tool for a collective assessment. Five posters

listed the questions and, simultaneously, the entire team took 30 minutes to 'walk' through the 30 questions, to provide input. By the fifth question, one member asked another: "Why did you score this one so low when I score it quite high? A lively conversation started over most of the questions, resulting in a high degree of exchange about different perceptions. This resulted in a high level of agreement on the fundamental issues that required attention.

**Removing interferences.** The three-hour workshop with the insights from the diagnostic exercise, and an enhanced, shared understanding of how 'knowledge people' work, led to the development of a programme to focus leadership on purpose rather than traditional 'management by objectives'. The task was to replace a management tool that was identified as the source of many organizational 'viruses' with interactive leadership, founded in a deep sense of purpose. To achieve this, leaders needed to increase the amount of time they spent with employees to help them raise their awareness of what matters and to sharpen their focus on the essentials, rather than hiding behind emails and management by objectives As a result, the organization became faster and more flexible in dealing with higher dynamics and the changing demands of its clients. By removing the tools, many of the interferences were immediately banished. Unblocking self-responsible people allowed the talent to use its full potential.

# Example: Leadership think tank | Switzerland

## People at the centre of attention

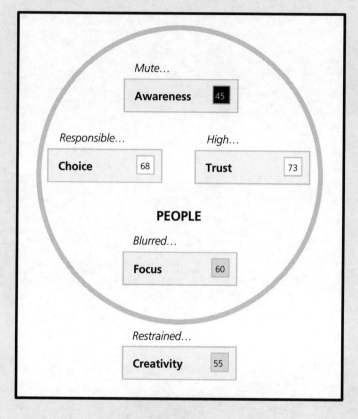

Mute...

**Awareness** 45

Responsible...

**Choice** 68

High...

**Trust** 73

**PEOPLE**

Blurred...

**Focus** 60

Restrained...

**Creativity** 55

H  High scores: above average

M  Medium scores: average

L  Low scores: below average

As one would expect, the support staff of a reputable leadership think tank only comprised employees who were among the most talented people in the field. To enable such employees to fully apply their talent, organizations must eradicate 'viruses'.

Looking inside the 'people frame', this is what the scores offered:

- People experienced high levels of trust and plenty of choice as a result of self-responsible work throughout the organization.
- However, awareness was muted and focus was blurred – symptoms of a lack of feedback and ongoing changes to agreed- performance plans.

Overall creativity was restrained, indicating that people could not apply their full potential. This is a costly deficit in a knowledge-driven organization. The good news was that it is easy to change: simply enable the 'inner game.'

The nature of the overall organizational structure determines much of its detailed operating environment.

# How do I coordinate work?

# ORGANIZATION

## The operating environment for greater agility and innovation

The organizational frame defines the operating environment that enables people to apply their potential, while coping with a turbulent environment.

The increasing importance of knowledge work with the opportunities of the 'inner game' to shift more control to employees, requires a different way to organize work. The good news is that agile organizations have a variety of advantages the most important being its ability to enable the self-organization of teams as a prerequisite for innovation supported by collaborative technologies.

Gestalt (German for shape or form) refers to the psychological theory that the mind forms a global whole with self-organizing principles. According to this theory, the human mind captures the 'whole', prior to perceiving the individual parts. 'Gestalt' psychology deals with our ability to acquire and maintain perceptions in a turbulent world.

The 'Gestalt' of an organization, with structure, systems, leadership, and culture adding up to more than the sum of its parts, helps leaders stretch beyond the fundamental choices between self-organized work and the coordination of work through bureaucratic procedures and rules. What assumptions about work determine my organization?

- What interferences prevent people from delivering productive work?
- How do I establish strong accountability?
- What are the implications of organizational structure on work design?
- How do I organize for agility and innovation?
- How do I coordinate work?

The nature of your operating systems determines much of the agility and innovation capacity in your organization.

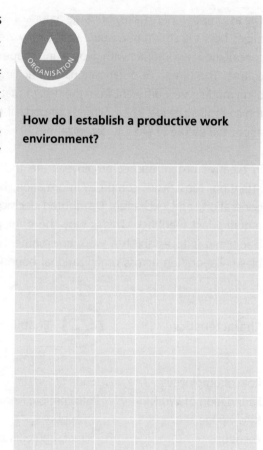

**How do I establish a productive work environment?**

# What assumptions about work determine my organization?

The assumptions we make about the nature of work determines how we structure accountability, how we organize control, how we interact with people and shape corporate culture. The design of organizations that achieve an enabling mode is very different from the design that facilitates the controlling mode. This is why it is important to be clear about the nature of work in organizations.

In creative organizations, employees are the centre of attention. Most work comprises information, knowledge generation, and exchange. Distributed decision-making requires fast feedback. This is why the primary task of leadership is to establish a work environment that enables collaboration across organizational boundaries with access to support from where the knowledge is. Controlling mode organizations are designed for efficiency. Centralized decision-making by management defines processes with workflows for materials. Employees are regarded a means of achieving production, guided by performance targets and tight control. The task of leadership is supervision and controlling goal achievement.

When the nature of work and organization fail to match, interferences hamper performance, prevent innovation, and lead to an inability to adapt to a changing environment. Hence, a 'virus-free' environment is vital to address the challenges of a turbulent environment.

| Characteristics |  Enabling mode: |  Controlling mode: |
|---|---|---|
| Role of employees | Ends | Means |
| Foundation of Work | Information, Knowledge | Material, process |
| Knowledge | Distributed | Concentrated, management |
| Feedback | Direct, immediate | Indirect, delayed |
| Purpose of leadership | Support | Supervision, control |
| Focus of control | Work | People |
| Location of control | Employee | Management |
| Leadership style | Collaboration | Command |
| **Principles** | **Self-organization** | **Bureaucracy** |

# The nature of work

## What interferences prevent productive work, greater agility and innovation?

Today, many organizations are still built on the principles of the controlling mode: a predominant control and comment style of operating. For organizations with dominant knowledge work, these principles lose their effectiveness or are useless altogether in a dynamic environment.

Typical interferences come from the following:

- **Detailed performance plans:** central guidance rather than self-organized work.
- **Process management:** tight control of flows rather than exchange of knowledge.
- **Abundance of key performance indicators (KPI):** detailed control rather than observation points for delegated decision-making.
- **Fixed budgets:** resource allocation based on pre-determined budgets rather than on demand for worthwhile projects.
- **Management by objectives:** bargaining for stretched goals rather than purpose and self-initiative.
- **Benchmarks for performance:** guidance for mediocrity rather t han what makes sense within the context.
- **Short-term goals:** focus on immediate returns rather than long-term value for stakeholder.

Today's turbulent environment requires organizations to adapt to new situations without delay. The challenge of keeping current customers happy and attracting new buyers requires organizations to innovate constantly.

Many of the management tools highlighted above were effective in a stable environment. When situations change fast, detailed plans require ongoing updating. By contrast tight processes and budgets that work on strict timelines cannot adapt and benchmarks direct the attention to the wrong things.

Removing such interferences is the priority when organizations move towards knowledge-based work, when agility is favoured over efficiency, or when innovation is required to stimulate growth.

# How do I establish strong accountability?

Questions around structure always start with accountability. When people are accountable, they are answerable for their own performance. This is why deciding on the structure of a new organization is not a democratic process. The principle decision regarding structure lies with the CEO. However, employees in 21st century organizations must have a deep understanding of what the organization is and how they can be successful (Simons, 2005). They must understand how they:

- Use resources effectively and efficiently
- Measure and report success
- Collaborate in the best way
- Use support for their own benefit

The focus of most organizational design is on job positions. Managers draw charts with 'boxes' of names. However, people come and go; systems and structures remain. Organizational design is the mechanism to structure authority and power through formal rights. Any structure requires the right of subordinates to, first, receive information, second, set specific goals and, third, influence the decisions of others. With rights come responsibilities. The right to receive information translates into responsibility for passing on information to the manager; the right to set goals involves responsibility for ensuring goals align with the organization's aims; and the right to influence involves responsibility for assisting others to support organizational purpose.

A new organization restructures responsibilities with different accountabilities and roles. Decisions and accountabilities for results are set in new places and with new people. These people are faced with the following questions:
- What resources do I control?
- What metrics are used to evaluate my performance?
- With whom do I have to collaborate and who influences my work?
- How much and what kind of support can I expect from others?

# Accountability

## Aligning structures, systems, leadership, and culture.

## Structures

**Resources**. Structural design follows positional clarity of strategy – the value proposition. The process starts with definition of the primary customer. Structure determines the resources available to serve clients. Organizational structure is the essential vehicle by which to place resources in the hands of responsible managers and employees.

Does structure clarify who the customer is?

Do I control few or many resources?

## Systems

**Metrics**. With clarity about unit structure, the task is to define the critical performance variables to support the implementation of the strategy.

A critical performance variable describes a state that must be achieved as part of strategy implementation on the way to success. Accountability requires clarity on the desired outcomes.

Does the structure strengthen accountability of individuals and teams?

Do my metrics allow few or many tradeoffs?

## Leadership

**Creative tension.** Structures and systems need a design that enables new ideas. Interactive networks are the means to facilitate the flow of information and knowledge to stimulate innovation.

One of the main purposes of an organization is to narrow people's focus and attention, but leaders must counterbalance the natural stability in any organization. This is why they need to interfere and create tension.

Does the structure facilitate or impede human interaction?

Do I need to interact within or across units to share and learn?

## Culture

**Commitment**. Structure, diagnostic systems, and leadership interaction in networks require people to collaborate and support each other.

Commitment requires the design of shared responsibilities embedded in corporate culture, with rights but also responsibilities, that hold people accountable for their responsibilities.

How do you reconcile the self-interest of people with the intent of the organization?

Do I have a strong commitment to helping others?

# How do I establish strong accountability?

Structure defines how accountability is distributed throughout an organization in line with a set of core processes that perform specific functions. Every organization performs all core processes. However, one of them usually dominates the others. What is your dominant core process?

**Operations**

**Examples:** Product and manufacturing. Such units produce and deliver products and services at best quality, lowest cost, and least amount of asset utilization. They want economies of scale, centralized and consolidated structures, and bargaining power for best practice exchange. However, resources may be far from what is required in this market, resulting in a lack of flexibility and speed.

**Customer**

**Examples:** Marketing and sales. These functions are responsible for top-line results. Their role is to identify customer needs, target profitable customers, market to these customers and translate transactions into lasting customer relationships. Such units prefer a high degree of autonomy for flexibility and speed with decentralized structures. However, this may result in duplicate functions and a lack of efficiency.

**Innovation**

**Examples:** Research and development. The purpose of this function is to develop new products and services to ensure clients return. Such units prefer horizontal structures, networks, Velcro-type arrangements, and favour collaboration to access information, knowledge and insights from within and outside the organization. However, the control of resources and outcomes is often a challenge.

**Support**

**Examples:** Development, governance, and service. Support functions combine organizational development, corporate governance and compliance, and shared services. They are functionally-orientated (such as HR, chief financial officer (CFO), communications, risk, legal) and prefer consolidated units for standardization and simplicity. However, resources may lack entrepreneurial spirit.

**Management**

**Example:** Corporate leadership. Its role is to establish, maintain, and develop the business by setting strategy, ensuring its implementation, and safeguarding the organization's assets.

Every organization creates boundaries. The design task is to limit the negative effects without increasing complexity. For example, organizing a business in divisions with adequate independence will always results in duplication of functions. Simplifying structures may reduce efficiency. Moreover, organizational design must allow teams to design their own structures while ensuring their reliability through shared standards and rigorous processes.

# Macro corporate structures

## The organization of accountability

Structural decisions usually follow strategy and have a variety of implications on the use of resources, performance measurement, creative tensions, and commitment. What is your dominant structure? What the implications on work design, systems, leadership, and culture?

| **Entrepreneurial organizations** | **Functional organizations** | **Profit-centred organizations** | **Segment organizations** |
|---|---|---|---|
| are driven by their dominant leader and entrepreneur. He or she is personally involved in business operations and makes most of the decisions. Functions are informally-and-flexibly-structured to remain agile. The organization's set-up reflects its small size and the need for creativity and growth. | are often of medium-size, established enterprises, managed by a small team of specialists. The CEO's role is to coordinate the various functions, to ensure collaboration, and limit autonomy. Often, these organizations face growing-pains. | are structured as a set of business units that span innovation, operations, and client facing processes. They are managed by a leadership team as a portfolio of business with assigned capital and strict performance targets. | are large, mature businesses that combine market and product combinations, often across various geographies, optimizing scale with local flexibility. As mature corporations, they develop a series of strong brands and combine the best mix of organizational features. |

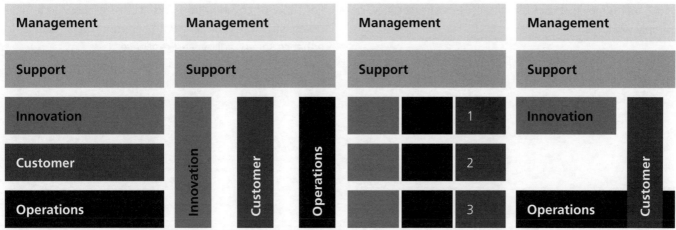

More often than not, your individual mix of projects, specialists, client segments, delivery mechanisms, and hierarchies will require a hybrid-type organization, combining macro corporate structures with micro work structures. Companies with less rigid cultures, multiple projects, and the need for agility and speed will choose some form of hybrid structure.

# How can I structure work for superior collaboration and knowledge sharing?

Corporate structures provide the 'grand design' for organizations, clarifying the alignment between account-abilities and strategy. However, hierarchies as top-down management structures and bureaucratic, vertical struc-tures are ineffective when people need to collaborate and access knowledge in networks. Organizational design is an important means of addressing speed, agility, and resilience. But central control structures have proven slow, inflexible, and fragile when it comes to changes in the en-vironment. Hence, we need to find the means of strength-ening accountability while at the same time allowing de-velopment of structures without the negative side-effects of silos such as duplication, inefficiencies, and blockages to knowledge sharing.

One of the promising solutions is to couple central corporate structures loosely with decentralized, self-organized teams. Such teams may be business units, centres of excellence, or simply work teams.

Network-type organizations, with hubs as cell-like struc-tures, guide the general model where decisions are made close to the market by sensing trends and responding flex-ibly to the needs of clients. Such natural structures should remain small to facilitate interactions and enhance trust. Rather than being functional jobs, they promote a gen-eralist's view. Moreover, networks establish strong bonds through shared values and principles. Managers take on roles as energizers, catalysts, and enablers.

So, how do you structure your business, organization or team? Tips, ways of thinking about it, and recommendations are readily available. The most prominent criteria are in line with strategy, the environment, context, clients, products, or size. My favorite is people. Different people need differ-ent structures with which to work.

For superior collaboration and access to knowledge, cor-porate structures combine with network type structures to enhance speed, agility, and resilience.

# Micro work structures

## Network-type structures

**The problem:** functional bureaucracies and hierarchies:
- Lack of speed: it takes too long to respond.
- Lack of agility: solutions are bound to central control.
- Lack of resilience: limited relationships and collaboration; purpose comes from the centre.

**The solution:** loosely-coupled network structures around a central core. Such organizations are fast-responders due to units that are closer to the market and centred on value creation. Such units are agile, sense opportunities and respond flexibly. Relationships and collaboration enhance overall resilience. Purpose comes from the client.

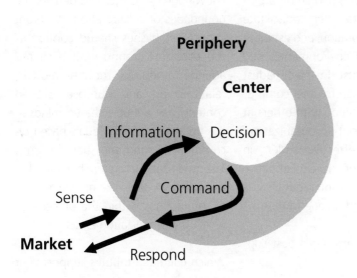

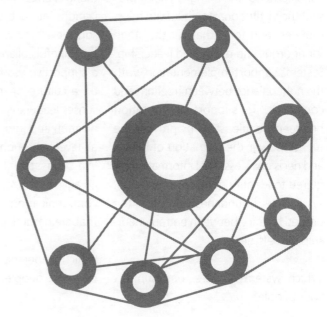

# How do I organize for superior agility and innovation?

The performance triangle model presents an organizational design framework representing the operating environment of an organization, linking people with leadership, systems, and culture.

## Systems

Systems are located at the lower right-hand corner of the triangle. They represent the institutional toolbox with rules, routines, and tools that set the stage for rigorous and disciplined leadership. Systems support implementation, with the right balance between freedom and constraint. To support collaboration between people, systems provide the fuel to power the formation of beliefs and decisions – essential information required to identify purpose. In addition, systems set boundaries to achieve the desired balance between entrepreneurship and efficiency.

Which systems features best support your people?

## Leadership

Leadership is a key component of the triangle. Effective leaders in agile organizations interact with people on a personal level, relate to others to facilitate meaningful collaboration, and establish a supportive work environment based on a culture of trust. In the broadest sense, leadership is effective communication and interaction with others at all levels, throughout an organization. We suggest that effective leaders, in an agile organization, develop effective communication and interaction skills that are natural and unique to them.

Which leadership attributes best support your people?

## Culture

The culture of an organization creates shared context, enables or inhibits knowledge exchange, and defines the boundaries of collaboration. A vibrant culture establishes shared context as the common ground with a shared agenda, language, thought models, relationships, and purpose. Shared context is all about a shared mindset, the behaviour of individuals based on common thinking and shared norms. The organizational culture becomes the invisible force that, like gravity, shapes all interactions within the universe in which the organization exists.

Which cultural attributes support your people best?

# The foundation for innovation

## The performance triangle model with systems, leadership, and culture

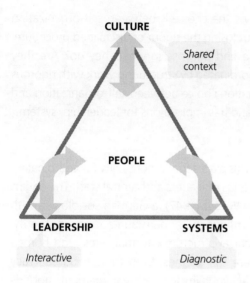

CULTURE

*Shared context*

PEOPLE

LEADERSHIP

*Interactive*

SYSTEMS

*Diagnostic*

Culture, leadership, and systems frame the corners of the triangle. Superior decision-making and effective actions require a culture that creates shared context. Leadership needs to be interactive and to facilitate the conversation around purpose, direction, and performance. Systems that work diagnostically, direct attention to those aspects that matter most and allow for self-directed action on deviations from the chosen path. Shared context, intense interactions, and diagnostic controls make organizations agile. They help people to detect weak signals early, allow for the interpretation of that information, and facilitate timely action. These are the features of an agile organization and the foundation for superior innovation.

**Systems**. Diagnostic systems represent the organizational toolbox with rules, routines, and tools for disciplined leadership. They represent the organization's control framework. Diagnostic controls work as closed loops and establish standards, information exchange, and feedback.

**Leadership**. In the broadest sense, leadership is interactive multi-directional communication encouraging people to collaborate. Interactions are the mechanisms by which people search, monitor, and exchange products and services. Interactions and communications are the tools of behavioural control.

**Culture**. The shared context and mindset shapes culture and enables knowledge exchange. It reflects and shapes the thoughts, decisions, behaviours, and actions of people.

The three elements of the triangle set the stage for 'knowledge people' to use their creativity as a means of achieving higher levels of innovation throughout the organization. There is a strong link between knowledge work and innovation (Tabscott and Williams, 2008). Innovation is directly related to value-creation in firms (Highsmith, 2009:31). Moreover, there is no doubt that innovation is important for the survival of any firm (Davila, 2006). Hence, organizations with people that create knowledge should focus their strategy on innovation. Systems, leadership and culture should create an environment in which people are able to use their creativity and knowledge.

# How do I coordinate work?

The coordination of work follows two principles that are not mutually exclusive: the choice is between self-organization and bureaucracy. The challenge is to facilitate delegated decision-making without losing the rigour of disciplined procedure. Do managers create an environment in which people collaborate? Do people find purpose in what they do? Are they encouraged to use their initiative? Or, do managers believe activities must be coordinated by structuring work with rigorous processes that tell people what and how things ought to be done? The coordination choice between self-organization and bureaucracy builds on a different set of assumptions about the nature of work and has implications for leadership, systems, and culture.

**Self-organization.** With this model, the primary responsibility for coordinating work lies with teams or individuals. Self-organization is all about spontaneous, self-initiated coordination by individuals or teams. It is obvious that delegated decision-making and self-organization go hand-in-hand. They enable agile and fast responses to challenges in a dynamic environment. A prerequisite for self-organization is that it requires guidance and structures that enable individuals to coordinate work without being distracted in all directions.

Self-organization is not about letting things go or losing control. Herman Haken's theory of the collaboration of elements within complex structures and dynamic systems states that collaboration and self-organization require constant outside energy (Haken, 1982). This means leaders should constantly invest time and attention in making self-organization and coordination work effectively in organizations. Self-organizing is not the same as self-directing. It is the task of management to provide direction for self-organized work. Moreover, complex systems can only self-organize when there is a boundary around it – the 'self' (Eoyang and Conway, 1999).

**Bureaucracy.** This places the responsibility for coordinating work into the hands of leaders and central staff. The origins go back to Max Weber (1947), a German sociologist, with his renowned writings on modern bureaucracy. Authority, control, hierarchical structures, formal rules, and human interactions were the themes. Even though bureaucracy has become the synonym for bad management, nobody would disagree with the need for efficiency through disciplined control, rigorous processes, clear rules, and simple coordination. The problem with bureaucracy is that it takes the individual, flexible, and fast approaches out of systems. This is especially challenging in a knowledge-driven work environment where creativity is required.

It is important to note that bureaucracies that force people to adhere to a set of principles, or that provide them with a set of methodologies and tools for consistent services, are needed in most organizations. The challenge with bureaucracy is less its existence than its interpretation by managers.

# Organization design principles

## The choice between self-organization and bureaucracy

The policy choice between self-organization and standardization is a choice of how businesses coordinate work. It has implications for how we interact and how we design systems:

**Individualization:** Coordination is the result of individuals taking the initiative. It promotes people to use initiative within clear organizational boundaries, supported by leaders who keep energy levels high.

**Markets/networks:** Coordination happens via competitive situations or networks. People are encouraged to contribute without the control of supervisors. This assumes there is sufficient choice and time to engage in projects when and where competencies are required.

**Formalization:** Leaders coordinate via structures and standardized procedures. This requires clarity of outcomes and transparency around the available competencies for specific initiatives.

In the new era, what can I do to promote self-organization without losing the benefits of bureaucracy?

**As an individual**
- Search for those areas where your initiative is appreciated and where you can add value.
- 

**As an organization**
- Create opportunities to self-organize through distinct projects and initiatives where creativity and knowledge are required.

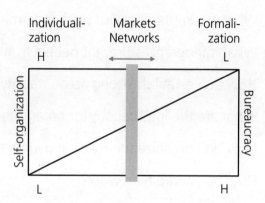

# How do I establish an organization built for people?

What assumptions about work determine the nature of my organization?

What interferences prevent people from delivering productive work?

How do I establish strong accountability?

What are the implications for organizational structure of work design?

How do I organize for agility and innovation?

How do I coordinate work?

# How do I establish a productive work environment?

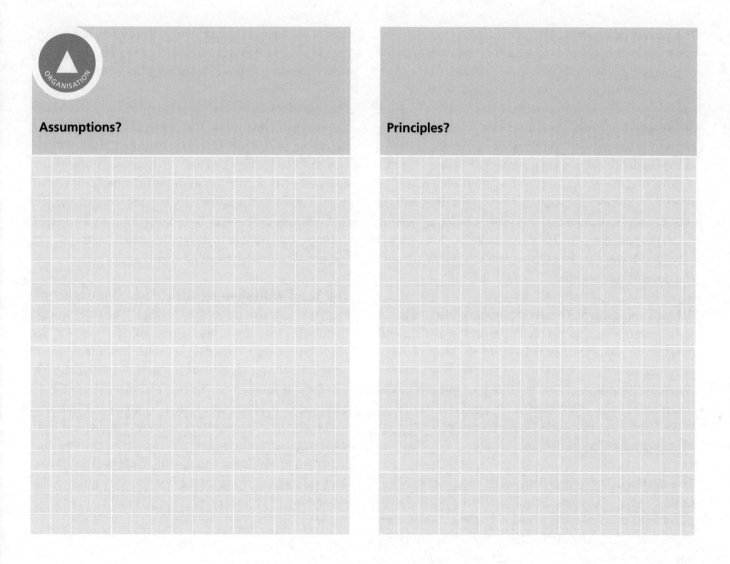

ORGANISATION

**Assumptions?**

**Principles?**

# From ongoing change to a superior ability to act

**The power of experts.** After restructuring his team, the newly-appointed leader of a global functional department of a major bank, with 500 employees located in every part of the world, decided to call in his leadership team for a strategy workshop to plan next steps. The complete renewal of this expert function was a deliberate decision following ongoing problems with line divisions conducting business at the border or beyond legal constraints. It was well recognized that the expert function had insufficient power to interfere in or overrule specific business deals. They had no ability to act in a culture that was toxic, with faulty systems leading to poor decisions. Hence, the new structure was the initial step toward increased power for this central support and governance function.

**Balance and control.** The ultimate purpose of a functional staff department is to design, implement, maintain, and manage the managerial systems of a firm. Most of these departments have to balance their support role with the demands of governance. To rebalance their role, the global leader called in his 25 top experts for a two-day workshop in the Swiss Alps. He needed to boost control over his inherited group of 'prima donnas'.

**The setting.** The instructions were clear: bring warm clothes and sturdy shoes. Shortly after landing in Zürich, the individuals were asked to take the train to a mountain village two hours away. From there, a postal bus (one per day) took them to a remote out-post where some people saw snow for the first time in their lives. They were then required to undertake a one-hour walk, each pulling a sled loaded with their luggage, to reach the mountain cabin,. Imagine a New York banker, a Singapore relationships manager and a German lawyer finding themselves in a remote area in which there was no signal for mobile phones and where the electricity was switched off after 9pm.

**Change of mindset.** The purpose of this exercise was clear and not up for discussion. The usual blame culture ("it was the others' fault") had to cease immediately. It was the only way to force the team to look at systems and members' approaches to leadership in order to completely rebuild ways of doing things. It was clear that this required a setting that was very different to the comfort of a banking office in Zürich. The aim was to gain some understanding of 'real life' and what banking was all about.

**The Team Workshop** provided a clear structure for the meeting: diagnosis rather than 'recipes'. The team worked through its diagnostic results presenting something like a shared mindset regarding its role. This strengthened accountability for its part in the overall organization. In essence it amounted to: creating and maintaining the organization's management system in a way that prevents the organization from getting back into trouble. The Team Workshop succeeded in bringing 'prima donnas' together to make a true difference to the future of the organization. And, for some, sledding for the first time was a memorable experience.

# Example: Functional department of a Global Bank I Switzerland

## Re-establishing a common glue

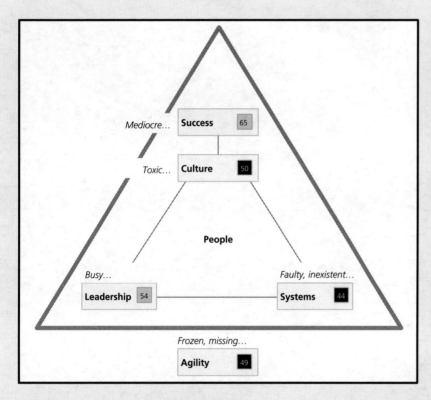

Mediocre... **Success** 65

Toxic... **Culture** 50

**People**

Busy... **Leadership** 54

Faulty, inexistent... **Systems** 44

Frozen, missing...

**Agility** 49

H   High scores: above average

M   Medium scores: average

L   Low scores: below average

Many traditional banks have experienced tremendous challenges in past years and it is not surprising to decode a pattern that is characteristic rather than unique. This is what the results of the diagnostic exercise mean:

- Positive financial results do not reflect the overall lack of success of the firm. Mediocrity prevails.
- A toxic culture prevents the organization from operating on automatic pilot. Too many interferences require leadership interventions resulting in a limited shared mindset.
- Busy leadership constantly runs on 'exception' mode, fixing some of the errors that the organization produces.
- The cause of many of these problems resides in poorly-designed managerial systems: the rules, routines, and tools leaders use to do their work.
- Overall agility is low or absent, resulting in an inability to cope with higher dynamics and changes in regulation and markets.

"Goals can provide some guidance – assuming that those that have set them put some thought in them!" - Peter Drucker

## Where does the energy come from?

# STAKEHOLDERS

## Stakeholder relationships as the sources of resilience and growth in a connected world

The 'stakeholder frame' defines the needs and expectations of an organization's constituents and provides a means of establishing its purpose. Organizations serve a variety of stakeholders: employees, clients, owners, suppliers, community, regulators, and many others. Stakeholder needs and wants are the starting point for an organization's mission and its goals. The way in which leaders establish the goals of their organizations, as a choice between broad direction and detailed performance targets, determines much of the relationship between stakeholders, how resources are allocated, and the nature of the development of the organization.

In a connected world beyond the boundaries of organizations, relationships, collaboration, and purpose are the bonding elements for superior resilience: the ability to withstand external changes and shocks. Connectivity becomes the primary means by which people to learn in organizations and connectivity stimulates growth.

- What assumptions about relationships determine my organization's goals?
- What interferences prevent people from seizing opportunities?
- How do we establish a strong mission?
- How do we establish an environment for high resilience and growth?
- How do I set goals?

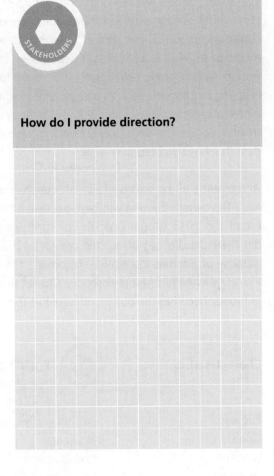

**How do I provide direction?**

# What assumptions about relationships determine my goals?

The assumptions we make about the nature of value-creation differ widely between the enabling mode and the controlling mode. These choices determine the nature of relationships with stakeholders, the purpose of the organization, and how we collaborate. The move towards the enabling mode represents a paradigm shift in management, whereas improvements within the assumptions of the controlling mode compare to spring cleaning; wiping away the dust that has collected over time.

At the centre of this shift is an age-old question: who comes first? The current thinking was best articulated by the speakers of the 2013 Global Drucker Forum in Vienna. What did Peter Drucker say about the priority? "The only valid purpose of a firm is to create a customer." The renowned Irish author and business philosopher, Charles Handy added: 'If money becomes the point, you have lost the point." The

mission becomes important. Steve Denning confirmed that "the purpose of an organization's mission is to provide purpose for its employees; to provide value for the very people who inhabit the walls and its organizational mission." Rick Goings, CEO of Tupperware, said: "Purpose is the glue that holds people together," and Tim Brown, CEO and president of IDEO, concluded: "An organization that thrives on a sense of purpose attracts talent naturally."

Regardless of your primary choice of stakeholder, it is important that your values and mission clearly communicate that priority. When the 'audio does not match the video', interferences prevent people collaborating, connecting, and finding purpose. Hence, a 'virus-free' environment is essential for coping with the challenges of a turbulent environment.

| Characteristics |  Enabling mode: | Controlling mode: |
|---|---|---|
| Purpose | Profitable client value | Shareholder Value |
| Goals | Resilience | Competitive advantage |
| Learning | Collaboration | Efficiency as the goal |
| Feedback | Multi-directional networks | Directional value chains |
| Control | Shared accountability | Steep hierarchies |
| Routine | Disciplined innovation | Control & bureaucracy |
| Relationships | Stakeholder relationships | Mechanistic leadership |
| **Principles** | **Broad direction** | **Performance goals** |

# Client value

## What interferences prevent people from seizing opportunities?

Knowledge-type organizations put people at the centre of attention, with the mission to add value for clients. However, the current reality in many organizations looks different. A variety of studies on employee engagement and satisfaction provide sufficient proof.

Typical findings show interference at alarming levels:

- Only 13% of employees believe they have trusted relationships at work. "How come trust-based industries such as banking and insurance firms don't have the trust from their employees?" John Hagel asked, in his speech at the 2013 Global Drucker Forum. "Organizations are failing people on humanistic terms." An absence of trust translates to a lack of speed.
- The AgilityINSights work with clients indicates that just 20% of employees have goals that are aligned with those of the organization. These are signs that classic management buy-outs don't serve the purpose in two ways: they fail to create 'pull' towards the mission and fail to help people find purpose. Missing direction prevents delegated decision-making.
- Statistics vary, but between 5% and 37% of employees know what their organization stands for: the lack of purpose has a direct link to motivation (Kaplan and Norton, 2006; Sprenger, 2010; Gallup, 2013). Purpose is a prerequisite for self-responsibility as an important source of motivation. Absent purpose means unused potential.
- A lack of collaboration tops most employee surveys: it is no secret that obstacles from a silo-type mentality prevent people working together, not just within, but also with, partners outside the organization. A lack of collaboration results in inefficiencies and work that does not get done.
- An alarming three-quarters of managers demotivate employees: faulty systems present abundant negative side-effects (Sprenger, 2010). An absence of motivation means poor performance.
- Only 11% of employees are passionate about work: it is time to rethink fundamentally the way in which we work. Speaking at the Drucker Forum 2013, Tim Brown, CEO of IDEO, said: "Fear-based environments kill any innovation."

As highlighted in a Deloitte study (2013), today's connected world requires an environment in which people find purpose, in which they can collaborate across organizational boundaries, and in which they build trusted relationships within and outside of the organization. Growth requires people to take risks and seize opportunities. Removing these 'viruses' establishes favourable conditions for growth; getting there requires more than just 'spring-cleaning'.

# How do I energize the organization?

**Expectations and contributions.** Stakeholders have expectations of organizations: investors want returns, clients expect quality products, employees expect employment. At the same time, stakeholders provide organizations with resources: investors provide capital, clients generate profit, and employees offer 'hands and hearts'. Value-creation in every organization requires the best match between stakeholder needs and their contributions to the organization. In reverse, stakeholders provide the resources that the organization need to conduct business.

Stakeholders are the source of purpose and the starting point for articulating organizational goals.

**Employees**. We put people first. This is why we have dedicated a distinct frame to people. People are involved in enacting strategy. While technology can help improve productivity, it cannot replace the knowledge and skills of people. People represent the collective intellectual capital with knowledge, skills, abilities, and motives – scarce resources in most organizations.

**Customers**. Without customers there is no business; work, without a customer, is no work. This is why customers are the inspiration for employees to do a good job. Customer want high levels of 'fast, right, cheap, and easy'. In return, the organization wants customers to trust it, to share information, and to allow it to achieve profitable growth. Labeling everyone a customer distorts the purpose of any organization. The choice of primary customer is the person or group the organization is designed to serve. It is important to limit that choice to those constituents that transact with the organization through markets.

**Investors**. Are they more important than customers? It is a frequent, but pointless, debate. It is more important to align values with your choice of 'primary customer'. Again, profit is a necessary condition for the existence of a (for-profit) business and not a means in itself.

**Suppliers**. Just about every organization has one or more suppliers. The nature of the relationship the organization has with its suppliers is the reverse of the one it has with clients. The decision regarding suppliers is a strategic decision that should not be left solely to the purchasing department.

**Supervision and community**. All organizations are subject to regulatory requirements. Regulators and the public are important stakeholders that influence the decisions and behaviours of managers. Pressure groups increasingly influence public opinion with an effect on reputation.

# Organizational goals

## Stakeholders as the origin of goals

The conversation about goals starts with two questions:
- What are my stakeholder's needs? What do I provide them with?
- What are my stakeholders' contributions? What do I need from them?

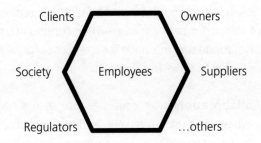

The following table serves as a list of ideas to initiate the conversation. The answers to the questions lead directly to organizational goals. The answers provide the key elements of your organization's mission.

The priority of the goals and statement is to communicate the things stakeholders value.

| Stakeholder | Needs | Contributions |
|---|---|---|
| Employees | Purpose, care, skills and pay | Hands, hearts, minds and voices |
| Customers | Fast, right, cheap and easy | Profit, growth, opinion and trust |
| Investors | Returns, rewards, figures and faith | Capital, credit, risk and support |
| Suppliers | Profit, growth, opinion, trust | Fast, right, cheap and easy |
| Supervision | Legal, fair, safe, true | Rules, reasons, clarity and advice |
| Public | Communities, jobs, fidelity, integrity, wealth | Image, skills, suppliers and support |

# How do I establish an environment that nurtures high resilience and growth?

Collaboration, purpose, and relationship represent the sides of the performance triangle. Their configuration for the enabling mode sets the stage for a resilient organization with the potential to grow from within.

**Collaboration** is an issue because of the complexity that increases with size. We keep adding functions, geographies, departments, services, client groups, and other structures to our organizations. In a complex and networked world, where knowledge matters, collaboration is more important than ever. Every structure creates barriers between people that need to work together, such as limited or distorted information flows. In addition, the very fundamental cooperation problem of employees and organizations having different, often conflicting, goals, needs to be resolved.

What does my organization do to facilitate collaboration?

**Purpose** connects systems and cultures to people. But "there is no administrative production of purpose" in the words of Jürgen Habermas (1988). What we often hear when the climate changes is: "When we lost sight of the purpose of our work, we started a discussion on motivation." When people experience their work as meaningful, they contribute with greater energy; they are physically, mentally, and emotionally fully-present. Purpose is created individually, subjectively. It is always 'me' that provides purpose to the world. It is called sense-making not sense-giving. Purpose cannot be delivered. It needs to be found or 'produced' individually.

What does my organization do to sense-make?

**Relationships** are the cornerstones of every business transaction. In individualized people-to-people relationship businesses, trust and agreement between employees and the organization is essential to the relationships with external stakeholders. As such, 'relationship capital' is essential to the value of a firm. But good relationships come at a price. They impose a challenge on every leader in organizations. Relationships also refer to connectivity. The greater the number of connections among people in an organization, the more restrictions and boundaries they place on one another. This limits their freedom of movement and their ability to perform (Stacey, 2000). This means relationships and connectivity must be tuned to an optimum level.

What does my organization do to enable trusted relationships?

# The prerequisite for growth

## Deep sense of purpose, trusted relationships and collaboration

**Purpose**, **relationships**, and **collaboration** connect the corners of the performance triangle. They are the bonding elements of every organization. For superior decisions, knowledge-work requires purpose. It is the driving force behind motivation.

'Knowledge employees' use internal and external relationships to share and expand their knowledge to create value for clients. Only knowledge that is shared and applied has value for any organization. New technologies facilitate the transfer of knowledge in a way that generates new knowledge.
Any knowledge-related task in an organization requires more than one individual for its completion. It is the combined knowledge and the shared experiences of collaboration that stimulate creativity, innovation, and growth.

**Resilience** results from a deep sense of purpose, trusted relationships among stakeholders, and collaboration to share knowledge. With these capabilities, organizations have a better chance of withstanding external shocks and change.

Moreover, this kind of working environment, paired with clarity of mission and goals, is a prerequisite for superior organizational development and growth.

# How do I establish goals?

Goals are an important communications tool among stakeholders. Goals articulate stakeholder preferences and provide indications of performance and growth. The nature of goal-orientation determines much of the relationship between an organization and its stakeholders.

Directing work in organizations follows two principles that are not mutually exclusive: broad direction and goal orientation. The challenge is to clarify goals and direction without becoming bogged-down in too much detail.

Do your managers pursue an oblique approach creating a framework with high-level and long-term directional and performance objectives? Or, do they determine a clear set of short-term goals for the organization? The goal-setting choice between broad direction and goal orientation has implications for how work gets done.

**Broad direction.** The foundation of this principle is obliquity (Kay, 2010). It assumes that goals are often achieved when pursued indirectly. Obliquity refers to the fact that many of today's problems are uncertain, complex, or 'wicked-like'[3] (Rittel and Webber, 1973; Courtney, 2008; Camilius, 2008). Circumstances change, rendering fixed goals obsolete faster than we appreciate. One way out is the model of broad direction. The challenge of indirect goals is that they need to be something to which people can relate. A broad strategy or vision helps employees to bridge their own agenda with an overarching goal. Broad direction does not mean performance does not matter. On the contrary, it requires organizations to measure performance on all aspects that matter. Often, organizations use 'meaning' when they talk about 'extrinsic motivated purpose'.

**Performance goals.** This model favours the alignment of goals, performance indicators and strategies. Alignment refers to the fit of one goal, with others based on a hierarchy of goals, or the need for collaboration (Kaplan and Norton, 2006; Labovitz and Rosansky, 1977). The idea is that everyone in the organization works towards common objectives. Alignment assumes individuals and organizations have the same agenda. However, it is well accepted that people are driven by their own inner purpose not by detailed performance contracts. Moreover, alignment requires objectives; measures that combine with incentives to block out everything that is not specifically included. Often, short-term perspectives with a shareholder-view prevail. This does not mean alignment is an inferior concept. Being aware of its consequences allows organizations to use the model in the correct context. Goals clearly relate to extrinsically motivated purpose.

---

[3] Wicket refers to problems that are hard to solve because information is incomplete and contradictory in a context where requirements often change.

# Relationship design principles

## The choice between direction and goals

The choice between broad direction and goal orientation determines the policy for establishing goals. It has implications for how we interact and design managerial decision-making systems:

**Purpose**: A broad set of objectives guides behaviours, actions, and decisions to enable people to align their ambitions with the goals of the organization.

**Direction**: Formal, long-term strategy, vision, and mission statements guide people. They leave room for individual alignment without the rigour of detailed performance goals.

**Targets**: Detailed, short-term performance targets prevail. They assume people align their personal objectives tightly with those of the organization.

In the new era, what can I do to promote broad direction without losing the essence of detailed goals?

**As an individual:**
- Search for goals that match your deep sense of purpose.

**As an organization:**
- Scan your organization's approach to management-by-objectives and unclutter those things that get in peoples' way.

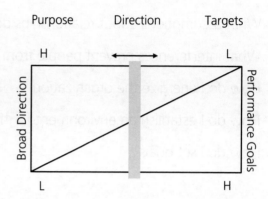

# How do I establish relationships for the right purpose?

What assumptions about relationships determine my organization's goals?

What interferences prevent people from seizing opportunities?

How do I energize the organization

How do I establish an environment for high resilience and growth?

How do I set goals?

# How do I provide direction?

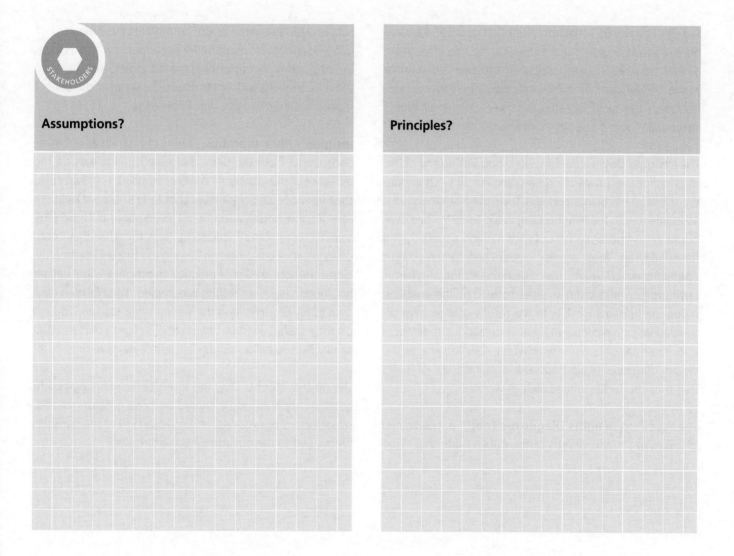

**Assumptions?**

**Principles?**

# The need for collaboration

At regular intervals, I organize INsights Days in various locations around the globe. One autumn, three executives from a retail bank in Sri Lanka attended the two-day seminar in the Middle East. All three participants performed independently the 'executive education' version of the INsights Diagnostic Tools™ prior to attending the seminar.

The **INsights Day** is a flexible, workshop setting and public offering for executives of organizations of all kinds. Before the event, participants conduct their own organizational assessment with the INsights Diagnostic Tools™. Their own business case becomes part of their individual work during the workshop. After a brief introduction to the current operating environment, the requirements for a dynamic environment, and what it takes to lead in the enabling mode, participants work with the results of their own organization to gain deeper insights, learn about interferences and potential, and determine where to intervene in the system. Participants work towards a 'laundry list' of issues that they can tackle immediately at work.

The Education **INsights Diagnostic Tool™** is a dedicated assessment for participants of the public leadership seminars on Management Design. It translates the INsights Days into a development platform for participants with their own business cases. By performing the diagnostic tool, they can share their results with peers during the seminar and benefit from the shared insights and knowledge.

**Insights rather than tips**. During the seminar, the three participants from the bank discovered their views on the resilience of the organization were comparable. In particular, their view of collaboration was not truly a surprise but initiated a conversation about what to do about it. During the seminar, they started collecting ideas for what they could do to improve collaboration among the three departments. Unsurprisingly, the list of practical things they could initiate got longer as the workshop progressed. They formed their own study group during the seminar and started working on their shared agenda. The setting created a mindset that simply illuminated a valuable corporate development path.

During the INsights Day, the three participants agreed to continue the work on a shared purpose, intense collaboration across boundaries, and open-access to relationships within and to the outside for the entire staff.

# Example: Retail bank I Sri Lanka

## Connecting related parts

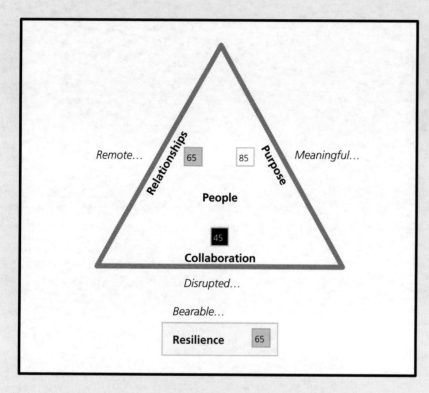

Three bankers merge their individual assessments to discover a high degree of overlap. This is what the aggregate result of their individual diagnostic exercise means:

- A high degree of purpose with lots of meaning for its people.
- Somewhat remote relationships indicating barriers around how people share and expand their knowledge through networks within and outside of the organization.
- Disrupted – or as they called it, inexistent – collaboration among the departments.

Resilience can be improved simply by fixing some of the collaboration issues. As the bank has successfully survived the past 50 years, the focus is solely on the collaborative element of resilience.

H | High scores: above average

M | Medium scores: average

L | Low scores: below average

Some things change faster than others. Some changes are visible, others are not. A glacier changes as we observe it, but for us to notice the change requires a long-term observation.

# How do I manage change?

# ENVIRONMENT

## The foundation for a high managerial ability to act in an uncertain era

The environmental frame defines much of how an organization operates, how it delivers performance, and how it adapts to cope with the challenges of the future.

There is no doubt that the current operating environment has changed for many organizations. Leaders are challenged by a 'wicked-like' (Rittel and Webber 1973, Courtney 2008, Camillius 2008) problem of how to deal with an uncertain future and concurrently meet the requirements of Generation Y with new ways of working supported by collaborative technologies. In line with Katz and Kahn (1987), "Changes in the environment have consequences for the internal setup of organizations." As humans, we are often our own biggest obstacle to change and interference in performance. The starting point for the scope of your organization's transformation into the enabling mode is the strategy and the required competencies to cope with the environment. Organizations with a high ability to act effectively use the knowledge of their people and combine this with dynamic capabilities to address challenges.

One of the fundamental choices that leaders have is whether they continue to use interfering, recurring change projects to adapt to the new era or build the capabilities for a superior ability to act. It is a choice between the principles of standardization or flexibility. The challenge is to go beyond that choice in order to establish an environment for superior performance.

- What assumptions about the environment determine my approach to change?
- What interferences prevent people from performing at their peak?
- What are the implications of your strategy for change?
- What are the competencies needed for change?
- What is the scope and nature of my organization's transformation?
- How do I establish an environment that provides a high ability to act?

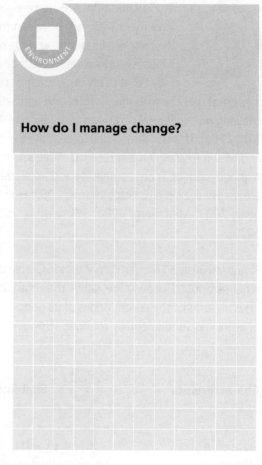

**How do I manage change?**

# What assumptions about the environment determine my approach to change?

The assumptions we make about the environment may vary between markets, industries, organizations, and the perceptions of leaders. However, there is a high agreement that many organizations operate in a 'hyperturbulent' environments (McCann and Selsky, 1984), challenging traditional corporate management (Emery and Trist, 1965). This has threatened to destroyed organizations and, in some cases, it has succeeded. Adequate responses to higher dynamics, more complexity and accelerated change are readily available (Castrogiovanni, 2002; Huy and Mintzberg, 2003; Mintzberg, 1994; Selksy et al, 2006; Stacey, 1999).

Simultaneously, in modern organizations, most of the work requires applied knowledge rather than the physical routines in terms of the contributions of its people. The nature of work has fundamentally changed. However, the results from my research indicate that the average organization uses only 67% of its talent effectively. This seems odd, given the scarcity of talent and a huge opportunity for improvement.

Technology contributes to the pace of change by enabling remote working, collaboration, and access to knowledge as never before. Education for modern talent has further removed knowledge asymmetries to eliminate the justification for traditional central control structures and the separation of thinking and doing.

It becomes clear that most business need to operate in both modes: the stable mode to manufacture goods and services; and the dynamic mode to access new markets and remain competitive. The challenge is to do both simultaneously in the same organization. Stress and tension is obvious when operating modes clash.

| Characteristics |  Enabling mode: |  Controlling mode: |
| --- | --- | --- |
| State of World | Complex and unordered | Order exists |
| Interactions | Infinite, networked | Finite elements, linear |
| Future view | Unpredictable | Predictable |
| Solutions | Emerging and self-organized | Predetermined, imposed |
| Institutions | Hubs and spokes | Traditional organizations |
| Management | Curate conditions | Create vision and implement |
| Approach | Emergence | Planning |
| **Principles** | **Flexibility** | **Standardization** |

# Four trends

## What interferences prevent people from performing at their peak?

Higher volatility, increasing complexity, greater uncertainty, and increasing ambiguities characterize the new dynamic era. These four trends affect us as individuals, with implications for how we manage our organizations. "In a dynamic environment, it becomes obvious that initiative, freedom to decide, innovation, and risk-taking become more important as compared to organizations in a stable environment with budgets (Kilman et al, 1995)."

**Higher volatility is norm.** Globalization, speed, real-time processes, faster decisions, synchronization, and immediate responses are required.

But when control fails, we implement more of it. We tighten the tools and reinforce alignment.

**Complexity increases with size.** Self-inflected complexity is the result of more of everything: the number of employees, places in which to operate, products on the shelf, segments we serve, functions that perform, stakeholders with interests.

But when we lack clarity, we ask for additional detail and more precise processes. We introduce additional bureaucracy.

**Uncertainty challenges strategy.** Shorter life cycles, less stable results, higher dependencies, more transparency, and higher reputation risks with sudden appearances challenge stability.

But when uncertainty rises, we second guess ourselves, mistrust people, and limit delegation. We give orders and prevent the use of knowledge.

**Ambiguity requires choice.** Rules of the game change, markets evolve, certainties dissolve, industries merge and change, loyalty vanishes, taboos are broken, and boundaries blur.

But when ambiguity creeps up, we set new rules and limit the degrees of freedom. We reinforce stability because we know how to deal with that.

Our normalized reactions to these challenges are human in nature, but not very effective when reflection is required. With higher challenges, we re-act (activate the sensory cortex of our brain) as the reflexive mode of operation. As a consequence, we lack sufficient energy to use the prefrontal cortex of the brain (the CEO). Hence, in challenging times, leaders need reflexive capacity and time to think rather than ineffective, knee-jerk reaction. We need flexible approaches to cope with change.

# In which environment do I operate?

Traditional organizations tend to resist change and are slow at implementing change. Traditional change, looking at something separate to a normal mode of operation, is in question. Change is seen as a reaction to its environment. Yet this view is being challenged (Kerber and Buono, 2005; McCann 2004; Weick and Quinn, 1999). A more proactive and deliberate approach to achieve competitive advantage demands continuous or fast change (Brown and Eisenhardt 1998; D'Aveni, 1999; Iansiti and Levien, 2004; Normann and Ramirez, 1993; Peters, 1987; Porter 1985). Discontinuity, as an unexpected disruption in the form of a disaster, crisis, or catastrophe needs to be considered (Beck, 2002; Mitroff and Alpaslan, 2003; Nathan and Kovoor-Misra, 2002).

In past, stable times, organizations implemented change programmes to prepare for external changes that normally escaped the strategy (Kerber and Buono, 2005) . Traditional change focused on coaching individual leaders personal behaviours and team-based approaches (Covey 1989; Mohrman et al, 1995; Senge, 1990;). Others relied on organizational design and alignment with strategy (Christensen and Overdorf, 2000; Galbraith, 1995; Nadler and Tushman, 1988, Porter, 1985). Moreover, culture change was emphasized to bridge organizational and individual interventions (Beer and Nohira, 2000; Gilmore et al, 1997; Molinsky, 1999). It is no secret that traditional approaches fail to perform in turbulent times because it is change that has changed.

Today, organizations need to balance the ongoing tension between stability and dynamics (March, 1991; D'Aveni, 1999). The challenge is to combine them in a meaningful way. Change is highly context-specific and depends both on the environment and the organization (Bennett A and Bennett D, 2004). In dynamic markets, it is essential to generate new insights and knowledge fast. At the same time, leaders need to manage their ongoing operation. For both, there is need for innovation in management.

The distinction between management in times of stability and dynamic situations helps us to clarify our minds on the fundamental choices between one-step change and continuous change. Stability relates to management that facilitates standardization and efficiency. In dynamic times, with ongoing, disruptive change, we need flexibility with managerial principles that facilitate ongoing change. As we will see, we may need to go beyond that choice to succeed in turbulent times.

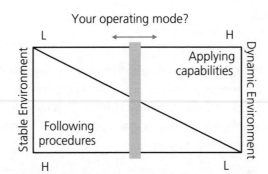

# Stability & dynamics

## The case for strategic competence management

We know from 'path dependence' effects, in social sciences and economics with roots in physics, that a likely development is not the result of a plan, as much as the combination of all possible paths. Path dependence explains that a set of decisions managers face for any given context is limited by their experiences, even though circumstances may have changed. As such, using the same approaches over-and-over again for strategy, planning, and implementation creates the path-effect or 'lock-in'. It limits our thinking about new ways of doing things.

Strategy is hard to identify, as it has to hit a moving target. This means that we have to build managerial competencies to address a changing future. We need tools to manage in an uncertain future and to support the transition into the enabling mode. This means simultaneously managing for stability and dynamic situations. This cannot be accomplished by a new set of linear tools. T. W. Gallwey (2000), author of The Inner Game of Work, points out that: "Following procedures is not the same as applying competencies."

Competencies represent the capability view of an organization (Eisenhard and Martin, 2000; Teece et al, 1997) and explain that the acquired potential of individuals for self-initiated and context-specific behavior requires knowledge (Erpenbeck and Rosenstiel, 2003; North and Reinhard, 2005; Prahalad and Hamel, 1990). Knowledge emerges with individuals, groups, organizations, and in networks. Individual competencies are a prerequisite for goal-oriented action.

Steinbeis University Professor Johanna Anzengruber (2013), in her pioneering work, ties employees', teams', organizations'

and networks' ability to act into an holistic concept combining the competence-based view of a firm with the required talent to cope within a turbulent environment. Organizations with a high ability to act use the knowledge in networks through people who engage themselves for the organization and simultaneously create the required capabilities to cope with the challenges of a turbulent environment. Her 'strategic competence management' helps leaders understand future organizational competencees in order to identify the required talent, teams, and networks. It is part of strategic management and takes an important role in adapting, integrating, and reconfiguring organizational capabilities, resources, and functional competencies for a changing environment (Teece et al, 1997). With this it becomes clear that building the managerial competence that enables a leadership team to cope with a turbulent environment becomes one of the most important features of successful management.

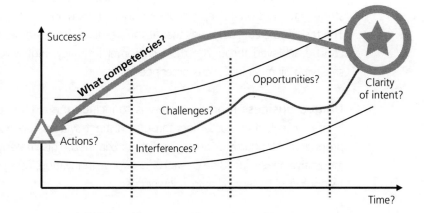

# What is the clarity of your strategic intent?

 Where do you start as a leader? Utmost clarity of strategic intent is what every leader aspires to but, as we now know, it is hard to attain. Every question about the business model starts with the strategy question. And, without a clear business model, it is useless to talk about how we manage our organization. A practical approach to overcoming an obscure future with more clarity of direction is to set the starting point as a value proposition.

Strategy is a decision about the strategic positioning of an organization (Porter, 1985). It describes how a firm competes in the market. There are three generic options (Hax and Wilde, 2001):

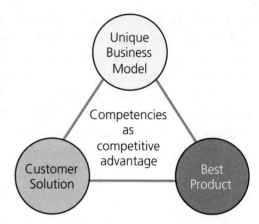

**Best product.** The best product-positioning represents the classical form of competition. Customers are attracted through low cost – a price advantage over competitors – or to a differentiated offering. Competitive advantage rests with product economics. Innovation comes from the product development process.

**Customer solution.** Rather than standardized products and services, this strategy focuses on a deep customer understanding and a strong relationship. The task is to create solutions that fit the needs of the customer precisely. This can be achieved through utmost customer intimacy, high value-adding, or satisfying all meaningful customer needs.

**Unique business model.** Its view is to include the extended value chain in a way to lock-in customers through distinct systems economics such as proprietary standards or access to distinct channels. This strategy may include innovative new value (Blue Ocean) or disruptive innovation, using cost-reducing technologies to serve clients at lower cost.

Every dominant strategy requires distinct processes as part of the business model. The choice of strategy further impacts structures, competencies, and the ability to adapt to a changing environment.

# Strategic intent

## More clarity through a meaningful value proposition

In most organizations, one of the three processes dominates the others. Operations is about delivering best products and services at the lowest cost and with least asset-utilization to customers. Customer targeting is about identifying specific needs. The innovation process includes developing new products and services. Every organization performs every process with a different priority. With clarity on the value proposition, leaders specify their business model and identify the competencies needed to address the strategy.

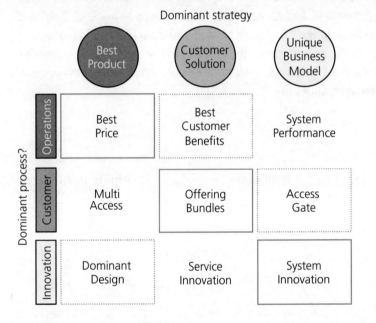

Dominant strategy

Best Product — Customer Solution — Unique Business Model

Dominant process?

| | Best Product | Customer Solution | Unique Business Model |
|---|---|---|---|
| Operations | Best Price | Best Customer Benefits | System Performance |
| Customer | Multi Access | Offering Bundles | Access Gate |
| Innovation | Dominant Design | Service Innovation | System Innovation |

**The following options serve as generic options to specify the strategy elements of the management model:**

- **Best price**: operational excellence to reduce cost.
- **Multi access**: customer-targeting with multi-channel access.
- **Dominant design**: stream of innovative products.
- **Best customer benefits**: excellence in customer economics.
- **Offering bundles**: combining channel/solution offerings.
- **Service Innovation**: improving customer value chain economics
- **Systems performance**: excellence in customer experience
- **Access gate**: channel and access control with product choice.
- **Systems innovation**: proprietary, open architecture with lock-in.

93

# How do I establish an environment that promotes a high ability to act?

It is increasingly recognized that firms need to be fast, agile and resilient (McCann, 2004; McCann and Selsky, 2005). Speed represents the capacity to implement strategy fast. Agility provides "the capacity to consistently change without having to change. It is the efficiency with which we can respond to non-stop change" (Haneberg, 2011:50-55) and resilience adds stability as the capacity to absorb, react to, and potentially reinvent the business model as a consequence of change. Speed, agility, and resilience describe the elements of an organization's ability to act. Such organizations enable people to perform the 'inner game' and create the capabilities to cope with a turbulent environment (the 'outer game') (Anzengruber, 2013). Such competencies refer to special dynamic capabilities (Schreyögg and Kliesch-Eberl, 2007; Teece et al 1997; Zollo and Winter 2002). Their purpose is to enable an organization to reconfigure its resources in order to quickly adapt to a changing environment. With increasing variety and higher dynamics in the environment, dynamic capabilities are a true competitive advantage (Augier and Teece, 2007:185). They enable sensing of change, seizing of opportunities, the management, maintenance, and transformation of an organization to remain competitive (Teece, 2007).

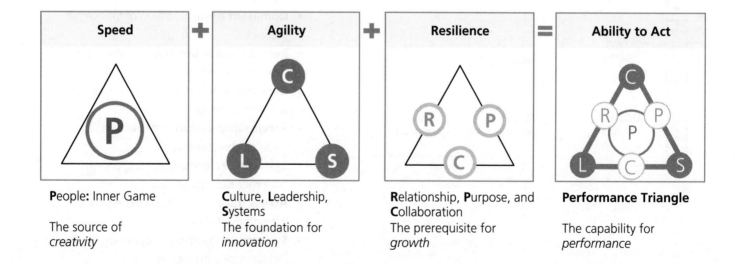

| Speed | Agility | Resilience | Ability to Act |
|---|---|---|---|
| **People:** Inner Game | **C**ulture, **L**eadership, **S**ystems | **R**elationship, **P**urpose, and **C**ollaboration | **Performance Triangle** |
| The source of *creativity* | The foundation for *innovation* | The prerequisite for *growth* | The capability for *performance* |

# The environment for superior performance

## Speed, agility, and resilience

The performance triangle, combining speed, agility, and resilience, represents an organization's operating environment which aims to help leaders increase their ability to act (Michel, 2013a).

**Speed**. The 'people frame' defines the policy of how we engage people. The 'inner game' is the tool that helps people translate knowledge into action. It transfers control to the learner. Learning is the solution for time critical action in dynamic times (Eisenhard and Martin, 2000:1115). Trust and choice further relate the 'people frame' to speed and creative capabilities.

**Agility**. The organization frame defines the policy of how we coordinate work. Agility is all about sensing opportunities early, taking action, and continuous change (Brown and Eisenhardt, 1998) through an integrated organization (Ghoshal and Gratton, 2002). It promotes self-organized work in teams with delegated decision-making for higher flexibility, effective adaptation to external change, improved problem-solving, and superior innovation as its benefits (Conrad 2004; Clegg et al 2006; Friedmann 1977; Hedlund 1986; Hendry 1992;). Agility requires the combination of dynamic managerial capabilities and managerial controls.

**Resilience**. The 'stakeholder frame' defines the policy of how we establish goals as a bonding element of relationships. It has a stabilizing effect through social controls and absorptive capabilities. Resilience is about the 'robustness' of systems (Beinhocker, 1999; Deevy, 1995). Organizations reach higher levels of resilience through collaboration (Doz and Baburoglu 2000), purpose, and relationships (Alpaslan and Mitroff, 2004) as cooperative strategies (Dyer and Singh, 1998). They are able to reinvent themselves and find new business models that preserve the core (Coutu, 2002; Hamel and Valikangas, 2003). The way we set goals determines much of the relationship with stakeholders and the growth of the organization.

# How do I manage change?

The new era, in a turbulent environment requires speed to capitalise on relevant opportunities, agility to sense weak signals early and continuously adapt, and resilience to withstand unexpected external shocks. The ability to act is the dynamic capability needed by leadership teams to enable them to manage organizations and people in today's challenging times and in an uncertain future.

Managing change follows two non-exclusive principles: flexibility as a dynamic capability; and standardization of one-time projects to alter an organization's resource base. Flexibility requires establishing a set of capabilities that is ready to use. Flexibility cannot be pulled out of a hat when needed. It requires an up-front investment. Standardization also refers to strategic restructuring and post-merger integration programmes. It requires ad hoc projects with a distinct change-purpose in mind. Do my managers build the required competencies to cope with future challenges or do they manage projects to alter the resources of the firm? The change model choice between flexible capabilities and standardization has implications for how an organization competes.

**Flexibility** refers to change as a managerial capability to learn, adapt, and evolve continuously. Flexibility assumes a dynamic environment. As a dynamic capability, it focuses on establishing the capabilities needed to cope with an ever-changing future. Dynamic capabilities use the knowledge of the talent as an individual approach to seizing opportunities and the proactive use of competencies to address a dynamic future. Ability to act is the management and development concept that leads to higher organizational flexibility. There is an obvious cost to this. It requires slack resources rather than high efficiency with no room to move. Organizations that lack capabilities for a high managerial ability to act are unable to cope with turbulent times.

**Standardization** refers to traditional, programmed change efforts as frequent, recurring one-time projects. Their focus is on single initiatives addressing specific change requirements, mostly determined by strategy, structure, or personnel changes. Their purpose is to fix 'results problems' quickly; they often serve the simple purpose of shaking up the organization. Standardization refers to normalizing people, processes, and cultures to eliminate undesired transaction costs. The underpinning assumptions of change projects are: a stable environment with clarity of objectives. While standardization works in a stable environment, many practitioners and researchers have found that most change projects fail due to a variety of reasons. Standardized change projects address problems with a timely quick-fix.

# Change design principles

## The stretch to move beyond the choice between flexibility and standardization

The choice between adopting flexibility or standardization is a change-management choice. It has implications for how we interact and design systems:

**Capabilities**: the organization has built agile structures, flexible systems, and dynamic capabilities to enable it to adapt continuously. Mental models (as images, beliefs, concepts, metaphors, …) guide the thinking rather than prescribing how things need to be done. They can cope with options and a variety of potential challenges and outcomes.

**Procedures**: the organization combines formal managerial routines with structured capability development, combining organizational development and talent development as a means of altering behaviours and outcomes.

**Instructions**: the organization adapts to changes in strategy, structures, or the environment through one-step, recurring change projects. Detailed instructions, tightened rules, rigid programmes, and excessive coaching promote different behaviours and outcomes as a quick-fix for pressing problems.

What can I do to stretch beyond in the new era?
**As an individual:**
- Develop and maintain individual capabilities, such as the 'inner game', to cope with change.

**As an organization:**
- Apply strategic competence-management to establish operational and dynamic capabilities.

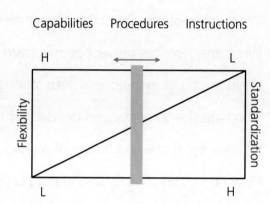

# How do I cope with a turbulent environment?

What assumptions about the environment determine my approach to change?

What interferences prevent people from performing at their peak?

What are the implications of your strategy for change?

What are the competencies needed for change?

What is the scope and nature of my organization's transformation?

How do I establish an environment that supports a high ability to act?

# What is my organization's operating environment?

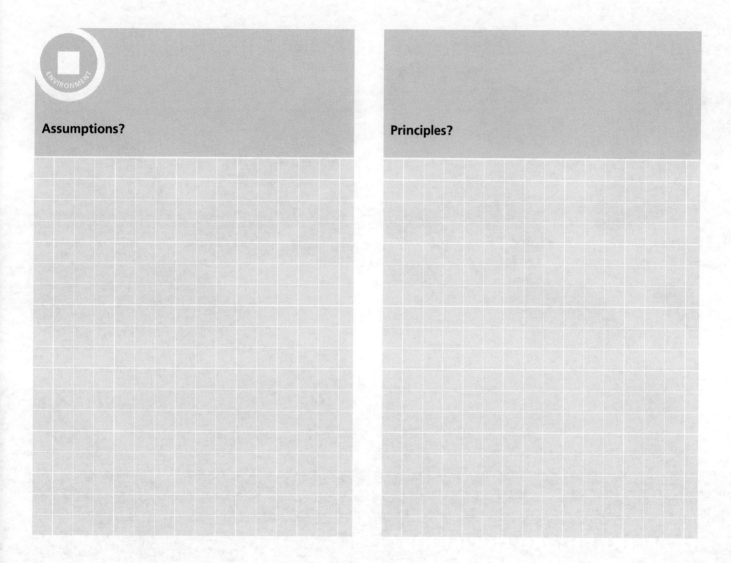

**Assumptions?**

**Principles?**

No two mountains are the same. As with dynamic managerial capabilities, mountains are specific and their appearance depends on the context.

# How do I make decisions?

# MANAGEMENT

## The operating model to make decisions, get things done, and lead the organization to success

The 'management frame' defines the operating model for the organization. It frames how people make decisions and gets things done.

Henry Mintzberg (2009) said that "management is, above all, a practice where art, science, and craft meet." However, "…control-and-command techniques do not suffice in a competitive environment, where creativity and employee initiative are critical to business success," according to Robert Simons (1995), professor at Harvard Business School. Roger Martin (2005), the Dean of the Roman School of Management and author, added: "It becomes obvious that decision-making needs design."

It is a choice between decision-making in line with the principles of power, or collective wisdom. The challenge is to go beyond that choice in order to lead the organization and people to success in turbulent times.

Why does it not happen? Our ability to suffer is well-developed, organizational 'viruses' interfere slowly and invisibly, and detailed insights on the workings of organizations are often missing. Moreover, bringing up this conversation requires a systematic approach: Management Design, with the following questions:

- What assumptions about management determines my approach?
- What interferences prevent the talent potential to apply its knowledge?
- How do I get things done?
- How do I delegate decision-making?
- How do I establish adequate control?

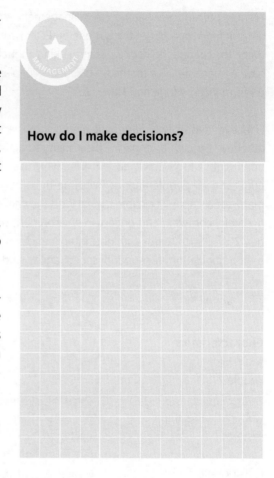

How do I make decisions?

# What assumptions about management determine my approach?

"Ninety percent of what we call 'management' is making it difficult for people to get things done." – Peter Drucker. However, "the changes on how we start thinking about leadership have a huge influence on the art of leadership, planning, and performance." (Hope and Player, 2012)

Effective leaders use diagnostic mentoring as a high-tech, reflective process to enhance their ability to act. Organizations with a high ability to act effectively use the knowledge of their people and, at the same time, have dynamic managerial capabilities able to deal with the challenges of a dynamic, complex, and uncertain environment (Anzengruber, 2013). Such teams eliminate interferences and manage their organizations for superior speed, agility, and resilience.

Their decision-making fits the enabling mode with adequate tools for highly-qualified talent.

Once established, the performance triangle established a rules-based view with the institution as an action-generating system. It programmes and controls goal-oriented action. Moreover, it stabilizes the order of systems through interpretations, relationships, and rules. But, at the same time, it is a dynamic model that adjusts to specific situations and the context of an organization. The triangle combines systems as the formal controls, leadership as the direct influence, and culture as the behavioral control mechanisms. It puts people into the center as the actors; purpose, relationships, and collaborative function as the bonding elements of an organization.

| Characteristics |  Enabling mode: |  Controlling mode: |
|---|---|---|
| People | | |
| Culture, leadership, systems | Speed: self-organization, multi-directional communications <br> Agility: enabling, feedback, interaction, transformation, transparency, innovation | Control, top-down <br><br> Bureaucracy with roles, rules, plans, reports, efficiency, predictability <br> Inward to outward view |
| Collaboration, purpose, relationships | Resilience: purpose, dynamic linking, networks | |
| **Principles** | **Collective wisdom** | **Power & hierarchy** |

# Interferences limit potential

## What organizational interferences prevent the talent potential to apply its knowledge?

In his legendary management book Levers of Control (2005), Harvard Business Professor Robert Simons states: "To unleash this potential [knowledge people], managers must overcome organizational blocks. Management control systems play an important role in this process." Over the years, organizational 'viruses' have invaded many firms unintentionally and unwillingly, interfering in the form of faulty leadership, erroneous systems, or an infected culture, preventing people performing at their peak. Or in line with Timothy W. Gallwey (2000), the creator of the concept of the 'inner game': "The greater the external challenges accepted by a company, team or individual, the more important it is that there is minimum interference occurring from within."

Such organizations are ill-prepared for both future challenges and knowledge work, and, at the same time, interferences keep them for using their full potential. As a result, organizations are slow in implementation, inflexible and unable to change, too fragile to withstand external shocks, and often unable to act. The symptoms are operating failures, lack of quality of services, misbehaviours, a lack of loyalty, a distorted brand, and eventually negative public attention driving the downwards spiral.

In most cases, it is not 'incompetent management' that causes these issues. Simply put, their management has a design rooted in the industrial age, effective only in a stable environment and management tools that have lost their impact or fallen by the wayside altogether in today's fast-moving environment. There are two ways to fix the problem: first, to increase the potential or, second, to remove the interferences. As most interferences stem from faulty systems, it is obvious that you should fix the operating system of an organization before investing in the potential of people.

The initial step is to identify the 'viruses' and pinpoint how they limit the potential of the organization and the talent.

# What interferences prevent the talent potential to apply its knowledge?

Management needs change. Here is how – starting at its origin. The sole purpose of management is success, but it is actions that deliver results (Sprenger, 2010). "Management is the art of getting things done."(Eccles and Nohira) The actions not visions, expectations, or solutions make the difference in organizations. Action refers to 'doing' as the interactions between stakeholders. Max Weber (1969), the German social philosopher, added a 'social' perspective to the definition. Actions always relate to people and their relationships. Moreover, subjective purpose means these actions need to make sense in the eye of the person taking action.

Peter Drucker (1996) related goal-orientation, as an attribute, to the economic purpose of an organization. Since most modern work requires more than one person for its completion, collaboration among stakeholders explains the existence of an organization. It needs to be noted that self-responsibility has its origin in European Humanism - self-responsibility being the foundation for people's motivation. As Professor Herb Nold (2011; 2012) expressed it, in his award-winning articles: "The task is to create an operating environment where people focus on purposeful, value-adding tasks, and share what they know to unlock creativity and accelerate growth."

Management is about allocating resources to customers. Resources include all assets, capabilities, processes, attributes, information, and knowledge that enable an organization to conceive and implement strategies for higher efficiency and effectiveness (Barney 1991:101). Resources have strategic importance when they contribute to competitive advantage. As such, they are valuable, rare, inimitable, non-substitutable – the VRIN criteria (Barreto, 2009).

The resource-based view of a firm explains how organizations create and maintain competitive advantage (Barney 1991; Penrose 1969; Prahalad and Hamel 1990; Nelson 1991; Wernerfelt, 1984). But, as Edith Penrose (1980) noted, "it is never resources that are the 'inputs' into the production process, but only the services that the resources can render." The client always judges the usefulness of these services. It is an organization's action-takers that determine the difference between resources and their use.

# The people – organization bridge

## Translating knowledge into action

Knowledge is the scarce resource as it relates to people, depends on the specific context, needs to be action-orientated, and is dynamic (Anzengruber, 2013). Knowledge is information, data, insights, results of cognition, methods, action-oriented construction (with constructivism at its core) and mental models (Rosenstiel et al, 2004). Knowledge relates to rules-based processes and, as a resource, to competence-based models. Individual action (doing) requires competence and is motivated by knowledge. Knowledge that is not used is of no value to an organization. The knowledge-doing (action) gap is a major issue in many traditional organizations. Organizations require the right tools to close the gap.

Knowledge as a resource always relates to people. But, people are not an asset in the legal sense – organizations cannot own people as suppliers and the service are indivisible. People, per se, are motivated. Self-responsibility is the dominant source of motivation. Purpose is a necessary condition for motivation. Moreover, people have the ability to reflect (pre-frontal cortex as the executive function of humans to initiate, engage and decide) and re-act (sensory cortex) as the reflexive mode of operation. As Peter Drucker (1967) concludes: "In times when knowledge is the critical resource, all people are executives …accept the fact that we have to treat almost anybody as a volunteer."

To cope with the challenges of a turbulent era (the 'outer game') and simultaneously benefit from the knowledge of the talent (the inner game), we need to build a bridge between the talent and organizations that cater to people. Management needs a design that enables that bridge to a superior ability to act. Some say management has only one client: the employee. The people – organization bridge, called management: three concurrent steps to translate knowledge into action:

1. Understand future capability needs and translate them into required talent, team, organizational, and network skills: **strategic competence management**.
2. Identify the managerial and organizational environment and decide on the management model: **Management Design**.
3. Transform management from old to new: **diagnostic mentoring**.

# How do you get things done?

To get things done, modern people require a high ability to act with competencies in five areas: the ability to think, understand, contribute, adhere, and engage. Action includes decision-making. In line with Peter Drucker (1967) "in the knowledge age, employees become executives", they make decisions.

**Think**: 'Knowledge people' have a set of metal maps. It helps them make sense of situations and make decisions. The benefits for an organization come not only from individual thinking, but from collective thinking. The thinking requires an opportunity to create meaning and asks for a deliberate choice to move in one direction.

**Understand**: Information and immediate feedback raise awareness of what is important. This helps people understand what matters and focuses attention. Superior understanding requires that sensors are not on mute and amplifiers work properly.

**Contribute**: Translating ideas into action. The task is to mobilize resources to get things done. People put their energy into things that they care about. And energy requires action to be meaningful. Contribution requires the opportunity to apply knowledge and support and balance freedom and constraints. Superior contributions build on the trust of people and in people.

**Engage**: Attention is a limited resource; energy is required to maintain it at a high level. Attention must be focused to prevent distraction from competing demands. A high level of engagement requires beliefs, motives, and purpose.

**Adhere**: Energy adds 'pull' and a positive tension to the boundaries of an organization. This tension requires a balance between entrepreneurship and efficiency. A high level of adherence maintains a good balance.

A well-developed ability to act, at individual-and-team-levels requires an 'enabling' operating environment; this allows things to get things done at an organizational level.

# From knowledge to action

## Five competencies to get things done

The 'inner game' techniques to translate knowledge into action require a different working environment. The following five questions initiate thinking on what is needed in organizations, to enable the (scarce, so precious) talent to act in line with the intent of the firm.

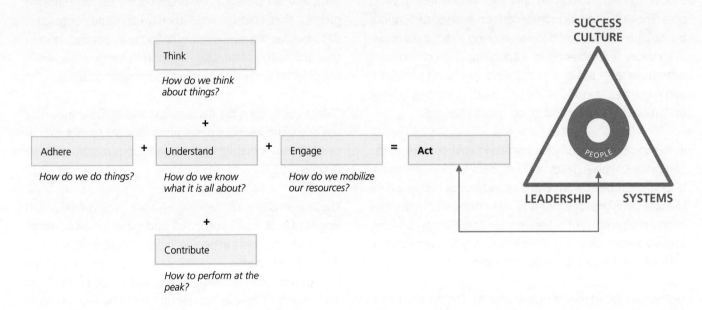

**Think**

*How do we think about things?*

**+**

**Adhere** + **Understand** + **Engage** = **Act**

*How do we do things?* *How do we know what it is all about?* *How do we mobilize our resources?*

**+**

**Contribute**

*How to perform at the peak?*

SUCCESS CULTURE

PEOPLE

LEADERSHIP          SYSTEMS

# How do you delegate decision-making?

Organizations with a high ability to act need good decision-making at all levels – from the centre to the periphery – tapping into the full potential of all people, the operating model, the information technology, and leadership practices. The task is to synchronize decision-making throughout the organization. Good decision-making needs a participative culture, entrepreneurial leadership, and collaborative systems as reflected in norms, beliefs, operating principles, and processes. It includes the balance of managing current operations effectively and doing new things well.

In the increasingly complex operating environment of organizations, where stakes are high, even for small decisions, leaders must be able to rely on employees at the periphery to make decisions. The task is to make delegation real, "creating an environment where people focus on purposeful, value-adding tasks, and share what they know to unlock creativity and accelerate growth" (Nold, 2012).

Leaders are faced with a dual challenge. On the one hand, they need to drive decision-making as far as possible down into the organization. For this, they need to be able to rely on people with good judgement. Good judgement means people know which signals from the market matter and which options are available, and can pick the right ones and act quickly; all this with substantial autonomy. On the other hand, leaders need to ensure rigour of thought, accountability, and discipline. It is the quality of the decision-making process that enables firms to have 'flexible footprints', described as the ability to reconfigure as needed, and to take advantage of new value opportunities as windows of opportunity open (Maitland and Sammartino, 2012).

"Most discussions on decision-making assume that only senior executives make decisions or that only senior executives' decisions matter. This is a dangerous mistake."- Peter Drucker (1967)

These trends are accelerating and are posing fresh challenges to leadership. Successful leadership means developing good judgement in people, helping them make sense of signals and knowing what it means for the strategy of the firm, to their business environment and to the firm's ability to compete. "I believe the real difference between success and failure in a corporation can be very often traced to the question of how well the organization brings out the great energies and talents of its people," said Thomas J. Watson (1963), former chairman and CEO of IBM.

# Decisions

## Decisions come in homeopathic portions – many frequent little decisions

Consider the following: executives make 20 decisions every day – some big, some small. In a decentralized and empowered environment, every employee makes 10 decisions per day – some important, others not: they are all 'executives'. In an organization of 500 'executives', this results in more than 5,000 decisions per day. For every year, this means more than one million decisions.

We invest millions of euros in the design of products, quality processes, change and incentive plans. And, in modern knowledge economies, products and services often comprise decisions; for example, a decision to invest, a decision for a medical treatment, a personnel-decision in management. Why do we not think about how we make decisions at scale? Decisions drive performance when most of these decisions are good decisions. As modern products are decisions, we need to spend the same amount of time on decision design as we do with traditional, physical product design. It is worthwhile re-thinking decision-making in your firm.

Not all decisions are the same. The following are four kinds of decisions to start the conversation on what, how, and when to delegate.

**Relationship decisions.** Their purpose is to define the contract that explains the social bonds between two parties. Shaping, maintaining and bonding a relationship requires such a contract. The employee – employer relationship is such an example: the people frame. the following: executives make 20 decisions every day

**Design decisions**. Social interaction requires space and time. The design of the frameworks, norms, and rules is what we call design decisions. Most of the organizational development decisions are examples: the organization frame.

**Goal decisions.** Their task is to balance competing demands: do we pay higher dividends, invest into growth or pay our employees? Goal decisions maximize value with limited resources. The decision describes a preference. Goal decisions demand further option decisions: the stakeholder frame.

**Action decisions.** They require a choice among alternatives to seize opportunities with their respective risks. Most strategy and policy alternatives require a decision on the way forward which requires action: the environment frame.

# How do I establish adequate control?

After the introduction of the competence-based view of an organization, we now need to turn to a rules-based view as the action-generating systems. Its purpose is to enable goal-orientated action. The structuring and management of attention is central to control processes in organizations. Organizations need to design and manage the process of attention and focus if they are to support the work environment for knowledge-driven talent.

Five managerial control systems enable action in organizations. The following metaphor should helps you to get the general idea: Imagine driving a car. You need five elements to control your driving. First, you need diagnostic information that informs you about speed and the state of your vehicle, for example, oil temperature. Second, a map or navigation system keeps you on track and helps you find the destination. Third, the engine generates the power with the wheels that translate energy into movement. Fourth, with the accelerator, you tell the engine to get moving. Fifth, you need brakes to control your speed; without brakes, one cannot operate safely a car at high speed. Imaging driving a good car: its engine, accelerator, and brakes are of equal quality. A poor car might have a huge engine but poor brakes, getting you in trouble if you have to slow down suddenly. There is a lack of alignment, with little symmetry between the parts.

**Managerial controls** work as a bonding mechanism in organizations. They create a variety of links that work like glue.

**Information** and feedback mechanisms tie every organizational unit and employee to the overall umbrella firm. For example, performance information is reported to the centre as part of the individual accountability of employees, whereas directional feedback information moves to the periphery of an organization – the duty of a manager to inform employees on strategy.

**Strategy** links the CEO with the board. Strategy development is also an important feedback mechanism within the organization if employees are encouraged to inform the strategy with their insights.

**Implementation** connects all organizational units with a conversation about their performance. As a rich communications process, it makes structures scalable, meaning that with it, organizations can grow without adding more infrastructure.

**Beliefs** link people to vision, values, and meaning to find purpose, and **norms** tie people to governance. Beliefs and boundaries set the frame for the things that are within or outside the limits. The nature of the challenges the organization has decided to tackle determines much of the design, the use, and the impact of these controls. This is why these control tools need to fit your specific situation in order to support people-centric leadership. As with a good car, the brakes and the engine need to meet the requirements of the path and the nature of your intended trip.

# Control

## Enabling superior decision-making and actions

I use the graphical representation of managerial systems in many figures as an integrated control mechanism, throughout the book, to reinforce the driving metaphor and the importance of the systemic links. The dashboard is in the centre, navigation on top, the tyres at the bottom, the accelerator pedal is right, and brakes are left. Keep this analogy and order of controls in mind as you continue reading. I will use the same structure for the presentation and the detailed discussion on the scorecard and tools leading to a people-centric culture. You will soon recognize a deliberate pattern.

The following five questions trigger the thinking on the need for control.

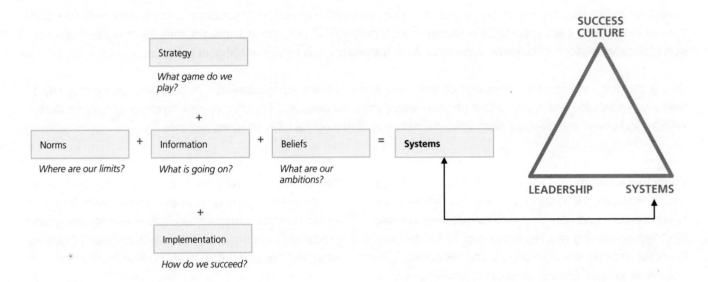

# How do I make decisions?

Decision-making is more than just the decision itself. It involves communication with people, gaining input on decisions, accessing knowledge to make decisions, and using external input to improve the decision-making.

Hierarchy is about managing up and down (in contrast to bureaucracy which is managing across) (Hedlund, 1993; Leavitt 2005). As such, hierarchy is absolutely essential in managing a large organization. In line with this, we have discussed the need to delegate decision-making to the periphery. Moreover, there is sufficient evidence that hierarchy attracts achievement-driven people and it is a mechanism to reduce complexity.

Collective wisdom uses the idea that large groups of individuals with a diverse set of perspectives often make better decisions than an individual. It gains importance in management through the use of web technologies. But, it is recognized that decision-making, in the form of collective wisdom, is still at the beginning in most management practices.

Do my managers tap into the knowledge of their employees, with shared responsibility for decisions? Or, do they rely on their own knowledge and insight to take personal responsibility for decisions? The decision-making choice between collective wisdom and power and hierarchy determines the nature of all managerial rules, routines, and tools.

**Collective wisdom** uses the brains of many to make decisions. However, it is important to note the difference between opinions and decisions. Crowds may have opinions, but decision-making requires accountability for decisions. Collective decision-making is popular and has potential, but also disadvantages. Crowds are good at providing input for structured decisions, but cannot be held accountable. The use of collective wisdom requires a significant shift of mind-set with many experienced managers in today's organizations.

**Power and hierarchy** are two of the oldest principles of management. Hierarchy provides managers with the power and accountability to make decisions. It assumes that greater experience and superior wisdom is with managers. However, information does not flow freely in hierarchical settings.

# Decision design principles

## Stretching beyond the choice of collective wisdom or hierarchy

The choice between delegation to use the collective wisdom and power/hierarchy is a choice of how we organize the decision-making in organizations. It has implications for how we interact and design systems:

**Delegation**: Decision-making is delegated to where the knowledge is. It assumes that distributed decision-making better uses the collective wisdom of many people at the client front.

**Involvement/structuring**: Leaders involve employees in their decision-making through various degrees of involvement in the process. Leaders may structure the decision-making process to gain sufficient control over key decisions.

**Command**: It is leaders who make decisions, based on the assumption that they are best qualified. They use hierarchical structures to access information required for their decisions.

What can you do to stretch beyond the choice in the new era?

**As an individual:**
- There are many ways of contributing to the decision-making by providing input, solving problems, innovating, and by accessing external sources for specific decisions.

**As an organization:**
- Taking a blended and structured approach, through delegation and involvement, often works best.

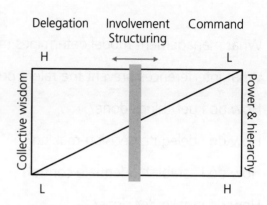

# How do I address the specifics of the operating environment?

What management model determines my approach?

What interferences prevent the talent potential to apply its knowledge?

How do I get things done?

How do I delegate decision-making?

How do I establish adequate control?

How do I make decisions?

# What is my managerial context?

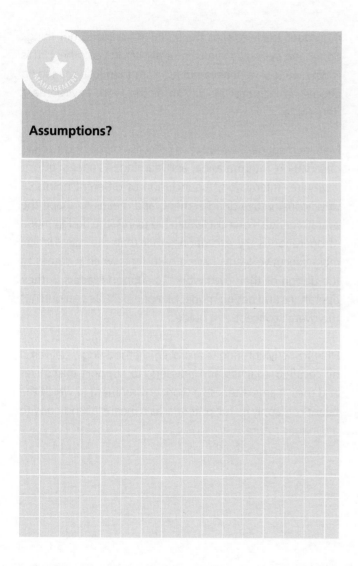

**Assumptions?**

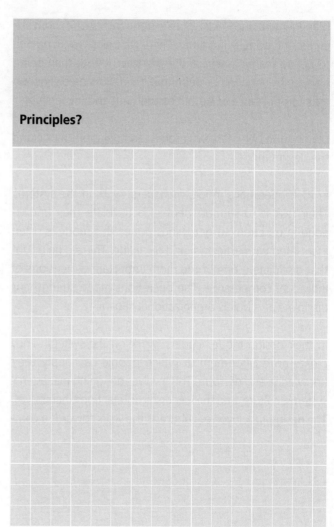

**Principles?**

# What is my dominant executive mode?

Management and leadership are frequent topics in both scientific and popular literature. There are many ways in which to define management and leadership. Rather than being trapped by yet another definition, the following distinction asks for a balance of both management and leadership.

I distinguish between two modes: an operations mode and the design mode.

In their operations mode, managers 'work in the system'. Their task is to support people to translate their knowledge into action, to get things done. This mode is often associated with efficiency and discipline. There is no doubt that discipline is one of the more important dimensions of individual competence. The operations mode strengthens discipline and builds organizational capability.

In their design mode, leaders 'work on the system'. They create an environment in which people can apply their knowledge and perform. This involves designing managerial systems, culture, and the leadership interactions themselves. The design task involves culture as the work towards a common goal, leadership as the social influence to get things done, and systems to maximize the efforts of others. This is why we look at leadership as more than just 'managing people'. It includes the design of the work environment for people.

Management design requires a reflective mode that involves observation, interpretation, and learning. As a team effort, it requires interaction, the inclusion of different points of view, constructive disagreement, and means to shape the overall agenda. For most leadership teams, the design mode of operation is the exception rather than the rule. Hence, most executive teams have a hard time when it comes to the design of their own work. To support leaders in their operations and design mode, Management Design outlines the overall concept as a guide.

Diagnostic Mentoring is a proven methodology, delivered by certified coaches and advisers, to support executives and their teams establish a work environment in which the talent can apply its full potential as a means of coping with a dynamic future.

# OPERATIONS AND DESIGN

## Enabling and managing the ability to act

*Management Design* is the 'think tool' for leaders to support them in developing their organization's competence to cope with a turbulent environment, boosting organizational 'ability' and creating an environment in which people have the opportunity to apply their thinking, understanding, contributing, engaging, and adherence.

Controls are the management tools for managers to support people to 'act' representing the organizational competence to translate knowledge into action.

**Work in the System**

**Management** as "the art of getting things done through people" as expressed by Mary P. Follet, an American social worker, management consultant and pioneer in organizational behavior. Or "transforming resources into utility", as described by Fredmund Malik (2008), Austrian management writer and consultant.

The rules-based view of the firm.

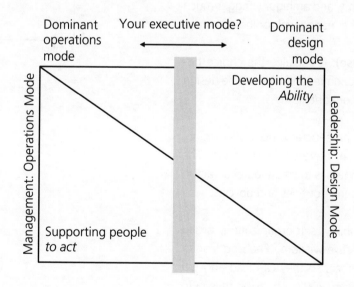

Dominant operations mode

Your executive mode?

Dominant design mode

Management: Operations Mode

Leadership: Design Mode

Developing the *Ability*

Supporting people *to act*

**Work on the System**

**Leadership** as "the duty to create an environment where people can apply their potential and perform at their peak" as described by business professor Herb Nold (2011) in his award-winning paper.

The competence-based view of the firm.

# What is my dominant mode?

The combination of the environmental challenges and the specific managerial responses explains four distinct operating modes. The purpose of the context model is to reflect on the current setting of an organization and what is needed to cope with future challenges. The gap indicates the nature of transforming the operation from the current approach to the desired model: it activates the design mode.

**The environment**: It explains how the various degrees of volatility, complexity, uncertainty, and ambiguity trigger much for the design of systems as the managerial toolbox.

**The management (response)**: It explains the choice between the plan and people economies and triggers the design of leadership interaction. In more detail, the...

**...controlling mode**: rules, bureaucracy, goal-orientation, market-power, standardization, hierarchy and power. The primary reason to establish control is to create bureaucracy in the sense of adequate managerial routines and policies.

**...enabling mode**: responsibility, self-organization, broad direction, flexibility, and collective wisdom. 'Enabling leadership' is about empowering others so they can lead and get work done (Marion and Uhl-Bien, 2007). The main reason to empower people is not to improve motivation, it is to improve the 'manageability' of the organization.

# Four archetypes

## What is your dominant context today and what will it be in the future?

Four dominant operating modes characterize the generic archetypal organizations. The purpose of these generic models is to facilitate the identification of your current mode and to discuss your future mode. Many readers ask why there are no examples for these modes. The answer is simple. The work from 10 years of research leading to Management Design clearly indicates that these patterns fit specific industries, businesses, and types of organizations. Because Management Design is a think tool that should not pre-format solutions, and as we know tips don't work, I have deliberately deleted examples from these archetypal models.

**Control context.**

Many organizations operate in a stable and predictable environment with clear deliverables and a high degree of standardization. Their management favours a rules-based approach with dominant control, detailed processes, and top-down decision-making. The preferred mode of operation assumes that people need to be extrinsically motivated to get things done. When things change, such organizations fix the specific gaps, tighten efficiency, and improve quality. (Simons, 1995; Forrester, 1961; Meadows, 2009)

**Market context.**

The business of various successful organizations in a turbulent market environment requires flexibility and speed to deliver specific outcomes. Their market-based approach assumes that distinct competitive advantages ensure enduring superior returns. These organizations apply rigorous targets, tying people to outcomes that align with the overall performance targets of the firm. Such organizations favour disciplined one-step change programmes to adapt their organization to changes in the environment. (Porter, 1982; 1985)

**Resource context.**

Organizations in a comparably stable environment, with scarce resources, are often driven by a strong mission and values. Their aspiration is to deliver reliable, consistent services through engaged people. When needed, such organizations adapt their resource base step-wise or continuously improve what they are doing. Most of these organizations have built resilience capabilities through a strong purpose, collaborative approaches, and relationships within, and with the outside. (Penrose, 1980; Barney, 1991; Prahalad and Hamel, 1990, Senge, 1990)

**Competency context.**

Organizations in a highly turbulent environment benefit from knowledgeable people to establish a high ability to act. They develop the required managerial competencies and build the talent base as a means to continuously innovate. Learning, and access to knowledge through networks, is as essential as their approach to reassessing their resource base continuously. Change is ongoing, but not as a disruptive process. It is the dynamic capability that makes these organization agile and nimble. (Anzengruber, 2013; Teece et al, 1997)

# What can I not delegate as a leader?

Four operating decisions are powers reserved for an executive who is responsible for a business: strategy, talent, reputation, and alignment. These decisions cannot be delegated for four reasons: they are 'big' decisions that require the experience of a seasoned executive; they impact the entire organization and nobody else in an organization has the accountability for the integration of the parts into the business as a whole; they belong together as they require alignment among the decisions; and these decisions can make-or-break the business. This is why the chief executive alone has these powers. He or she can make these decisions without asking anybody. Five groups of questions guide the work in the system.

1. **Talent**. Relationship decisions –establishing contracts between people and the organization.
2. **Capabilities and alignment**. The many design decisions – creating the right environment for people to work.
3. **Resources and reputation**. The balance of competing goals – setting goals that make sense to stakeholders.
4. **Environment and strategy**. The choice, among alternatives, to deliver value – deciding on the opportunities and challenges to address.
5. **Management**. Your choice on how to lead the organization.

The management decision is unique to the role of the CEO. Their role is to set the principles and policies for his or her professionals that, in return, recommend the best design of management.

Five groups of questions guide the work on the system.

# The integration framework

## How do I manage my organization?

**Questions to work in the system:**

**Questions to work on the system:**

**What talent?** What talent do I need? What knowledge, ideas, and skills do I need to address a turbulent future?

**How to engage?** What assumptions about people determine my leadership? What principles help me engage people?

**What capabilities?** What capabilities do I need? What organization do I need to build and maintain competitive advantage?

**How to coordinate?** What assumptions about work determine my organization? What principles help me coordinate work?

**What resources?** What resources do I need to serve our clients? What do our stakeholders want from us?

**How to set goals?** What assumptions about relationships determine my goals? How do I set goals?

**What challenges?** What are the challenges my organization faces? What is our strategy as a response to these challenges?

**How to change?** What assumptions about the environment determine my change approach? How do I manage change?

**What leadership?** What leadership do I need manage my organization and create value for stakeholders?

**How to decide?** What assumptions about management determine my leadership? How do I make decisions?

# The five frames unfold into the Management Design Framework

The five frames on people, organization, stakeholders, environment, and management turn into a practical framework as notepad to capture ideas on your management design.

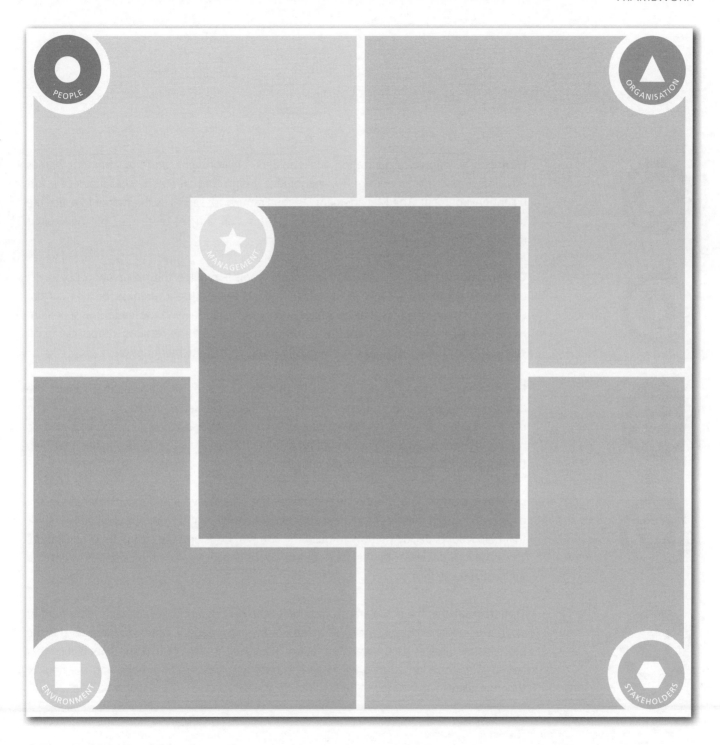

# How do I manage my organization?

**Frames**. The people, organization, stakeholders, environment, and management frames establish a shared language for a management design that meets the challenges of a turbulent environment. The Management Design Framework serves as the model to articulate the assumptions and principles. The result of this step is a set of choices on the desired managerial competencies.

**Observation points**. The INsights Diagnostic Tools™ provide the observation points on managerial competencies and the model for leaders to raise the awareness for their current situation. The performance triangle serves as a dynamic model with the leadership scorecard and a variety of other tools to review current competencies. The result is utmost clarity on where to start the transformation towards the desired management design.

**Focus areas**. A variety of design tools help leaders focus on those areas that require the attention. Key issues address gaps between current and desired managerial capabilities. The context frame guides the design to a set of tools with choices on organizational behavior, culture, leadership, and the management model. The result is a set of key issues that help the organization to close the identified gaps.

**Leverage points**. The change step identifies the critical leverage points to transform the organization from the old to the new design. Systems roles and change levers are two tools that help leaders decide on how to build the competencies and transform the organization. The result includes clarity on the development needs and decision on the initiatives to develop the required capabilities.

**Transformation**. The actual transformation to the new design requires the development of distinct managerial competencies as a competitive advantage. Diagnostic Mentoring is the process that initiates such a transformation. The result is a set of dynamic capabilities that help the organization address its challenges based on the enabling mode and the help of superior talent.

# Management Design

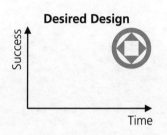

## Framework.

What is my desired management design? What assumptions and principles determine my choice of design? What managerial capabilities are needed? Unfold the performance pyramid and use the triangles to identify the desired model.

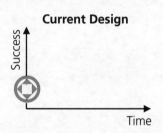

## Insights.

What is my current management design? Where is the potential? What interferences does my organization face? What are my current managerial capabilities? Use the INsights Diagnostic Tools™ questions to identify the current model and capabilities.

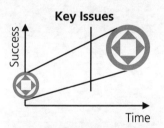

## Design.

What are the gaps to be addressed? What are the identified key issues to close the gaps? What competencies does my organization need to develop? Use the set of design tools to identify the gaps and key issues to develop the desired capabilities.

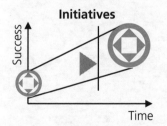

## Change.

How do I enact the new management design? What initiatives are needed to transform towards the new model? What capabilities support the new model? Use the set of change tools to establish the roadmap initiative for the transformation.

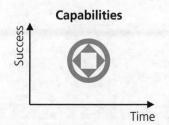

## Mentoring.

How do I manage with the new design? How do I transform to a new set of capabilities? How do I continue to develop the capabilities? Use Diagnostic Mentoring to maintain a high ability to act and cope with a turbulent environment.

OBSERVATION POINTS FOCUS THE ATTENTION ON THE THINGS THAT NEED TIME AND ENERGY

# INSIGHTS

## What is my current management design?

# The assessment of current capabilities

## Observation points

Organizational learning

The INsights Diagnostic Tool™

**The Self-assessment**
- Success
- Speed
- Agility
- Resilience
- Ability to act

**The Leadership Scorecard ™**
- Action

Organizational capabilities

Insights identifies the current potential and the interferences to managing the organization for a superior ability to act. The INsights Diagnostic Tools™ support the self-assessment to establish the critical observation points for leaders to identify the current managerial and organizational capabilities.

Diagnostic Mentoring guides the interpretation of the review by establishing a facts-based starting point to transform towards the desired capabilities.

**Current Design**

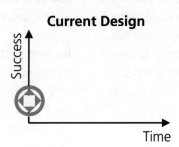

# How do I remove the 'viruses' to unlock the potential?

The performance triangle model serves as an initial overview and starting point for a detailed review of all critical elements of an organization. It is a simple, but powerful concept with a variety of indicators that help leaders develop a superior ability to act.

Effective leadership and systems are prerequisites for a productive culture. The combination enables good decision- making and supports employees to translate knowledge into action; purposefully, collaboratively, and based on sound relationships. Trust translates to faster speed, awareness amplifies weak signals increasing flexibility, and choice speeds up decisions to react to unforeseen challenges. The results are superior 'work in the system' and a higher agility without interferences from infected corporate management.

When 'viruses' interfere with a poisoned culture causing faulty leadership, or erroneous systems, then the senses are likely to be 'on mute', mistrust prevails, and tight rules prevent people from capitalizing on opportunities. As such, people face an adverse 'outer game' beyond their abilities. Challenged by both the 'inner and outer game', performance takes a break and people are unable to realize their full potential.

Examples of 'viruses' are:
**A toxic culture**: Faulty procedures, values without consequences, cynics dominating, backwards delegation, waiting for decisions, faulty decisions, egotism…
**Faulty leadership**: Control prevailing, busyness without results, drowning in details, senselessness, or a focus on numbers…
**Broken systems**: Bureaucracy or non-existent routines, formalism, faulty controls, decisions being reverted, rules only applying to some…

The list is long and seldom the same for every organisaton. The task is to ensure that leadership and systems are free of 'viruses' so that employees are enabled to handle the challenges of the 'outer game' and unfold their potential.

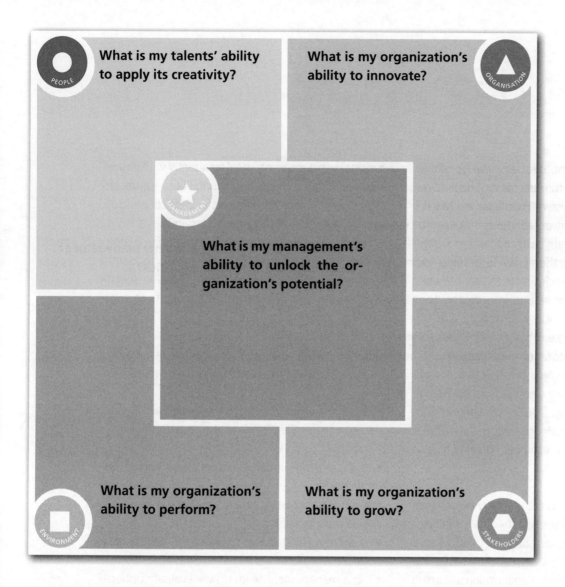

Where is the potential?

What interferences prevent a superior ability to act?

What are the current capabilities?

Where are the gaps?

# What is the reflective capacity of my organization?

As the features of competencies may be similar among firms, it narrows the spectrum of distinct dynamic capabilities to very few (Eisenhard and Martin, 2000:1109-1110): innovative, adaptive, and absorbing competencies. Innovative capabilities require the creativity of people and the ability to develop and learn. Adaptive competencies refer to organizations with the ability to change. Absorbing competencies include routines to accumulate, distribute and use knowledge (Cohen and Levinthal, 1990; Zahra and George, 2002) Furthermore, an organization's network connections, for example, through alliances, are hard to copy and therefore a competitive advantage (Sharma and Blomstermo, 2003). Networks reduce risks, facilitate new knowledge accumulation, and the development of own resources (Weerawardena et al, 2007)

An organization's ability to act is largely determined by ongoing critique and the variety of perspectives. Moreover, organizations are often looked at as a black box modelled with processes and routines but its 'actors' are not considered. Organizational learning adds the 'people perspective'. The idea is that organizations have a routine to deal frequently with innovation and change of existing capabilities: accumulate experience, codify and articulate knowledge (Zollo and Winter, 2002:350). Dynamic capabilities are not a variation of current capabilities. They require a choice of the right capabilities. The challenge is to identify these experiences, filter them from situation-specific knowledge, and generalize these insights to revise existing routines.

Here are some initial questions to find out whether your organization owns such reflective capabilities.

- Does my organization have the mechanisms and routines to reflect on how it manages the organization?
- Is there institutionalized observation and self-reflection?
- Does it provide systematic feedback with an outside perspective?
- Is there a constructive conversation on the feedback?
- As a management team do we evaluate options?
- Do we develop credible alternatives?

# Organizational learning

## Management as a dynamic capability

To develop dynamic capabilities, organizations need two concurring and balancing processes: a dual process model (Schreyögg and Kliesch-Eberl, 2007). This combines the selection of competencies as a structured process with an early environmental warning system to compensate for the risk of ongoing changes (systems viewed as controls).

Process one is about the selection of the right managerial competencies.

Process two includes the control of these competencies.

The logic for the separation of the two comes from the inability of individuals to observe their own actions simultaneously. The separation enables the reflection on action as double-loop learning. Hence, double-loop learning needs to be applied if process two is to be an effective [control] mechanism (Agyris, 1992:9).

As managerial competencies are all context-specific, the task of Diagnostic Mentoring becomes one of operationalizing the performance triangle model, providing the ability to review managerial competencies, and facilitating its appropriate design. The selection and development of managerial capabilities is what we call management design. The INsights Diagnostic

Tools™ serve the monitoring of managerial competencies, and the triangle model turns into a managerial control tool.

Focus of attention is known as an effective approach for people to learn. This is why Management Design uses the INsights Diagnostic Tools™ to provide the critical observation points that initiate the conversation about its design.

The observation of a neutral-but-critical variable helps us to perform and improve an activity without any instruction. It is like magic; by using a critical performance variable at work, people steadily improve their performance. Learning takes place and performance increases.

As a mentor, your only responsibility is to maintain non-judgemental observation, to provide an opportunity to learn, and to ensure people regain their focus once it is lost.

Awareness is learning by translating data from observation into information without a judgement about performance. It combines the skills, knowledge, and experience of the learner.

Diagnostic Mentoring applies organizational learning techniques to help leaders establish dynamic capabilities.

# What are your observation points?

A competence is a resource or capability defined by its use for a goal-orientated purpose. It is the perspective of leaders that determines the difference between a capability and a competence. The diagnostic exercise provides leaders with a self-assessed perspective of their organization's managerial capabilities.

Reports document the responses from the participants in the diagnostic exercise as scores for a variety of resources & capabilities. These scores translate resources and capabilities into 'competencies in use' on a scale between 0 (worst score) to 100 (best score). A distinctive handicap system (as in golf) makes the scores comparable among similar firms (thresholds that change the colors from pink [or black] to yellow [or yellow] and green [or pink]). The qualification is a code for the meaning of the score as related to the specific competence. The handicap colors add a qualitative perspective to the scores. The color code on the scores indicate missing competencies (pink or black), average competencies (yellow or grey), and superior competencies (green or white).

The Leadership Scorecard™ and the Leadership Toolbox™ include 30 broad categories of competencies with an origin in self-organization (Foerster, 1984; Luhmann, 2008; Meadows, 2009; Senge, 1990;), systems theory (Kappelhoff, 2006), and managerial control (Simons, 1995). The vertical view of the tools represents the control perspective –'work in the system' whereas the horizontal view reflects the competency based view of a firm and 'work on the system'.

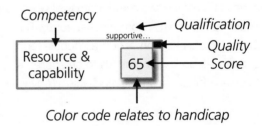

132

# The INsights Diagnostic Tools™

## The tool to review an organization's management model

The INsights Diagnostic Tools™ provide the online organizational self-assessment delivering a variety of results reports and presentations for the conversation of management teams on the capabilities for turbulent times. The diagnostic test reviews current state (provides observation points) and guides the design through a variety of think tools.

The tools are based on institutional reflection as an analytical means of assessing management concepts and methods in view of their ability to absorb new insights, to review the toolbox, and to innovate current views and practices. Participants in the online management survey include the executive team and managers with people responsibility. It takes between 10 and 30 minutes of their time to answer the set of questions.

To provide a contrast with the management view, a complementary online employee diagnostic test uses the same Performance Triangle model, which allows a leadership team to compare management and employee views in their organization.

The diagnosis needs to span an entire organization and is independent of individuals. It is a non-routine assessment to prevent organizations becoming accustomed to answering the questions. The unit of analysis always is 'the organization' – defined as an operational unit that shares the same leadership, values, and principles. This may be a firm, a department of a larger organization, or a team.

Diagnosing managerial practices and systems prevents organizations from using the same proven routines and competencies that create path-dependency. As such, the assessment prevents the lock-in phenomena known from applying the same procedures over and over.

The following self-assessment represents the most simple but fully functional offline version of the various online INsights Diagnostic Tools™.

# The Self-assessment

## Instruction

Answer the questions starting with 1 on the left side up to 30.
Circle the score as 0, 25, 50, 75, or 100 in line with your self-assessment.


For questions 1 to 16, use the following handicap system to color code your scores:

**H**  Green (or white) scores above 75: We are among the best.

**M**  Yellow (or grey) scores between 45 and 75: We are in the middle ground.

**L**  Pink (or black) scores below 45: We lack relevant capabilities.

Use a color marker for the analysis with all following tools.


For questions 17 to 21, use the following handicap system to label your scores:

**H**  High for 75 and higher: demanding challenges, high clarity

**M**  Medium for between 45 to 75: Average scores

**L**  Low for 45 and below: little challenges, low clarity

With some practice, you might use your own thresholds to create your own handicap system, e.g. change the thresholds for changing the color rating.

| | **For yourself, your team or your organization, to what extend do the following statements apply?** | Fully disagree | Disagree | Neirther /nor | Agree | Fully agree |
|---|---|---|---|---|---|---|
| 1 | My organization has a successful strategy and delivers on its promises. It attracts the right stakeholders. | 0 | 25 | 50 | 75 | 100 |
| 2 | My team shares the same intent, agenda, attitude, and beliefs. It does what it says through a supportive culture. | 0 | 25 | 50 | 75 | 100 |
| 3 | Leaders support employees through productive conversations and enable them to perform. | 0 | 25 | 50 | 75 | 100 |
| 4 | Our organization has policies in place that clarify the rules and make people accountable. | 0 | 25 | 50 | 75 | 100 |
| 5 | Our organization maintains processes that help people raise the awareness for what matters most. | 0 | 25 | 50 | 75 | 100 |
| 6 | Our organization's controls and decision-making tools help everyone maintain the focus on important things. | 0 | 25 | 50 | 75 | 100 |
| 7 | We/I can freely collaborate across boundaries, exchange information, and support each other. | 0 | 25 | 50 | 75 | 100 |
| 8 | We/I are/am encouraged to build relationships within the organization and to the outside to access knowledge. | 0 | 25 | 50 | 75 | 100 |
| 9 | Our/my work is purposeful, I/we can commit to the organization's goals that establish strong bonds. | 0 | 25 | 50 | 75 | 100 |
| 10 | Our organization continues to capture relevant opportunities and steadily grows its customer base. | 0 | 25 | 50 | 75 | 100 |
| 11 | Our organization is well known for its innovations as products, services, and approaches. Ideas turn into value. | 0 | 25 | 50 | 75 | 100 |
| 12 | I have sufficient access to information and get the feedback to raise my awareness for what matter most. | 0 | 25 | 50 | 75 | 100 |

| **For yourself, your team or your organization, to what extend do the following statements apply?** | Fully disagree | Disagree | Neirther /nor | Agree | Fully agree |
|---|---|---|---|---|---|
| **13** I am able to focus my attention on important things without being interrupted or distracted. | 0 | 25 | 50 | 75 | 100 |
| **14** I have sufficient choice to determine what I do and how I get things done. I am encouraged to stick to my path. | 0 | 25 | 50 | 75 | 100 |
| **15** I have the trust in my abilities, my colleagues, and my manager. I can access plenty resources to get work done. | 0 | 25 | 50 | 75 | 100 |
| **16** I can fully apply my full potential, skills, talents, and knowledge to the benefit of the organization and its clients. | 0 | 25 | 50 | 75 | 100 |

| **For yourself, your team or your organization, to what extend do the following statements apply?** | Very Low | Low | Neirther /nor | High | Very High |
|---|---|---|---|---|---|
| **17** The volatility in our market environment are… | 0 | 25 | 50 | 75 | 100 |
| **18** The complexity in our organization is… | 0 | 25 | 50 | 75 | 100 |
| **19** The uncertainty in our organization is… | 0 | 25 | 50 | 75 | 100 |
| **20** The ambiguities from the external environment is… | 0 | 25 | 50 | 75 | 100 |
| **21** The clarity of the intended strategy of our firm is… | 0 | 25 | 50 | 75 | 100 |

| Which statement best fits your organization? | Fully disagree | Disagree | Neirther /nor | Agree | Fully agree | |
|---|---|---|---|---|---|---|
| **22** I work long hours because I love what I do and identify with what I do. | 0 | 25 | 50 | 75 | 100 | I work here because of an attractive salary and the ability to get ahead. |
| **23** I have the information needed to get things done through informal coordination. | 0 | 25 | 50 | 75 | 100 | I get things done through formal routines and get access to information on request. |
| **24** I perform based on a broad direction with a long-term perspective. | 0 | 25 | 50 | 75 | 100 | I perform based on detailed set of short-term targets. |
| **25** My job requires on going flexibility and I act based on what makes sense. | 0 | 25 | 50 | 75 | 100 | My job is subject to ongoing change with a focus on productivity and efficiency. |
| **26** We make decisions based on the knowledge and insights from employees. | 0 | 25 | 50 | 75 | 100 | Leaders make decisions as they have the knowledge and information. |
| **Who gains respect in your organization? Someone who…** | | | | | | |
| **27** …takes rational decisions formally, follows guidelines, and gets things done. | 0 | 25 | 50 | 75 | 100 | …is flexible, takes decisions naturally, improvises, and adapts to situations. |
| **28** …decides while having a controllable, comprehensive future in mind. | 0 | 25 | 50 | 75 | 100 | …decides while having an unpredictable, confusing future in mind. |
| **Your manager can be best described as someone who…** | | | | | | |
| **29** …structures the work environment, follows routines, and clarifies accountability. | 0 | 25 | 50 | 75 | 100 | …is flexible, frames ideas, motivates, and provides broad guidance. |
| **30** …takes decisions, communicates them and ensures their implementation. | 0 | 25 | 50 | 75 | 100 | …involves others in decisions, asks for opinions, and leads through a vision. |

# When 'viruses' interfere with growth

Here is an example of a typical growth organization – combining high, medium, or low scores from the online diagnostic tool with insights from a discussion with the CEO on his experience and reaction to the results. Here is the story of the results: the organization hits its own brakes with growing formalities (medium systems score) and flawed leadership (low score). The system hurdles have names such as TQM, process-orientation, forms, BSC, objective agreements, and so on.

When organizations grow fast, most entrepreneurs install a leadership team and introduce professional tools and routines. The organization works through functional structures, certification, detailed procedures, leadership manuals, extensive measurement and more. These tools are designed to support leadership to cope with the challenges of growth and increasing size. In fact, too much of this creates leaders who hide behind the institution or take shortcuts to get things done.
This is practical and keeps everyone from getting in trouble: "We follow rules rather than to get things done". In the medium-term, this results in flawed leadership with a poisonous impact on culture. It destroys the creativity and increases uncertainty. Results will start to deteriorate if 'viruses' are not removed.

It is important to interpret the scores in line with the reader's own experience. The best way to do it is to share observations and insights with someone else – your team – to correct the natural bias towards your favourite cure method (the things that you are comfortable with) – the typical advisor problem.

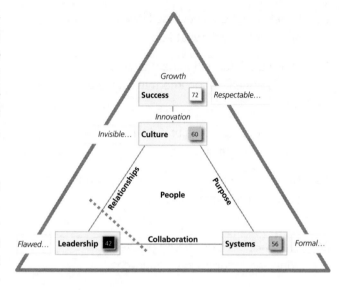

**H**   High scores: above average

**M**   Medium scores: average

**L**   Low scores: below average

# Potential and interferences

## The performance triangle

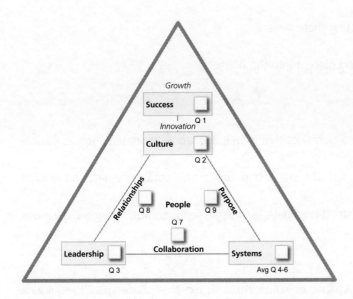

Instruction: place your scores into boxes in line with the respective questions. Then use a green-yellow-pink colour marker to code your scores in line with your handicap.

This is how you read the results: the colour-coding key is as follows:

**H** If you see a lot of green, congratulations! You are on the best track to unlocking the potential of your people. They demonstrate entrepreneurial behaviors, intense collaboration, and a high client-focus. Your task is to keep it at that level. Use the diagnostic to frequently check where you are.

**M** If yellow dominates, it is time to break out of the middle ground. Check your organization for how it perfects the art of decision-making, intensifies people interactions, and closes the knowing-doing gap. Ensure you don't miss an opportunity.

**L** If you see a lot of pink, immediate action is required. Continue the work on your Management Design.

# Ready for the future?

What is the future of my organization? What prevents me getting there faster?

Instruction: select the label in line with your score/handicap and place it into the figure.
This is what your scores mean:

## Success

**H** High [green/white] = respectable: an organization with few interferences that is well aligned with strategy, reacts flexibly to challenges, and has the capabilities to cope with the future.

**M** Medium [yellow/grey] = mediocre: an organization that is satisfied with status quo, delivers acceptable results, and refrains from changing things too much.

**L** Low [pink/black] = failing: an organization where cynics and mistrust dominate, leadership sends confusing signals, decisions are slow and unreliable, and 'viruses' take over.

## Environment

**H** High [green/white] = extreme: an organization that faces a dynamic environment with extreme challenges. It requires a management model and competencies that can cope with such challenges.

**M** Medium [yellow/grey] = considerable: an organization with considerable challenges that each require attention and managerial capabilities to address them adequately.

**L** Low [pink/black] = normal: an organization in a stable environment where traditional managerial approaches are effective. Though situations can change and it needs to be monitored.

## Clarity of direction

**H** High = predictable: an organization with utmost clarity on the strategic direction and intent. I can clearly identify the capabilities needed to address future challenges.

**M** Medium = blurred: an organization with a blurred strategy and direction. This requires dynamic capabilities that help to address a changing environment.

**L** Low = uncertain: an organization with difficulties in clarifying strategy and intent. It requires distinct dynamic managerial capabilities and monitoring with a diagnostic tool.

What are the implications on your management design, systems, and capabilities?

# Success

## The future model

Where do I start as a leader? Leadership is the capacity to translate vision into reality. It is the ability to envision the future, to make decisions in line with the intent, and to implement them that is critical to the success of any organization. But we know that reality never follows plans. New opportunities arise, challenges change, and interferences prevent us from using our full potential. It is therefore important to build dynamic capabilities to remain fast, agile, and resilient. The future model provides an overview of the challenges leaders face in translating the future into managerial capabilities to address their challenges.

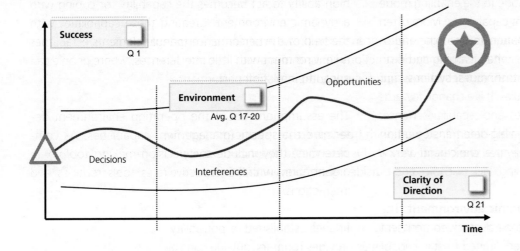

Success does not rely on serendipity:

- What keeps my organization from succeeding in the market?
- What prevents me from clarifying strategic intent?
- What challenges does my organization face?
- What opportunities are worthwhile pursuing?
- What interferences require attention?
- What competencies do my organization need to address the challenges?

# What is your talents' ability to apply its creativity?

This is what your scores mean:

### Awareness

**H**   High [green/white] = alert: people have observation points, and non-judgemental feedback enables clarity.

**M**   Medium [yellow/grey] = obstructed: blurred signals, noise, and limited or faulty feedback limit clarity.

**L**   Low [pink/black] = mute: signals are on mute. Erroneous feedback leads to disengagement.

### Focus of attention

**H**   High [green/white] = intense: self-initiated learning and concentration draws attention to important things.

**M**   Medium [yellow/grey] = blurred: limited learning and distractions limit performance.

**L**   Low [pink/black] = congested/wrong: distraction or wrong focus lead to inexistent performance.

### Choice

**H**   High [green/white] = responsible: self-determined work with freedom creates space for creativity.

**M**   Medium [yellow/grey] = limited: limited choice and work that is determined by limits creativity.

**L**   Low [pink/black] = inhibited/missing: lack of choice and outside control prevent creativity.

### Trust

**H**   High [green/white] = reliable: a high trust environment and confidence established responsibility.

**M**   Medium [yellow/grey] = formalized: limited trust in capabilities provides room for outside control.

**L**   Low [pink/black] = interfered/missing: mistrust results in a control-dominated work environment.

### Creativity

**H**   High [green/white] = unfolding: people apply their full potential, knowledge, skills, and talent.

**M**   Medium [yellow/grey] = restrained: interferences prevent people from using their full potential.

**L**   Low [pink/black] = inhibited / unused: people are unable to tap into their resources.

### Speed

**H**   High [green/white] = in the flow: the organization has the full capacity to react and implement fast.

**M**   Medium [yellow/grey] = keeping up: the organization hesitates and has limited capacity to implement.

**L**   Low [pink/black] = left behind: the organization is unable to act and misses opportunities.

What are the implications on your management design, systems, and capabilities?

# Speed

## The 'inner game'

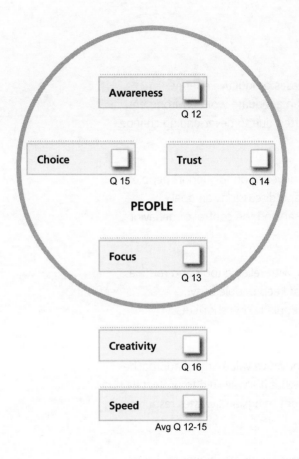

Speed is the essential capability in a turbulent, fast-moving environment. The elements of the 'inner game' are the clues to higher speed in organizations. With the 'inner game', people anticipate and react to higher dynamics in markets and the environment in a timely manner.

The 'inner game' provides the technique through which people can cope with higher challenges, using the art of relaxing distorting thoughts (Gallwey, 2000). Doubts, stress, fear, biased focus, limiting concepts or assumptions distort our thoughts, decisions, behaviors, and actions. These interferences keep people from always operating at our full potential.

Awareness, choice, and trust help people to focus their attention on what counts. The result is flow – the state where learning, performance, and creativity are at their peak (Csikszentmihalyi, 1990).

How do I engage people?

What keeps people from playing the 'inner game'?

What is my organization's potential for speed from 'within'?

# What is my organization's ability to innovate?

This is what your scores mean:

### Culture

**H**
**M**
**L**

High [green/white] = vibrant: people share the same mindset that releases productive energy.
Medium [yellow/grey] = invisible: the culture is 'unnoticed'; it enables an adequate work environment.
Low [pink/black] = toxic: people are tired and lack a shared mindset often due to never-ending change.

### Leadership

**H**
**M**
**L**

High [green/white] = interactive: leaders interact through productive conversation to support people.
Medium [yellow/grey] = busy: leaders are occupied by administration and discussions on goals.
Low [pink/black] = flawed or missing: leaders focus on targets, appraisal, and the control of behaviors.

### Systems

**H**
**M**
**L**

High [green/white] = diagnostic: control follows a systemic framework with reliable tools and routines.
Medium [yellow/grey] = formal: control is an administrative burden that keep people busy.
Low [pink/black] = broken or missing: control produces friction with people taking shortcuts.

### Innovation

**H**
**M**
**L**

High [green/white] = prospering: the organization is recognized for innovative value-added approaches.
Medium [yellow/grey] = preserving: the organization continued to do what it always did to protect its turf.
Low [pink/black] = missing/wasted: the organization is unable to reinvent things and wastes resources.

### Agility

**H**
**M**
**L**

High [green/white] = anticipating: the organization has the competencies to address higher challenges.
Medium [yellow/grey] = passive: the organization has limited competencies to cope with turbulence.
Low [pink/black] = freezing: The organizations fails to cope with a dynamic environment.

What are the implications on your management design, systems, and capabilities?

# Agility

## Culture, leadership, and systems capabilities

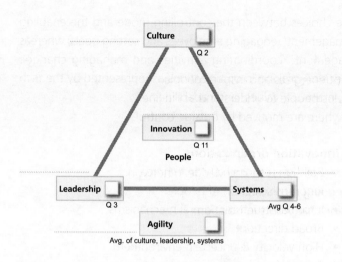

Agility is the ability of an organization to anticipate changes without have to change.

Agility requires a working environment with a culture based on a shared mindset, leadership that interacts with people, and systems as diagnostic controls.

Culture works like a social control mechanism where people act based on deep values and shared principles. Leadership represents the interactive control mechanisms as the direct influence on people and work. Finally, systems function as managerial controls with diagnostic tools that help the organization to capture higher challenges.

How do I coordinate work?

What keeps my organization from being agile?

What is our potential to capture opportunities to address a dynamic environment?

# What is your organization's ability to grow?

This is what your scores mean:

### Purpose

**H** High [green/white] = meaningful: a purposeful work environment energizes and inspires people.
**M** Medium [yellow/grey] = formalized: formalized sense-making helps people to understand act in line.
**L** Low [pink/black] = missing/wrong: a meaningless environment where are motived by outside control.

### Relationships

**H** High [green/white] = intense: a connected organization where people access to knowledge in networks.
**M** Medium [yellow/grey] = remote: Remote relationships require ongoing reconnecting.
**L** Low [pink/black] = destroyed/missing: a disconnected organization that works in isolation.

### Collaboration

**H** High [green/white] = intensive: a work environment where people exchange knowledge in networks.
**M** Medium [yellow/grey] = organized: leaders coordinate work and facilitate the sharing.
**L** Low [pink/black] = disrupted: a disconnected organization where silos prevent collaboration.

### Growth

**H** High [green/white] = developing: people capture opportunities and grow the business.
**M** Medium [yellow/grey] = maintaining: an organization with people that hesitate to capture opportunities.
**L** Low [pink/black] = restraining: an organization that does not grow with people not taking any risks.

### Resilience

**H** High [green/white] = robust: an organization with developed competencies to withstand turbulent times.
**M** Medium [yellow/grey] = bearable: an organization with sufficient purpose, relationships, and collaboration.
**L** Low [pink/black] = fragile: Inexistent capabilities put the organization at risk.

What are the implications on your management design, systems, and capabilities?

# Resilience

## Relationship, purpose, and collaboration capabilities

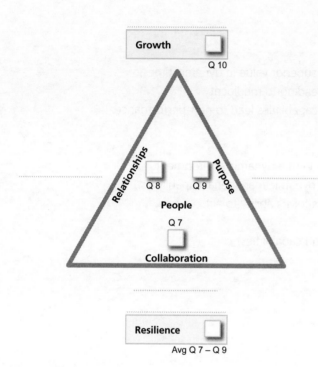

Resilience is the ability to withstand shocks and resist interferences in response to a turbulent environment.

Resilience requires an operating environment in which people find purpose in what they do, where they access knowledge in the network, and freely collaborate across organizational boundaries. These are the essential features of an organization able to withstand external shocks and survive despite ongoing changes in its operating environment.

Purpose is the prerequisite for responsibility, and trusted relationships are hard to break with people who collaborate to establish strong bonds as the capabilities of a highly resilient organization.

Goals determine the nature of purpose, relationships, and how people collaborate.

How do we set goals?

What are the interferences to resilience?

What is the robustness potential of the organization?

# What is my organization ability to perform?

This is what your scores mean:

**Performance**

High [green/white] = peak: people use their full potential to deliver superior value in dynamic times.

Medium [yellow/grey] = mediocre: interferences limit the potential leading to mediocrity.

Low [pink/black] = weak/missing: the lack of potential and missing capabilities lead to non-performance.

**Ability to act**

High [green/white] = extensive: Well-developed competencies cope with a dynamic environment.

Medium [yellow/grey] = restrained: 'viruses' interfere with available dynamic managerial capabilities.

Low [pink/black] = missing: the organization lacks the competencies for its ability to act.

What are the implications on your management design, systems, and capabilities?

# Ability to act

## Combining speed, agility, and resilience

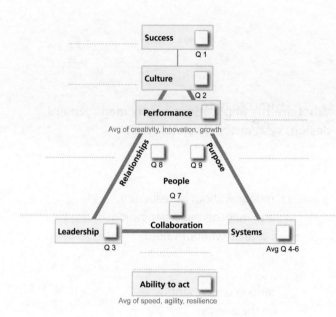

'Ability to act' is the capability to successfully manage an organization in a fast-moving environment. It combines speed, agility, and resilience into a dynamic capabilities with features to cope with disruptive change fast and, at the same time, to assure superior stability and robustness to external shocks.

How do I manage change?

What are the inferences to managerial ability to act?

What is the potential of my organization for a superior ability to act?

# What is my managerial ability to unlock the organization's potential?

Imagine driving a car. You need five things to do this successfully: first, the navigation system shows you where to go to (strategy); second, reading the dashboard, you know how fast you are going (information); third, the engine and tyres (implementation) make the vehicle move; your judgement, based on available information and the destination in mind, will tell you whether to push the accelerator (fourth, beliefs) or hit the brakes (fifth, boundaries).

In line with the driving metaphor, reading the table vertically reveals the following: good information systems help employees to make sense and raise the awareness of what is important. This increases the agility of the organization as employees can react on changes in the environment. Clarity of strategy supports leaders in providing direction and establishing a shared intent. This enhances the overall alignment of the organization. Rigorous implementation and performance conversations establish the shared agenda to address the capabilities of the organization. Strong beliefs enable the conversation on the contribution of every employee. This creates the shared aspirations and purpose for higher motivation. And clear boundaries with a conversation about risks help the organization to set its norms. As a result, the organization ensures that it is smart about how it uses its playing field.
The performance triangle provides the meaning of the 20 capabilities in more detail (Michel, 2013b).

What are the implications on your management design, systems, and capabilities?

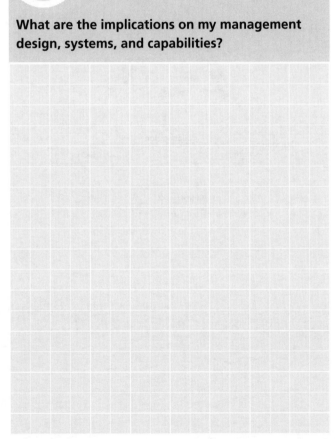

**What are the implications on my management design, systems, and capabilities?**

# The Leadership Scorecard™

The Leadership Scorecard™ summarizes 20 capabilities as observation points, with 15 questions, into a table for leaders to 'work in the system'. It offers a template for generic dynamic managerial capabilities (Michel, 2007). They become context-related and specific through the answers to these questions. The horizontal view of the scorecard represents the competence view (success, culture, leadership, systems) whereas the vertical view (information, strategy, implementation, beliefs, and boundaries) establishes the systems and control framework in organizations (Michel and Seemann, 2005). With the appropriate design, these capabilities turn into distinct organizational competencies.

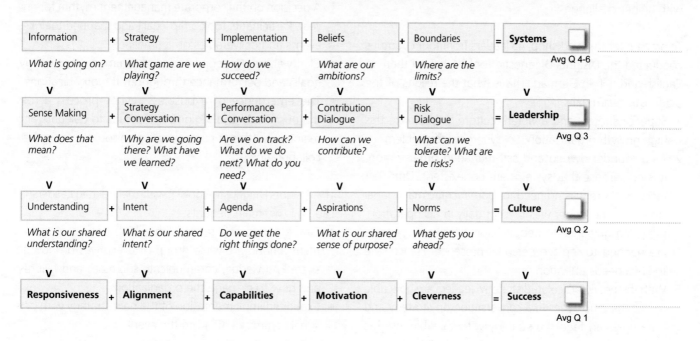

| Information | + | Strategy | + | Implementation | + | Beliefs | + | Boundaries | = | **Systems** | |
|---|---|---|---|---|---|---|---|---|---|---|---|
| *What is going on?* | | *What game are we playing?* | | *How do we succeed?* | | *What are our ambitions?* | | *Where are the limits?* | | | Avg Q 4-6 |
| v | | v | | v | | v | | v | | | |
| Sense Making | + | Strategy Conversation | + | Performance Conversation | + | Contribution Dialogue | + | Risk Dialogue | = | **Leadership** | |
| *What does that mean?* | | *Why are we going there? What have we learned?* | | *Are we on track? What do we do next? What do you need?* | | *How can we contribute?* | | *What can we tolerate? What are the risks?* | | | Avg Q 3 |
| v | | v | | v | | v | | v | | | |
| Understanding | + | Intent | + | Agenda | + | Aspirations | + | Norms | = | **Culture** | |
| *What is our shared understanding?* | | *What is our shared intent?* | | *Do we get the right things done?* | | *What is our shared sense of purpose?* | | *What gets you ahead?* | | | Avg Q 2 |
| v | | v | | v | | v | | v | | | |
| **Responsiveness** | + | **Alignment** | + | **Capabilities** | + | **Motivation** | + | **Cleverness** | = | **Success** | |
| | | | | | | | | | | | Avg Q 1 |

# Structures and tools to manage growth and transitions

The leadership team of a specialty food company decided to articulate its successful strategy and revisit the structures in view of ongoing high growth and the need to deal with increasing complexity. A two-day workshop was intended to review the effectiveness of management in view of high growth and the requirements on structures capable to cope with higher challenges.

To prepare for the workshop, 45 leaders from four countries conducted the INsights Diagnostic Tools™, half of them in English and half in German. This is what the results of the diagnostic test means:

1. Superior success and a vibrant culture characterize this high growth organization. So, where is the problem?
2. As a founder-owned and self-managed organization, it is no surprise that systems are nonexistent. Until just recently, there was no need for bureaucratic managerial system as the leader was present daily in his operation, providing guidance to people. Going forward, systems are needed to replace personal presence. Hence, the toolbox needs attention.
3. With the newly-articulated strategy, leaders are now able to engage employees in a conversation on strategy and how they can feed the strategy with valuable insights from clients.
4. Going forward, it will become important to make rules and boundaries explicit for leaders to coach employees on critical decisions. As the founder delegates more accountability to the management team and employees, it is necessary to install the appropriate 'braking' system.

**The Leadership Lab** served as a corporate development platform and simultaneously as an individual development effort for all leaders involved in the development process. The aim was to determine the key elements of corporate management and to initiate the necessary changes on site. The workshop served as a platform for the following:

- A decision on the corporate management rhythm for one year. Participants took a flip-chart and mapped their key events and deliverables on a timeline.
- Clarity about the tools needed to communicate strategy, goals, and performance throughout the organizations.
- The emergence of a business review process across the businesses and regions as a means to delegate and maintain sufficient control, and as a tool to strengthen collaboration.

The INsights Diagnostic Tools™ with their related Leadership Lab had two main benefits:

- Strengthened coherence with a high degree of agreement among a diverse group of executives on how to share knowledge, communicate successes and failures, and how to manage the organization.
- Expedited implementation of the new strategy with personal commitments from the event.

# Example: Specialty foods I Italy

## Fixing the toolbox to enable growth

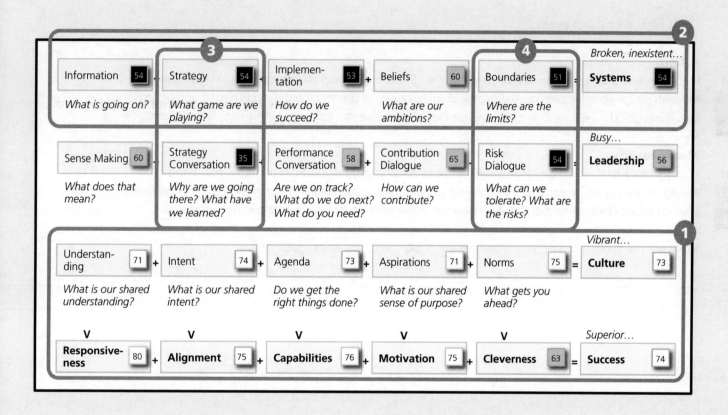

| | | | | | |
|---|---|---|---|---|---|
| Information `54` | Strategy `54` | Implementation `53` | Beliefs `60` | Boundaries `51` | **Systems** `54` *Broken, inexistent…* |
| *What is going on?* | *What game are we playing?* | *How do we succeed?* | *What are our ambitions?* | *Where are the limits?* | |
| Sense Making `60` | Strategy Conversation `35` | Performance Conversation `58` | Contribution Dialogue `65` | Risk Dialogue `54` | **Leadership** `56` *Busy…* |
| *What does that mean?* | *Why are we going there? What have we learned?* | *Are we on track? What do we do next? What do you need?* | *How can we contribute?* | *What can we tolerate? What are the risks?* | |
| Understanding `71` | Intent `74` | Agenda `73` | Aspirations `71` | Norms `75` | **Culture** `73` *Vibrant…* |
| *What is our shared understanding?* | *What is our shared intent?* | *Do we get the right things done?* | *What is our shared sense of purpose?* | *What gets you ahead?* | |
| **Responsiveness** `80` | **Alignment** `75` | **Capabilities** `76` | **Motivation** `75` | **Cleverness** `63` | **Success** `74` *Superior…* |

**H** High scores: above average

**M** Medium scores: average

**L** Low scores: below average

# What is my organization's ability to think, understand, contribute, adhere, and engage?

This is what your scores mean:

### Action

High [green/white] = superior: the organization has the competencies to support people decide and act.

Medium [yellow/grey] = average: the organization struggles in guiding the decision-making and actions.

Low [pink/black] = faulty/missing: the organization misses essential competencies to get things done.

### Manageability

High [green/white] = well-developed: interactive leadership and diagnostic systems support people.

Medium [yellow/grey] = demanding / time-consuming: busy leadership and formal systems limit actions.

Low [pink/black] = missing / defect: faulty leadership with erroneous systems work like 'viruses'.

What are the implications on your management design, systems, and capabilities?

# Action

## The work environment for getting things done

The five competencies that sum up the vertical view of the Leadership Scorecard ™ are: think, understand, contribute, engage, and adhere. They closely relate to what it takes for people to play the 'inner game'. For example, the organization's capacity to understand represents the result of superior information, sense-making, understanding, and responsiveness. The leadership and systems features, as the two competencies that can be directly influenced, provide an indication of the overall quality of the management as the 'manageability' of the firm.

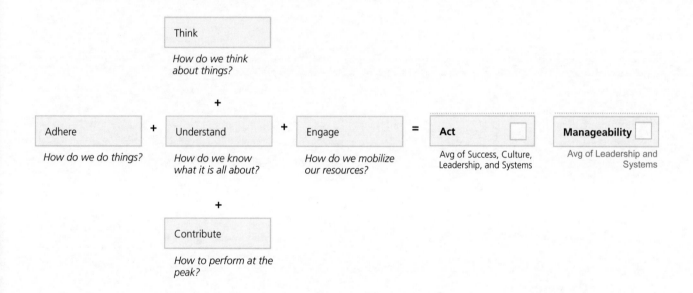

# What are my current organization's managerial capabilities?

The INsights Diagnostic Tools™ provide the observation points for the leadership team to understand current managerial capabilities. So far, we have explored the potential and interferences to a superior ability to act.

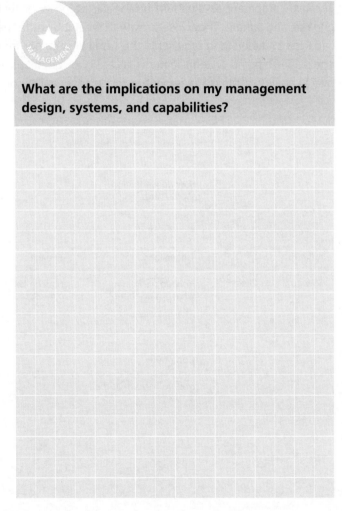

**What are the implications on my management design, systems, and capabilities?**

# Organizational capabilities

## The work environment for getting things done

The people, organization, stakeholder, environment, and management frames combine the organizational capabilities needed to compete in a dynamic environment.

The following table decomposes the Management Design Framework into its five parts:

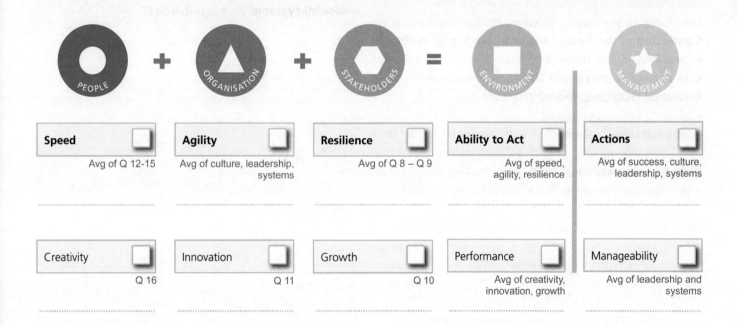

| Speed | Agility | Resilience | Ability to Act | Actions |
|---|---|---|---|---|
| Avg of Q 12-15 | Avg of culture, leadership, systems | Avg of Q 8 – Q 9 | Avg of speed, agility, resilience | Avg of success, culture, leadership, systems |

| Creativity | Innovation | Growth | Performance | Manageability |
|---|---|---|---|---|
| Q 16 | Q 11 | Q 10 | Avg of creativity, innovation, growth | Avg of leadership and systems |

# What is my current management model? In what dominant mode do I operate?

The five areas frame the management model of an organization: people, organization, stakeholders, environment, and management. In every area, leaders have the choice between the principles of the enabling mode and principles of the controlling mode.

The choice of the management model has implications on the design and the use of the systems Leadership Toolbox™.
- How do I engage people?
- How do I establish goals?
- How do I coordinate work?
- How do I manage change?
- How do I make decisions?

What is my dominant management model?

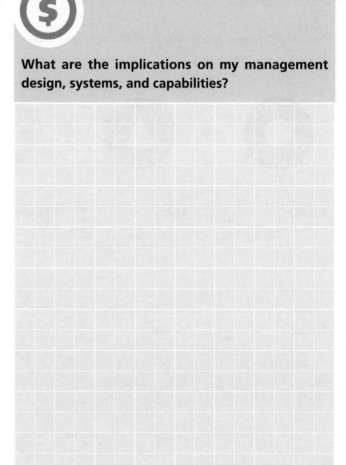

**What are the implications on my management design, systems, and capabilities?**

# Management model

## The principles that determine how work gets done

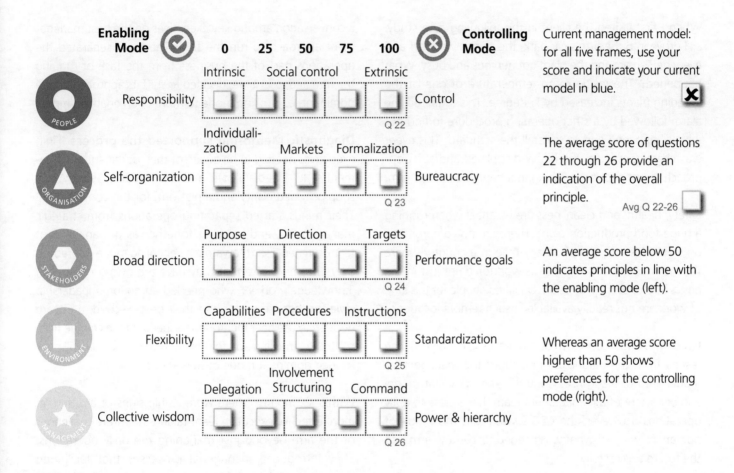

| Enabling Mode ✓ | 0 | 25 | 50 | 75 | 100 | Controlling Mode ✕ |
|---|---|---|---|---|---|---|
| | Intrinsic | Social control | | | Extrinsic | |
| Responsibility | ☐ | ☐ | ☐ | ☐ | ☐ | Control |
| | | | | | Q 22 | |
| | Individuali-zation | | Markets | | Formalization | |
| Self-organization | ☐ | ☐ | ☐ | ☐ | ☐ | Bureaucracy |
| | | | | | Q 23 | |
| | Purpose | | Direction | | Targets | |
| Broad direction | ☐ | ☐ | ☐ | ☐ | ☐ | Performance goals |
| | | | | | Q 24 | |
| | Capabilities | Procedures | | | Instructions | |
| Flexibility | ☐ | ☐ | ☐ | ☐ | ☐ | Standardization |
| | | | | | Q 25 | |
| | Delegation | Involvement Structuring | | Command | | |
| Collective wisdom | ☐ | ☐ | ☐ | ☐ | ☐ | Power & hierarchy |
| | | | | | Q 26 | |

**PEOPLE**

**ORGANISATION**

**STAKEHOLDERS**

**ENVIRONMENT**

**MANAGEMENT**

Current management model: for all five frames, use your score and indicate your current model in blue. ✕

The average score of questions 22 through 26 provide an indication of the overall principle.  Avg Q 22-26 ☐

An average score below 50 indicates principles in line with the enabling mode (left).

Whereas an average score higher than 50 shows preferences for the controlling mode (right).

# The management model in an environment where control is key

When I first visited the client in the following case study, as I drove into the firm's car park, the alarms went off and every person around the plant got nervous and busy. What happened? The inside room temperature of one of the breeding plants increased by ¼ degree. This triggered the alarm followed by a strict operating procedure to find out why it happened and to reinstall the standard. This event was characteristic for the highly-disciplined and strict approach to just about everything that happened in this firm.

Safety, health, and cleanliness are essential when running a huge food production plant. There are no compromises on standards and quality at any time in a country where the firm has to train much of its workforce not just in the basics but for every profession. Qualified people for this kind of work are not readily available in such remote locations.

**No compromise on control**. Under these conditions, the results from the diagnostic test about the management model are not a surprise. Control is the dominant model and behaviour of a management team that is close to daily operations. However, the CEO sensed that this mode of operations was not what was needed to lead the firm into the future successfully.

**Rethinking the management model**. With the results from the INsights Diagnostic Tools™, the workshop initiated

a conversation among key executives on the best management approach to run the firm. The team separated the operations part of the business from the task of running the firm and, over time, decided to shift its approach from a dominant, controlling mode to more of an enabling mode.

**Diagnostic Mentoring supported the process**. First, executives needed to be aware of their dominant management style. The diagnostic and the executive Team Workshop provided clarity and a platform for this conversation. Their minds started separating operations from strategic management, and working together as a management team initiated a shift towards the enabling mode. Moreover, they became aware that they have a growing number of 'knowledge workers' who needed an adapted leadership style for them to perform at their best. Second, the team decided to use peer mentoring to speed up the change from control to enabling and to prevent that they would fall back to their dominant mode of operations.

Within six months, there were visible signs of a different, more effective executive team taking the future challenges of the firm beyond just managing the daily operations. They introduced managerial processes that facilitated learning and initiated the development of capabilities that allowed them to cope with the increasing volatile market environment.

# Example: Farming | South Africa

## From control to include the enabling mode of operations

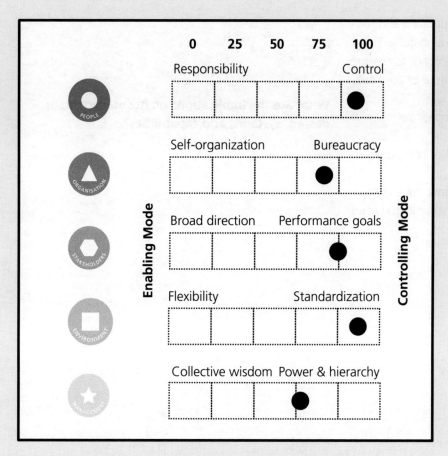

Eighteen executives reviewed their management model. This is what the aggregate result of their individual diagnostic means:
- Overall, the management model is based on control: all principles scored on the right side.

The question arises: is this the best way to manage an organization when 'cleanliness and food safety' is a key competence and a non-debatable quality standard.

# What are the challenges my organization faces?

Four challenges frame the nature of the operating environment: volatility, complexity, uncertainty, and ambiguity. These challenges determine much of the overall approach to change in organizations, and they determine the nature of the Leadership Toolbox™.

- How does my organization cope with higher volatility of markets?
- How does my organization address higher complexity in my organization?
- How does my organization overcome higher uncertainty?
- How does my organization deal with higher ambiguity and weak signals?

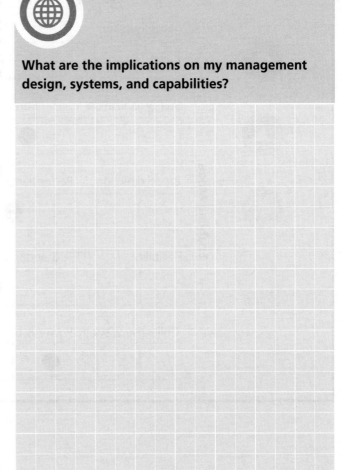

**What are the implications on my management design, systems, and capabilities?**

# Environment & challenges

## The nature of the challenges that determine the approach to change

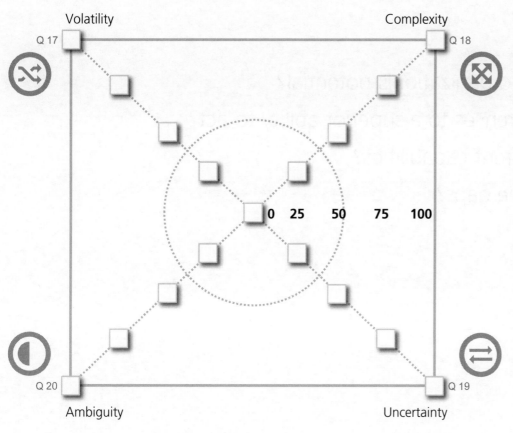

Current challenges: use your scores on volatility, complexity, uncertainty, and ambiguity and mark your respective scores in blue.

The average score of questions 17 to 20 provides an indication of the overall nature of the environment.

Avg Q 22-26

An average score below 50 indicates a stable environment (inside the centre).

Whereas an average score higher than 50 shows challenges of a dynamic environment (outside the centre).

## What capabilities support your management model?

Checklist: Did I…

- ☐ Identify the organization's potential?
- ☐ Spot interferences to a superior ability to act?
- ☐ Evaluate current capabilities?
- ☐ Articulate the gaps?

**What is my talents' ability to apply its creativity?**

My interferences?
My potential?

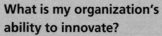

**What is my organization's ability to innovate?**

My interferences?
My potential?

**What is my management's ability to unlock the organization's potential?**
My interferences?
My potential?

**What is my organization's ability to perform?**

My interferences?
My potential?

**What is my organization's ability to grow?**

My interferences?
My potential?

FOCUS AREAS HIGHLIGHT THE ISSUES THAT REQUIRE ATTENTION AND CARE!

# DESIGN

**What are the key issues to close the gaps?**

# The tools to design the future capabilities

## Focus areas

Work on the system
- When 'viruses' interfere

Context frame
Four management models
- The people-organization bridge
- The Leadership Scorecard™

Management capabilities
- The choice of tools

Change culture
- The design of tools
- The use of tools

Design identifies the key issues that need to be addressed with the new model, new capabilities, and adapted systems to close the capability gaps.

The context frame guides a variety of think tools with choices on how to implement the desired management design.

The list of key issues helps to close the gaps on the way to a Leadership Toolbox™ that fits the specific context of your organization.

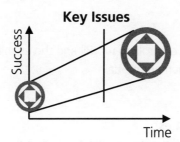

# How do I design management structures in line with the principles of choice?

A variety of think tools support leaders address the design of management with a set of key issues to close the gaps and to implement the design choices.

**Desired model and capabilities**: the Framework guides the identification of the desired management approach.
**Existing model and capabilities**: Insights establishes the base line showing gaps of the current approach.
**Key issues** identify the gaps between the desired and existing management approaches as the focus areas that require attention.

### Context frame
Both, the nature of management and the environment trigger the conversation on the specific context, the desired operating mode, and the required capabilities.

### Management model
The choice between the controlling model and the enabling mode has implications on the nature of the management model.

### Management capabilities
The different characteristics between the stable and the dynamic environment and the clarity of the strategy trigger the need for capabilities that fit the specific context.

### Operating modes
The difference between 'espoused theory' and 'theory in use' explains the specific changes for the design of management.

### Leadership styles
The need for the fit between leadership, culture, and the management model initiates a conversation on style.

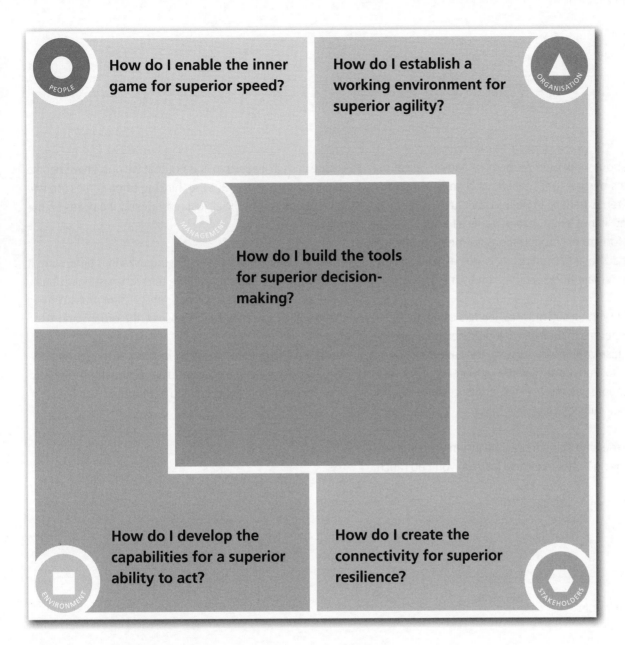

What are the key areas that need my attention to close the gaps?
What is the context of my operation?
What management model meets my industry?
What capabilities are needed for my environment?
What is the design of my toolbox?
What leadership style is required?

# What are the key areas that need my attention to close the gaps?

Design is all about work on management and organization with a systems perspective. Leaders who enter a new organization often experience bureaucracy. But just keeping routines going is not what leadership is all about. Great leaders transform their organizations to meet the needs of people and the organization. It is not acceptable for institutions to remain bureaucracies run by mediocrities.

To cope better with turbulent times, leaders create the best conditions for people to perform, and outdated bureaucracy isn't one of those conditions. As such, they ask themselves what it takes to transform hierarchical bureaucracies into agile organizations in which excellence is celebrated and people use their full potential.

This means leadership being more than just making individuals better. Having better individual leaders won't do much for the crisis in leadership. It is not that we don't have people thinking systemically. But the thinking often comes too late and change is superficial; just rearranging the boxes on the organization chart.

Effective leaders find ways to run organizations differently. It is not enough to get things done through existing routines, rules, and tools. Leaders 'work on the system' transforming their toolbox to serve the purpose of the organization.

'Work on the system' starts by looking at the current potential and the interferences as diagnosed with the self-assessment tool and as articulated in Insights.

# Work on the system

## What are the gaps between your current and desired speed, agility, and resilience?

To recap, the performance triangle model provides a high level summary of the potential and interferences in organizations.

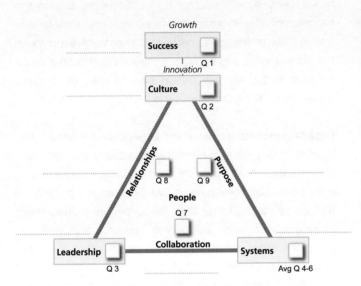

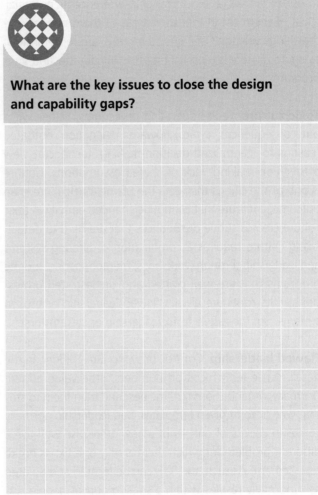

**What are the key issues to close the design and capability gaps?**

# What is my approach to removing 'viruses'?

Consider 'viruses' as blockages or interferences in potential. Most of them are in the 'soft' areas of the organization - the things we don't see and, therefore, are more difficult to address. Here is a partial hit list to initiate the 'anti-virus program':

**Toxic culture**: Faulty operating procedures, values without consequences, cynics, upwards delegation, outdated reasons for centralized decision-making, technocrat view of decision-making, lack of shared assumptions. Culture is one of the things that gets the blame, but culture is an outcome, a feature that cannot be changed directly. A toxic culture creates subtle dissonances that are hard to detect. Fixing culture requires a combination of altering systems and leadership through workshops, mentoring, or corporate programs that are well crafted and orchestrated professionally. Its roots are always flawed leadership or broken systems. So, the task is to fix leadership or systems first.

**Flawed leadership**: Control, busy, no time, hidden in the detail, sense-less, focus on numbers, little value added. Normally, organizations hire the best and train them to stay that way or to fit given templates. Bad leadership normally comes in counts of one – not many, otherwise we have a different problem for which there is only one fix: its entire replacement. As such, the flaw can be located and isolated as it normally resides within a small group of people. Ex-

changing a leader is an option but normally comes late. And 'viruses' spread. An immediate reaction is evident. Fixing a leader takes time and toxins might still spread for a while. It is expensive, and success is questionable, despite the promises of a huge 'leadership-fixing industry'. Coaching or training flawed leaders is ineffective. I normally recommend the performance and behaviour matrix. Performance problems can be fixed where there is a will to learn. Behavioural problems or any mix requires a different choice of action.

**Broken systems**: Bureaucratic or inexistent routines, formalism, faulty design, revisiting past decisions, slow implementation that slows decision-making, infected rules, erroneous tools. Normally, it is a selected set of systems that cause flawed leadership. Favourites are management buy-outs, incentives, budgeting, resource allocation, or communications. When it's broken, then it affects the entire organization. Systems weeds have huge leverage. HR, chief financial officer, chief risk officer, chief growth officer, CEO are often the cause but not the symptom – individually-optimized but not aligned. Fixing systems is critical, affects the entire organization, and is often a risk. But not doing anything is not an option. It is comparatively cheap to fix broken systems; it is a free choice and it can be done fast. But just fixing the toolbox might not be good enough. It might require a new design: a fundamental rethink of the way you lead the organization.

# When 'viruses' interfere

## A simple formula: performance=potential-interference

In many organizations, the unwritten and informal rules are the biggest obstacles to performance. Informal rules develop through cultural norms, habits, and shared experiences to cover all areas: thoughts, decision-making, behaviours, and actions. When rules don't fit the needs of people, they turn into 'viruses' and directly limit the potential. Such 'viruses' spread over time and infect the entire organization.

"So much of what we call management consists in making it difficult for people to work." - Peter Drucker

When the Leadership Scorecard™ is broken, effective leadership is impossible. Both extreme outside 'control and command' or ineffective bureaucratic cultures limit potential. Similarly, solely quasi-democratic and unguided, consensus-driven decision-making develops 'viruses' over time that prevent people from getting things done.

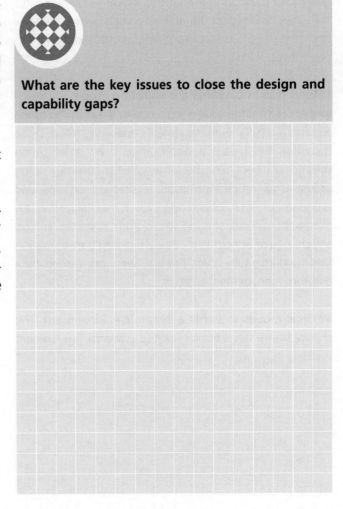

**What are the key issues to close the design and capability gaps?**

# What is the context in which my organization operates?

The move towards the enabling mode as a means for managers to develop the ability to cope with a dynamic environment; often requires simultaneous lateral and vertical moves:

**Lateral moves towards the enabling mode**: the transformation from the controlling mode to the enabling mode requires a change in management capabilities. More often than not, this means a step-change in an organization beyond just becoming better at what is currently doing or just acquiring different tools, techniques, systems, and processes, or just following new rules. It is a change towards a different mindset, attitude, values, and capabilities. Hence, any change of operating mode is a big-step transformation that fundamentally alters the way we work guided by a different management toolbox.

**Vertical moves towards a dynamic environment**: The change from a stable environment to a dynamic environment

with higher volatility, complexity, uncertainty, and ambiguity requires the development of dynamic capabilities such as management, innovation, agility, and resilience. The aim is to create such capabilities in order that the organization can cope with an ongoing dynamic environment without always having to change to enhance its ability to act. As such, a high ability to act becomes the capability for coping with a dynamic environment. Creating these capabilities with the help of the performance triangle elements establishes an environment with little interferences, where people can apply their full potential.

The assumptions about the operating environment determine the specific management capabilities. As competencies, they include the decision-making toolbox in organizations with the respective rules, tools, routines, and interactions.

# Context frame

## Mapping the current and future context in four operating modes

**My current context:** in line with the two scores for environment and management, as identified in Insights, mark your current context as market, competencies, rules, or resources in blue.

**My desired context:** in line with your choice, as identified in the Framework, mark your desired context as market, competencies, rules or resources in green.

- What is my current context and operating mode?
- What is my desired context and operating mode?

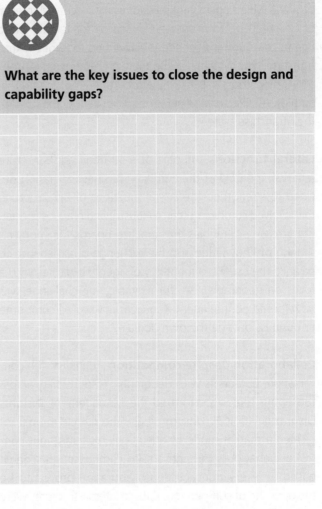

**What are the key issues to close the design and capability gaps?**

# Moving from a market to a competency context

Executive search in its tradition is a transaction-oriented business where agents are paid for every successful referral of an executive to a business in search for talent. These agents are quasi-independent actors tied together with a franchise-type system. Calling them entrepreneurs is probably going too far but they are certainly not traditional employees. Executive search firms differ in how they design their franchise system.

**Lateral functions**. As part of a strategy and structure renewal, the CEO of the European business operation decided to strengthen the lateral functions of his structure; this involved combining scarce industry and practice specialists across geographies into practice boards for improved sharing of knowledge and the exchange of experience to balance the usual silo mentality of agent structures with a focus on geography. So, for example, the challenge was how 'prima donna' agent X in Germany would contribute to business outside the own domain.

**Collaboration despite competition**. To initiate the conversation, 65 agents with geographic responsibility across the entire region performed the Management INsights Diagnostic Tools™. Unsurprisingly, the current model indicated a market mode of operations meaning tight control of behaviours through a sales compensation scheme based on every transaction. Collaboration proved to be the opposite of competition. If these lateral structures were

ever to work to promote collaboration, the organization had to deviate from its dominant market mode. However, this plan did not progress without interference. During the one-day team workshop about the diagnostic results, it was not just hinted at but explicitly said that two of the key agents would immediately switch to competitors if the sales commission structures was changed in their disfavor. I know many readers now smile as this is quite common in sales-driven business models.

**Diagnostic Mentors**. The executive management had to make a decision on a change of culture – a larger transformation that would slowly tilt the organization sideways without losing sales power (the ambitious targets were not to be compromised). With the help of the chief operating officer, the experienced Diagnostic Mentor crafted the transformation program that included the revised commission structures that included a better mix of factors to facilitate the lateral sharing. A new set of tools was required to facilitate the experience exchange and strict formal business reviews were needed to strengthen control.

After just one business cycle, the results showed clients gained better candidates. The organization shared its practices and insights across geographies which turned into a competitive advantage as recognized competencies in a variety of their segments. And, yes, several head-hunters that could not deal with the change left!

# Example: Professional Services I UK

## The shift towards competencies as the operating mode

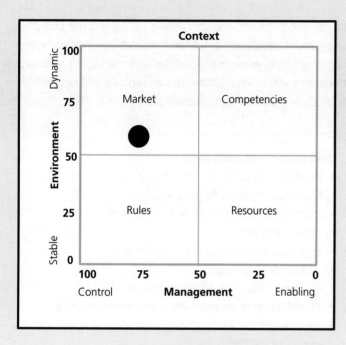

With a new strategy and a revised structure, the management team of a human resources professional services firm revisited its approach to management. They engaged 45 of their leaders in the European and Middle East markets to conduct the diagnostic with the following result:

- Overall, the 'market' context combines a highly dynamic environment and a controlling management mode.

The question they asked themselves was what operating mode best supports their strategy and structure.

# What is the management model that meets my choice of industry?

Four generic management models (Birkinshaw, 2012) frame the choices between the controlling mode and the enabling mode. (Employees) and stakeholders combine to the 'ends of management' (engaging employees and setting goals) whereas organization and environment represent the 'means of management' (coordinating activities and managing change). These combinations result in four different approaches to the decision-making in organizations as represented by the fifth 'management frame'. All four models imply different mind-sets, attitudes, values, and capabilities.

## Professional organizations
- Rigorous, tight, formal processes, clear rules
- Knowledge management, collaboration
- Inspiring place
- Encourage people to search for new opportunities
- Build on broad goals and intrinsic motivation

**Examples**: engineering type offices, foundations, consultancies

## Innovation organizations
- Build on responsibility and choice.
  Rigorous selection of people
- Informal structures, lateral mechanisms
- Broad direction
- High velocity & uncertain environment
- Default for start-ups
- Project, ventures in larger organizations
- Fun place to work but messy and often complex

**Examples**: Start-ups, high-tech operations, entrepreneurial firms, …

## Control organizations
- Awards, celebrations, promotions
- Standard operating procedures, automation, quality control
- Work in a stable environment with routine and linear approaches

**Examples**: large, established manufacturing organizations, …

## Prima donna organizations
- Internal markets, best people, rewards
- Tight goals
- Loose coordination, opportunistic
- Collective wisdom
- Highly informal – freedom on how to get things done
- Tension between control and freedom, personalization and formalization

**Examples**: Investment banking, insurance agencies, holding firms, …

# Four management models

## Mapping current and desired people, stakeholders, organization, and environment model choices

**My current model:** in line with the average scores of people and stakeholders as well as organization and environment, as identified in Insights, mark your current model as professional, innovation, control, or prima donnas in blue.

**My desired model:** in line with your choice of management model, as identified in the Framework, mark your desired model as professional, innovation, control, or prima donnas in green.

- What is my current model?
- What is my desired model?

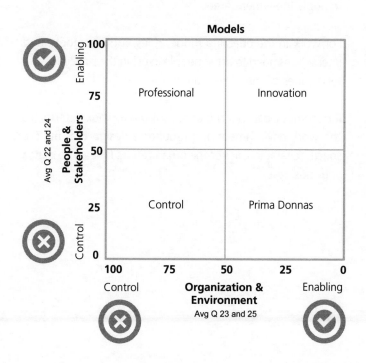

**What are the key issues to close the design and capability gaps?**

# How do I enable the 'inner game' for superior speed?

With the people frame, we now turn to matching individual with organizational capabilities.

Organizations in the enabling mode favor self-responsibility as the principle to engage people. Organizations in a stable environment tend to use control as a means to manage people.

**Self-responsibility** builds on choice, awareness, focus of attention, and trust.

**Control** results in standardization, command, aiming at goals, and mistrust.
For the enabling mode or the controlling mode, rules, routines, tools, and interactions follow different principles:

**Rules** determine the game. As explicitly-articulated or implicitly-assumed 'ways things need to get done', rules trigger much of the behaviors of people. The design of rules means to enable choice or standardize how things are being done. Often, rules are articulated in a negative manner –excluding the things that are 'off-the-list'.

**Routines** determine the pace through raising awareness or command for plan fulfillment. We all hate overly strict routines. But facts are that they free our creativity and foster efficiency. Skipping routines and discipline makes us slower not faster (Weinberg, 2001).

**Tools** as a means to frame decisions, enable focus of attention, and goal alignment. People use tools to increase productivity, quality, and efficiency. But they do more. They work like a human coach to reach higher levels of rigor and discipline.

**Interactions** are the most direct means of influence managers have on employees. Interactions signal trust and as such enable trust or spread mistrust.

For higher levels of creativity, speed, and employee engagement, the work environment needs to enable people to apply the 'inner game'.

For work in the enabling mode, rules, routines, tools, and interactions need to assist people in using the principles and techniques of the 'inner game'.

It becomes clear that the design of the toolbox determines the work environment and requires a design that fits the specific characteristics of the organization. It needs to match your business.

# The people – organization bridge

## Designing the work environment for the 'inner game'

Culture, leadership interactions with rules, routines, and tools as systems frame the work environment of every organization. Rules, routines, tools, and interactions strongly influence the culture of an organization and widely differ between organizations that operate in a different context. Choice, awareness, focus, and trust represent the 'inner game' as the necessary capabilities for people to perform at their peak.

For organizations that operate in the enabling mode with the choice of self-responsibility as the preferred model, the bridge between people and organization needs careful design.

Rules, routines, tools, and leadership interactions frame the Leadership Toolbox™. Over time, the toolbox becomes a meme - the idea, concept, belief, theory, ideology or fashion of how things are and how things are being done in organizations (Dawkins, 1989). Employees use these pieces of information and copy it through interaction and learning (Stacey, 2000). The toolbox translates into an important means to design "how things are being done around here". This is also why the design of the toolbox matters as it results in different behaviors in the enabling or the controlling modes.

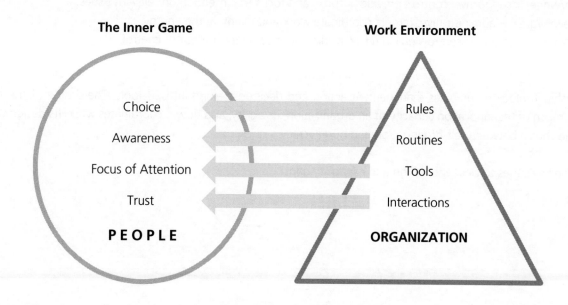

# How do I establish a more agile working environment?

With the organisation frame, we now turn to the working environment.
This is what your scores mean:

### Rules

**H** High [green/white] = effective: a simple set of rules supports discipline and responsibility.
**M** Medium [yellow/grey] = regulated: policies as prescriptions on how to do things.
**L** Low [pink/black] = infected/missing: inconsistent rules that nobody follows.

### Routines

**H** High [green/white] = enabling: a flexible set of processes to help us establish rigor without bureaucracy.
**M** Medium [yellow/grey] = conserving: consistent processes for a rigorous cycle to manage the organization.
**L** Low [pink/black] = bureaucratic: cumbersome processes for control and compliance without value.

### Tools

**H** High [green/white] = supportive: controls provide purpose and focus the attention on relevant issues.
**M** Medium [yellow/grey] = administrative: targets coordinate work and maintain the energy.
**L** Low [pink/black] = erroneous: controls pull in different directions or things are out of control.

The Leadership Toolbox™ combines management action and decision-making into 20 tools. The design of the toolbox determines much of the innovation capacity of an organization, its agility, and how it coordinates work. Its design varies in line with the choice between self-organization and bureaucracy.

What are the key issues to close the design and capability gaps?

# The Leadership Toolbox™

The Leadership Toolbox™ includes 20 broad categories as capabilities with an origin in self-organization (Foerster, 1984; Luhmann, 2008; Meadows, 2009; Senge, 1990), systems theory (Kappelhoff, 2002), and managerial control (Simons, 1995). The vertical view of the tools represents the control perspective –'work in the system' where as the horizontal view reflects a competency view based on the performance triangle model and 'work on the system'.

These 'big systems' represent categories as bundles of capabilities. Their labels and how they are used in organizations are context and situation specific. Examples include employee engagement, how we inspire employees to perform, might be called a different thing in any individual organization. These categories represent capabilities with generic, universal functionalities (Michel, 2013a). This makes the toolbox fit any size organization in the profit and non-for-profit sectors.

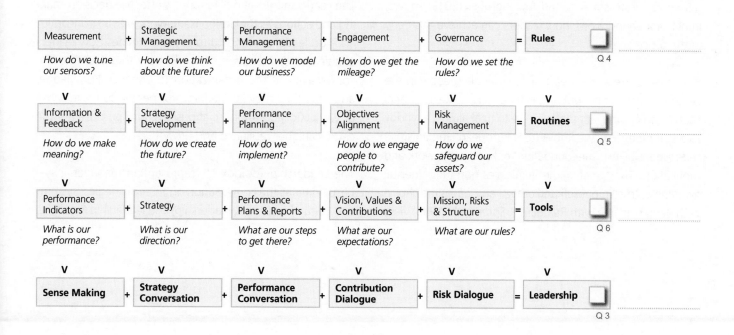

# How do I create the connectivity for superior resilience?

Still using the stakeholders frame, we now turn to goal setting and the nature of relationships.

The performance triangle serves as the model and bridge between the competencies of people and the challenges organizations face. It uncovers the managerial capabilities organizations need to achieve peak performance levels.

In the enabling mode with predominant self-organization, a preparatory step towards organizations' superior ability to act is to gain a deep understanding of future organizational capabilities in order identify the required talent, teams, and networks. Professor Johanna Anzengruber (2013) shows, in her pioneering work, how leaders can achieve this early in the process.

Such talents are at the heart of the triangle (people in the centre). In many of his writings, Peter Drucker advises leaders should "accept the fact that we have to treat almost anybody as a volunteer." As we know from European Humanisms , self-responsibility is the foundation for knowledge work and motivation. The 'inner game' reinforces non-judgemental awareness, trust in oneself and others, and leaves the choice with people. In line with Reinhard K Sprenger's (1995) view that "trust is the fastest management concept", the 'inner game' promotes speed in organizations through decisions at the client front, through applied knowledge, and leaders who do not interfere.

Culture, leadership, and systems frame the corners of the triangle. The Leadership Scorecard™ combines 20 capabilities into a framework that serves both effective management and the design of the work environment. Shared context, intense interactions, and diagnostic controls make organizations agile.

The Leadership Toolbox™ supports effective decision-making and actions as the design framework with a strong influence on leadership and culture. It determines how leaders enable the coordination of work, how they facilitate the connectivity of the organization to enhance knowledge, and how they provide meaning for people to make sense of work. Collaboration, relationships, and purpose are the clues to higher resilience and growth.

The Leadership Toolbox ™, representing managerial systems, initiates the conversation on three strategies: systems and culture; systems & leadership; and leadership & culture.

# Meaning, coordination and connectivity

**Purpose**, **relationships**, and **collaboration** are the bonding elements of the triangle. For superior decisions, knowledge work requires purpose. Purpose is another dominant source of motivation. Empowered employees use internal and external relationships to share and expand their knowledge to create value for their clients. Only knowledge that is shared and applied has value for any organization. New technologies facilitate the transfer of knowledge in a way that generates new knowledge. Any knowledge-related task in an organization requires more than one individual for completion. It is the combined knowledge and the shared experiences that stimulate creativity, innovation, and growth.

To illustrate this, the image of the Borg society in the *Star Trek, Next Generation* TV series, where millions of individuals were connected mentally through a vast neural network so the experiences of any single individual were immediately shared with the entire collective, may lead the future (Michel and Nold, 2013).

Collaboration across boundaries is essential to tap into the collective intelligence of people and deal more effectively with a turbulent environment. Shared purpose, relationships across networks, and boundary-free collaboration are the organizational capabilities to withstand external shocks and defend against unexpected outside influences. They are the building blocks of a resilient organization, the glue that keeps culture, leadership, systems, and people at the centre together.

# How do I establish superior purpose?

The following four positions indicate your current and desired source of meaning:

**Short-sighted**: low focus and high energy. Being busy and doing productive work becomes confused , intensity often results in inefficiencies or progress in the wrong direction; apparent short-sighted habits and ineffective behaviours dominate. In a crisis, action dominates reflection, often changing themes and initiatives.

**Purposeful**: high focus and high energy. Characterised by stepping back and reflecting, explaining goals and intent, people are convinced they are contributing something and feel accountable for what they do, self-determined and experience a high level of freedom.

**Distant**: high focus and low energy. Teams are exhausted, they lack their own resources, defensive reactions prevail and people have been trained, over time, to focus on their point, ignore reality, justify, constantly destroy energy; uncertainty takes over.

**Paralyzed**: low focus and low energy, Teams conduct routine work – administration, don't show initiative to tackle new things, busy all the time with something.

The generic strategy, to reach the flow line ( flow being the zone where people perform at their peak). It begins with a lateral move: increasing focus through systems. Systems establish the desired culture over time. Hence, culture will adjust, with a time lag, to alterations of the Leadership Toolbox™. Energy will build up and shape the culture. Diagnostic systems and shared context culture will establish superior meaning.

**What are the key issues to close the design and capability gaps?**

# The systems-culture strategy

## Mapping energy levels and the ability to focus attention in four positions

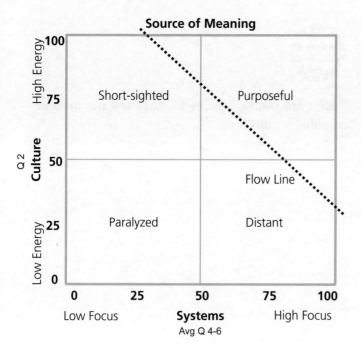

**My current position**: in line with the two scores for culture and systems, as identified in Insights, mark your current position as short-sighted, purposeful, distant, or paralyzed in blue.

**My desired position?** Mark your choice as short-sighted, purposeful, distant, or paralyzed in green.

- What is my current position?
- What is my desired position?
- What is my strategy?
- How do I get from the current position to the desired position?

# How do I establish superior collaboration?

The following four positions indicate your current and desired coordination of work:

**Scattered**: low focus and high attention. Leaders compensate for broken systems by paying attention to the things that matter most for themselves, missing out on synergies and walking in different directions. Missing feedback and information results in scattered attention, where it is difficult to collaborate on too many things.

**Collaborative**: in control – high focus and high attention. Diagnostic systems support interactive leadership to focus leaders and employees on important things. As a result, employees collaborate to solve the shared problem.

**Ill-focused**: high focus and low attention. Diagnostic systems guide managers, without reflection, to pay attention to things that don't matter, missing out on relevant opportunities and risks. With managers not interacting to come to a consensus on a shared problem, employees cannot cooperate to address challenges, despite clarity on what needs to be done.

**Undermanaged**: little focus and low attention. Broken systems lead to faulty decisions and leadership not paying attention to what matters most. Without any interaction and information on what matters, employees cannot collaborate on anything.

The generic strategy, to reach the flow line, is clear. It comprises a lateral move: increase focus through systems. Systems enable superior leadership over time. Second, leadership will adjust, with a time lag, to alterations of the Leadership Toolbox™. Attention will increase as part of leadership interactions and diagnostic systems. Diagnostic systems and interactive leadership establish superior collaboration.

**What are the key issues to close the design and capability gaps?**

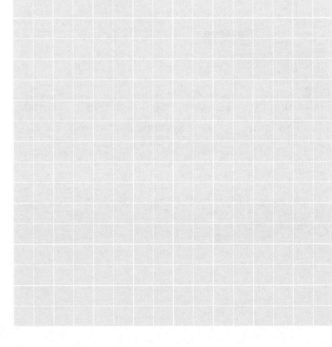

# The leadership-culture strategy

## Mapping attention levels and the ability to focus in four positions

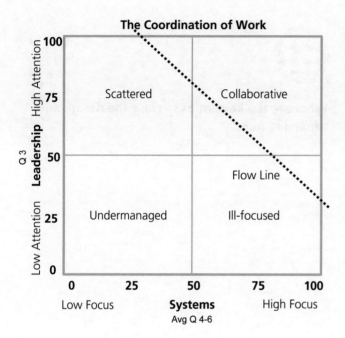

**The Coordination of Work**

*Leadership* — High Attention / Low Attention (Q 3)

- 100
- 75 — Scattered | Collaborative
- 50
- — Flow Line
- 25 — Undermanaged | Ill-focused
- 0

0    25    50    75    100

Low Focus    **Systems**    High Focus
Avg Q 4-6

**My current position**: in line with the two scores for leadership and systems, as identified in Insights, mark your current position as scattered, collaborative, ill-focused, or undermanaged in blue.

**My desired position?** Mark your choice as scattered, collaborative, ill-focused, or undermanaged in green.

- What is my current position?
- What is my desired position?
- What is my strategy?
- How do I get from the current position to the desired position?

**189**

# How do I establish superior relationships?

The following four positions indicate your current and desired source of meaning:

**Wasted**: low attention and high energy. People are continuously busy, low activity bores, there is a need for ongoing motivation, lots of action but little impact, people are blind to inefficiencies, miss opportunities or the right time.

**Connected**: high attention and high energy. High awareness of energy and time and a good balance of operational work with strategy, strong bonds among people and with the organization. Collective leadership prevails.

**Administrative**: high attention and low energy. People work long hours but with little impact, get things done; there is little room to tackle additional things as they use all their reserves – concepts constantly change, teams are often bored.

**Hesitant**: low attention and low energy. People stand in each other's way, do just the necessary, resist change, are mobilized by others, have a hard time escaping the negative spiral. Individual leaders dominate through command and control.

The generic strategy, to reach the flow line, is clear. It begins wth a lateral move: increased attention through interactive leadership. Superior leadership improves the culture over time. The culture will adapt, with a time lag, to alterations of leaders using the Leadership Toolbox™ interactively. Energy will increase as part of leadership interactions. Interactive leadership and a shared context culture will establish superior relationships.

**What are the key issues to close the design and capability gaps?**

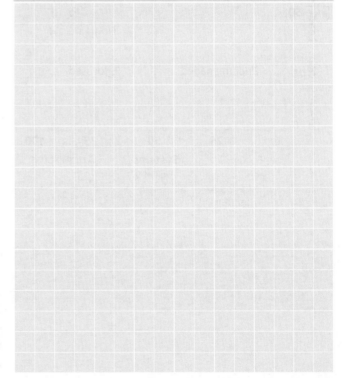

# The systems-culture strategy

## Mapping energy levels and attention in four positions

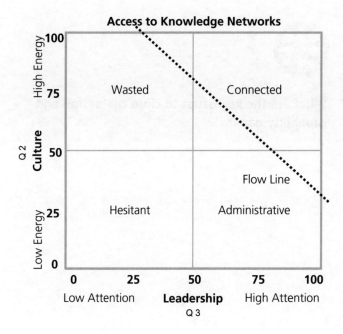

**My current position**: in line with the two scores on culture and leadership, as identified in Insights, mark your current position as wasted, connected, administrative, or hesitant in blue.

**My desired position?** Mark your choice as wasted, connected, administrative, or hesitant in green.

- What is my current position?
- What is my desired position?
- What is my strategy?
- How do I get from the current position to the desired position?

# How do you develop capabilities for a superior ability to act?

With the 'environment frame', we now turn to managerial capabilities. The combination of environment and strategy results in four generic approaches to manage an organization:

- **Learning**: managing as learning from patterns and themes.
- **Experimentation**: managing in line with options and models.
- **Mapping**: managing by looking at an organization as a system with levers.
- **Rationalizing**: managing analytically and standardizing for efficiency.

In situations with high clarity and great stability, rational approaches to management work fine. Classic standard operating procedures are effective in supporting leaders to manage strategy, performance, and risks. It is critical that leaders pick controls that best support their specific task and set their standards.

With higher challenges, or little clarity on strategic intent, traditional operating systems are no longer sufficient. Higher market and internal challenges require the organization to continuously learn and search for new patterns. When the strategy is difficult to articulate, a systems-view helps to create maps and define critical levers. Operating systems with these features require a different design.

With both, higher challenges and little clarity on strategy, options and models help leaders establish their agenda. This requires a structured approach to management.

Ir becomes clear that every response to the challenges requires a different toolbox. Effective management in line with the specific context is a prerequisite to maintain a superior ability to act.

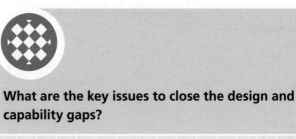

**What are the key issues to close the design and capability gaps?**

192

# Management capabilities

## Mapping challenges and strategy in four responses

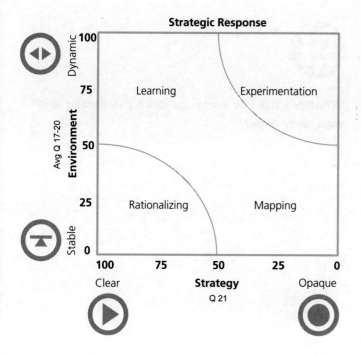

**My current response**: in line with the two scores for environment and clarity on strategy, mark your current response as learning, experimentation, mapping, and rationalizing in blue.

**My desired response?** Mark your choice as learning, experimentation, mapping, and rationalizing in green.

- What is my current response?
- What is my desired response?
- How do I get from the current position to the desired position?

# What is the toolbox of your choice?

It is a new management era for two reasons: one, confusing signals, more to manage, faster change, and less clarity dominate our daily work. But we want maximum impact with least effort. Two, the nature of work has shifted from hands to knowledge. Yet we still try to manage our organizations the way we have always done it: it is time to update the tools in the toolbox to the requirements of the new era.

The controlling toolbox is designed for predominant outside control. However the requirements for the enabling toolbox designed for greater challenges and the needs of the knowledge age differ with self-responsibility as the dominant principle.

**The enabling toolbox** is an inside-out toolbox. Its design enables people to apply the 'inner game' with awareness, trust, choice, and focus of attention as the principles that establish relationships, enable collaboration, and help people find purpose in what they do. It builds on self-responsibility to get things done. Its foundation initiates with people that energize the organization.

The **controlling toolbox** is an outside-in toolbox. It assumes that managers control work, motivate people, set goals and define jobs in a detailed manner. As such, the energy clearly resides with managers.

Each toolbox describes the opposite ends of a continuous line between the needs of the enabling mode and those of the controlling mode. However, there are many shades in between. This is why the Leadership Toolbox™ needs the design that fits the specific organizational context.

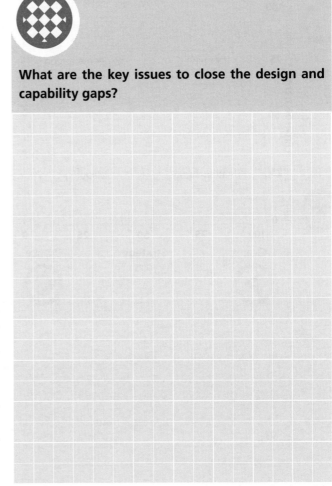

**What are the key issues to close the design and capability gaps?**

# The enabling and the controlling toolbox

## Two options for different managerial capabilities

Management teams use the Leadership Toolbox™ with rules, tools, routines, and interactions to manage their businesses. To meet the challenges of a business context with higher dynamics, changes in the business model, and varying strategic responses, the toolbox needs a design that meets the specifics of the context.

To simplify, the **controlling toolbox** works well in a stable environment with clarity on strategy and the setting of a controlling mode.

The **enabling toolbox** applies a context in a dynamic environment, an opaque strategy, and organizations in the Enabling mode.

The toolbox for a dynamic environment, an opaque strategy, and the enabling mode.

The toolbox for a stable environment, clarity in strategy, and the controlling mode.

The differences between the two toolboxes not only include different rules, tools, routines, and interaction mechanisms, they imply different mindsets, attitudes, values, and capabilities.

The switch from the plan to the people toolbox is a transformation that results in fundamentally different behaviours.

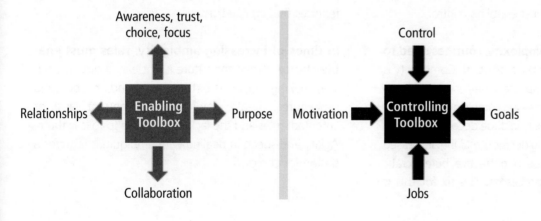

# What are the capabilities of my toolbox?

When challenges arise, speed, agility, resilience, and a superior ability to act are essential:

1. **To address greater volatility, tools must focus attention rather than aim.** When things change fast, people need something they can hold on to. Use tools that focus attention on what is important. With increasing volatility and market dynamics, it is important to get the control policy right as a balance between enabling self-initiative and fostering goal-achievement. The way to fix erroneous tools is to address their appropriate design for purpose and collaboration. Prevent focus on the wrong things by using tools that help people to focus their attention rather than just enabling control.

2. **To cope with growing complexity, routines need to create awareness rather than control.** Complexity is like water; it cannot be compacted. Better awareness is the only way to deal with increased complexity. Traditional ways of addressing complexity include deconstructing it, setting goals, and delegating decision-making. Increased complexity is a frequent cause of ineffective, bureaucratic routines and managerial processes. The fix for this is

appropriate design that re-establishes the lack of rigour. Prevent an emphasis on control by designing routines that enable higher levels of awareness.

3. **To cope with rising levels of uncertainty, leadership needs to trust rather than command.** The only way to deal with uncertainty is to trust in your own capabilities. With increasing uncertainty, it is important to define a leadership policy that balances responsibility and outside control. The fix for flawed leadership is to design interactions better to improve relationships and support collaboration. To prevent creeping uncertainty from hampering performance, interactions require a design with features that enable trust.

4. **In times of increasing ambiguity, rules must enable choice.** When the future is unclear, choice in decision-making performs better than standard operating procedures. Greater ambiguity is a frequent cause of 'infected' rules and the lack of discipline to follow them. Agility and speed in dealing with ambiguities requires a design for choice.

# The environment – toolbox bridge

## Mapping challenges and tools with the challenge matrix

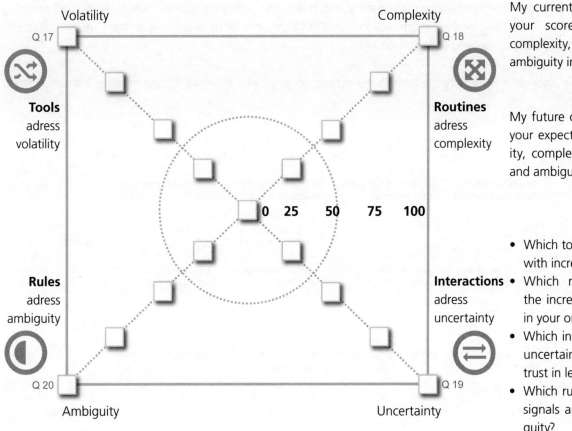

My current challenges: use your scores on volatility, complexity, uncertainty, and ambiguity in blue.

My future challenges? Mark your expectations on volatility, complexity, uncertainty, and ambiguity in green.

- Which tools help me cope with increasing volatility?
- Which routines address the increasing complexity in your organization?
- Which interactions reduce uncertainty and increase trust in leadership?
- Which rules amplify weak signals and reduce ambiguity?

# Which are the tools that help me cope with higher challenges?

To cope with the challenges of higher dynamics, complexity, uncertainty and ambiguity, leaders need to design their toolbox, e.g. the rules, routines, tools, and leadership interactions need to fit their choice of desired capabilities, the management model, the nature of their industry and the environment.

Use the Leadership Toolbox™ to identify the tools that meet the needs of your changed or new mindset, attitude, values, and capabilities.

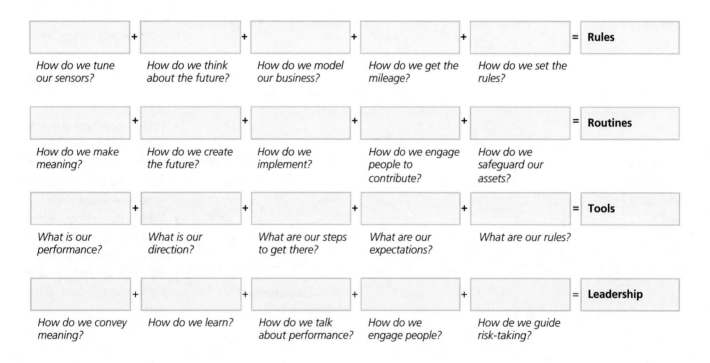

| | | | | | Rules |
|---|---|---|---|---|---|
| How do we tune our sensors? | How do we think about the future? | How do we model our business? | How do we get the mileage? | How do we set the rules? | |
| | | | | | Routines |
| How do we make meaning? | How do we create the future? | How do we implement? | How do we engage people to contribute? | How do we safeguard our assets? | |
| | | | | | Tools |
| What is our performance? | What is our direction? | What are our steps to get there? | What are our expectations? | What are our rules? | |
| | | | | | Leadership |
| How do we convey meaning? | How do we learn? | How do we talk about performance? | How do we engage people? | How de we guide risk-taking? | |

# The choice of the toolbox

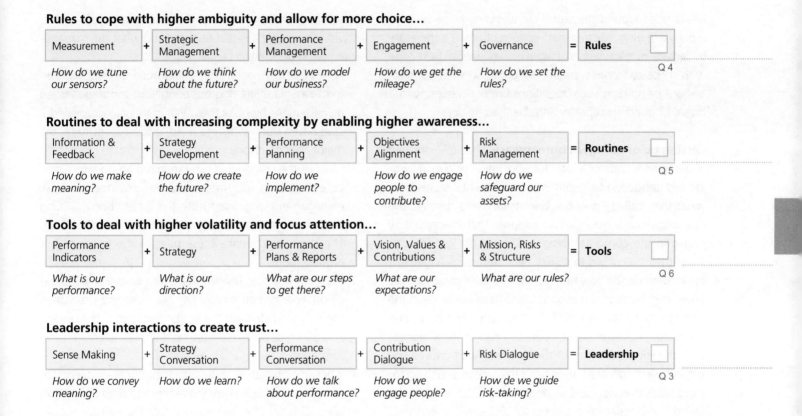

**Rules to cope with higher ambiguity and allow for more choice...**

| Measurement | + | Strategic Management | + | Performance Management | + | Engagement | + | Governance | = | **Rules** | ☐ |

How do we tune our sensors? — How do we think about the future? — How do we model our business? — How do we get the mileage? — How do we set the rules?

Q 4

**Routines to deal with increasing complexity by enabling higher awareness...**

| Information & Feedback | + | Strategy Development | + | Performance Planning | + | Objectives Alignment | + | Risk Management | = | **Routines** | ☐ |

How do we make meaning? — How do we create the future? — How do we implement? — How do we engage people to contribute? — How do we safeguard our assets?

Q 5

**Tools to deal with higher volatility and focus attention...**

| Performance Indicators | + | Strategy | + | Performance Plans & Reports | + | Vision, Values & Contributions | + | Mission, Risks & Structure | = | **Tools** | ☐ |

What is our performance? — What is our direction? — What are our steps to get there? — What are our expectations? — What are our rules?

Q 6

**Leadership interactions to create trust...**

| Sense Making | + | Strategy Conversation | + | Performance Conversation | + | Contribution Dialogue | + | Risk Dialogue | = | **Leadership** | ☐ |

How do we convey meaning? — How do we learn? — How do we talk about performance? — How do we engage people? — How de we guide risk-taking?

Q 3

# Designing a toolbox to support the transformation

Many cities around the world are investing huge sums of money in their public transport infrastructures. It is therefore legitimate to ask which management model can best cope with these challenges: traditional public services administrations or running such operations like businesses, with a board of directors representing the shareholders.

**Letting go of stringent bureaucracy**. The newly formed management team of a local transportation system in Switzerland decided to transform its management systems from what they called "public administration" to running the operation like a business. To support that change, they engaged the corporate INsights Diagnostic Tools™ with 25 of their executives to review their current management system and decide how to make the change throughout the entire organization. To explain the differences, here is the example of what they called "bureaucracy": to hire a clerk, the manager of the traffic operation had to file a request with the HR department of the city, then wait until all signatures were collected, then hand the task of searching for candidates over to another department that handled the hiring… a standardized process for just about everything. Many of the managerial tools were built to prevent errors rather than to enable good work.

The Leadership Toolbox™ offered a perfect platform for a conversation during the Team Workshop about entrepreneurial behaviors. This summed up their desire to change things and become more agile and fast in responding to competitors that had none of the bureaucratic legacy. This is what the diagnostic test revealed and what the management team decided to tackle:

1. They were convinced they could build on superior performance planning, rigorous budgeting and standardized management by objectives. While this area provided a save haven upon which to build, it turned out to be the major change effort.

2. Most of the managerial rules required an update. Competencies such as strategising performance, and risk management originated from the school book, lacking any tailoring to the specific context of the organization. The task was to make these rules fit the needs of this organization.

3. Rigorous business reviews were introduced to redo traditional performance reporting practices and strengthen the conversation with the major divisions of the organization. These reviews ended up guiding the entire transformation.

4. It became obvious that the management team needed to perform a strategic planning exercise to map its way forward. This became the tool to initiate the transformation.

After just three years, the city transportation systems was recognized, way beyond the country borders of Switzerland, for its innovative approach to meeting the challenges of a dynamic environment, with highly professional people working in an organization that is a fun place to work.

# Example: Transportation | Switzerland

## From public administration to running a commercial business

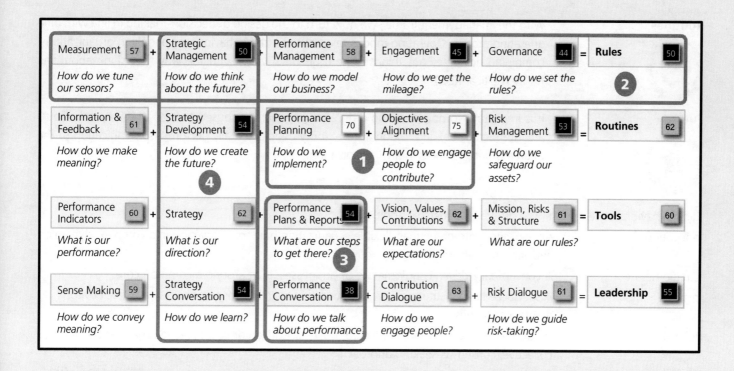

| | | | | | |
|---|---|---|---|---|---|
| **Measurement** `57` + | **Strategic Management** `50` + | **Performance Management** `58` + | **Engagement** `45` + | **Governance** `44` = | **Rules** `50` ② |
| *How do we tune our sensors?* | *How do we think about the future?* | *How do we model our business?* | *How do we get the mileage?* | *How do we set the rules?* | |
| **Information & Feedback** `61` + | **Strategy Development** `54` + | **Performance Planning** `70` + | **Objectives Alignment** `75` | **Risk Management** `53` = | **Routines** `62` |
| *How do we make meaning?* | *How do we create the future?* ④ | *How do we implement?* ① | *How do we engage people to contribute?* | *How do we safeguard our assets?* | |
| **Performance Indicators** `60` + | **Strategy** `62` + | **Performance Plans & Reports** `54` + | **Vision, Values, Contributions** `62` + | **Mission, Risks & Structure** `61` = | **Tools** `60` |
| *What is our performance?* | *What is our direction?* | *What are our steps to get there?* ③ | *What are our expectations?* | *What are our rules?* | |
| **Sense Making** `59` + | **Strategy Conversation** `54` + | **Performance Conversation** `38` + | **Contribution Dialogue** `63` + | **Risk Dialogue** `61` = | **Leadership** `55` |
| *How do we convey meaning?* | *How do we learn?* | *How do we talk about performance?* | *How do we engage people?* | *How de we guide risk-taking?* | |

**H** High scores: above average

**M** Medium scores: average

**L** Low scores: below average

# Designing a toolbox to support the transformation

**Routines**

With the 'management frame', we now turn to the design of decision-making in line with nine operating modes. Operating modes take routines (the behaviours of people in organizations) combining how they get things done (horizontal view) with the way they think about the future (vertical view).

**Future**

It is important to note that the difference between 'espoused theory' (the way behaviours are intended to be) and 'theory in use' (how people actually perform) is an indication of the degree of interferences in any organization.

Each behavioral style represents a different Leadership Toolbox™:

| | |
|---|---|
| Innovation | An evolving, entrepreneurial, flexible organization built for innovation in a complex, dynamic and venturing environment. |
| Conglomerate | A conceptually-driven conglomerate of businesses, built around a common core. |
| Institute | A specialized and institutional organization that searches for responses to specific environmental challenges. |
| Political | An aggressively-controlling, conflicted, politically-driven or collaborative organization with collective, consensus-seeking approach. |
| Mission | A strongly mission-driven organization with distinct values, myths, culture or ideology, often lead by a dominant leader or idea. |
| Clients | A customer-orientated, adaptive organization. It transforms deliberately and frequently to improve focus. |
| Vision | An entrepreneurial organization with dominant and visionary leadership. |
| Service | A service-orientated organization with distinct competencies. It must be well-aligned to demonstrate its unique perspective. |
| Position | A scale-orientated organization with a clear, generic strategy and perhaps commodity-type products or services. It strives to be best in its field. |

# Operating modes

## Mapping the future and routines with nine operating modes

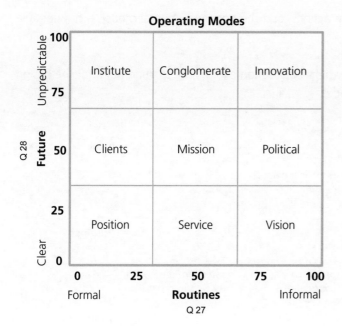

**Operating Modes**

| | Formal | Routines | Informal |
|---|---|---|---|
| **Unpredictable** (100–75) | Institute | Conglomerate | Innovation |
| **Future** (50) | Clients | Mission | Political |
| **Clear** (25–0) | Position | Service | Vision |

Q 28 / Q 27

**My current (theory in practice) behaviours**: in line with the two scores for routines and the future, mark your current behaviors in one of the nine boxes in blue.

**My desired behaviors (espoused theory)?** Mark your choice in green.
- What are my organization's current behaviors?
- What are my organization's desired behaviors?
- How do I get from the current behaviors to the desired behaviors?

# What is the ideal design of my toolbox?

The dominant organizational behaviours –how people perform actions, and the dominant mental models – how people think about the future, determine the design of the toolbox.

Use your selected tools and apply the design principles for your behaviour-action choice. The starting point for the design always is your choice of operating mode and management model.

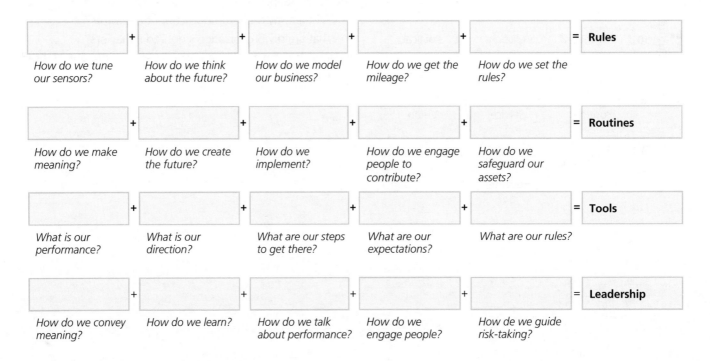

|  | + |  | + |  | + |  | + |  | = | **Rules** |
| How do we tune our sensors? | | How do we think about the future? | | How do we model our business? | | How do we get the mileage? | | How do we set the rules? | | |

|  | + |  | + |  | + |  | + |  | = | **Routines** |
| How do we make meaning? | | How do we create the future? | | How do we implement? | | How do we engage people to contribute? | | How do we safeguard our assets? | | |

|  | + |  | + |  | + |  | + |  | = | **Tools** |
| What is our performance? | | What is our direction? | | What are our steps to get there? | | What are our expectations? | | What are our rules? | | |

|  | + |  | + |  | + |  | + |  | = | **Leadership** |
| How do we convey meaning? | | How do we learn? | | How do we talk about performance? | | How do we engage people? | | How de we guide risk-taking? | | |

# The design of tools

## Selected design principles

| | Generic model | Thinking – about the future | Doing – the routines |
|---|---|---|---|
| **Innovation** | Images or tag lines | Models | Framing |
| **Conglomerate** | Thought processes and models | Patterns | Learning |
| **Institute** | Standard operating procedures | Programs | Coping |
| **Political** | Campaign | Cooperation | Defending |
| **Mission** | Frames with values, expectations | Content | Uniting |
| **Clients** | Guiding principles for value creation | Relationships | Integrating |
| **Vision** | Images of the future | Ideas | Envisioning |
| **Service** | Service advantages | Capabilities | Aligning |
| **Position** | Results, standards or projects | Positions | Analyzing |

# How do I match the toolbox to the dominant leadership style

Effective leaders use a well-designed Leadership Toolbox™ to 'work in the system'. Ideally, the leadership style needs to match the design of the toolbox and vice versa.

Four styles characterize different leaders. Every style is equally effective in its specific context:

**Cultivating style**: cooperative, tangible, strategic, learning, modelling, developing, idea-generating

**Outbound style**: visionary, values-driven, brand-focused, change-demanding, communicative

**Systemic style**: Process-and-systems-oriented, accurate, detail-focused, analysis-driven, plan-driven, fostering stability, continuation, and consistency

**Situational style**: Strategizing, innovative, visionary, ideas and concept generating, idealistic, welfare of people, creative

In knowledge-driven organizations with considerable challenges, it is important that the leadership style fits "the way things are being done around here". Diverging styles often lead to stress, tensions, or the loss of control. For example, when leaders with a dominant structuring style meet an organization that favours informal approaches, tensions are likely to occur. The leaders demand a style that the organization cannot deliver. In reverse, when a formal organization meets a little-structured leader, stress is the result. The leader demands speed and flexibility that the organization is not able to deliver. High speed, agility, and resilience require styles that the styles match the desired culture.

In general, the following principles apply: Structuring relates to routines (systems) and involvement to interactions (leadership)
- High structuring styles work well in organizations with formal routines.
- Low structuring styles work well in organizations where informal dominates.
- Highly involving styles are needed in an uncertain future where intense interactions are needed.
- Low involving styles work well in in clear situations where direct influence is effective.

# The use of tools

## Linking the leadership style with change culture

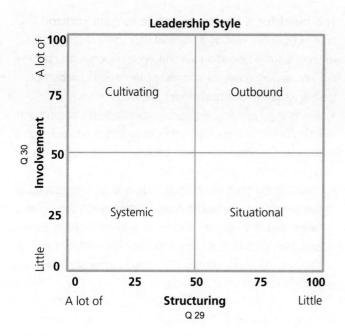

**Leadership Style**

**My organization's current style**: in line with the two scores for structuring and involvement mark your current response as cultivating, outbound, situational, or systemic in blue.

**My organization's desired style?** Mark your choice as cultivating, outbound, situational, or systemic in green.

- What is my current style?
- What is my desired style?
- How does my organization's dominant style match the culture change preferences?
- How does the structuring match the routines (the 'doing' capacity)?
- How does the involvement match the future (the 'thinking' capacity)?

# The case of over-engineered management

**The CEO office**. One Saturday morning, I received an email from the CEO of a utility firm serving a large geographic region, stating: "I have read on your website about the CEO office, can you help us to become better organized?" I agreed to pay a brief visit to talk to them about this. A week later, I took the train to meet the client. The receptionist directed me to his office. Walking through the building felt like walking through a hospital with all doors closed and dead silence. I approached the secretary's office which had a 5cm-thick door and heavy looks. With a friendly greeting, I was escorted to the CEO' office through another heavy wall with a think door. After offering me a coffee, she closed the door and it felt like someone had closed me inside a refrigerator.

**When the CEO's style transmits culture**. Well-prepared, the CEO eloquently explained his problem: "We do not seem to be well-organized. Work does not get done. I have tried everything, introducing new processes, training the secretary, and tightening goals." His desk was stacked high with papers. I asked what these piles were all about. He then selected some folders: 'new concept for energy 2050'; 'proposal for a new business segment'; 'request for a new position in department X'; … most of these dossiers were dated months ago. On a cynical note, 'Dossiers', in Switzerland, refer to issues that administrators work on until the problems disappear without action taken. It sounded like politics. In essence, I faced the ultimate example of a 'perfect' CEO who controlled every part of the organization. His style did not meet the needs of the organization. It was a difficult message to communicate; it did not need much analysis.

**The need for a less formal style to gain control**. The energy business was in a state of flux. It was obvious that running a small operation via concepts, papers, and dossiers did not enhance overall communication and collaboration. Here is what the diagnostic work showed:

- A dominant systemic leadership style: high structuring and little interaction. The CEO introduced lots of processes and tools and requested analysis papers but without sufficient conversation to engage people.
- The existing operating mode indicated an unpredictable future and very formal routines. It transmitted the leader's belief that the industry would be very different in future and that getting there required discipline and formal procedures. All tools, routines, and rules were designed for perfect control.

**A tough message**. The executive briefing was short and simple. As a diagnostic mentor, I went in there to guide the CEO through the findings. The message was clear:

- He could dramatically improve overall effectiveness by switching from structuring to greater interaction.
- The organization would run more smoothly if routines that catered to a less formal style were designed.

A wise decision. After reflection, the CEO decided to alter his direct reporting structures and hired a chief of staff to handle the daily operations and free the CEO to focus on his strengths on strategy and industry foresight. Today, the firm is well-recognized for its superior customer service and professionalism – a strong brand in an industry in change.

# Example: Utilities l Switzerland

## Sometimes less is more

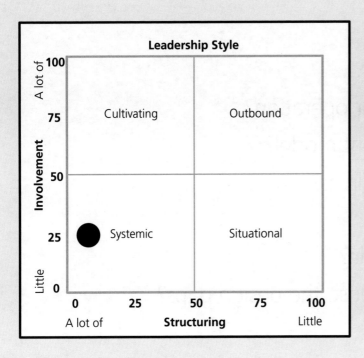

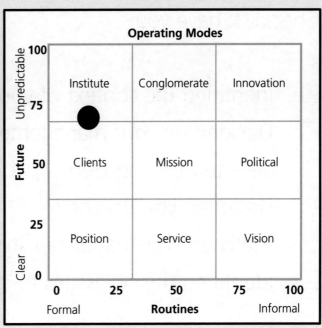

What are the key issues to close the gaps?

Checklist: have you…

☐ Identified the context of your operation?

☐ Decided on your management model?

☐ Selected the required capabilities?

☐ Designed your toolbox?

☐ Matched your leadership style?

☐ Identified the key issues to close the design gaps?

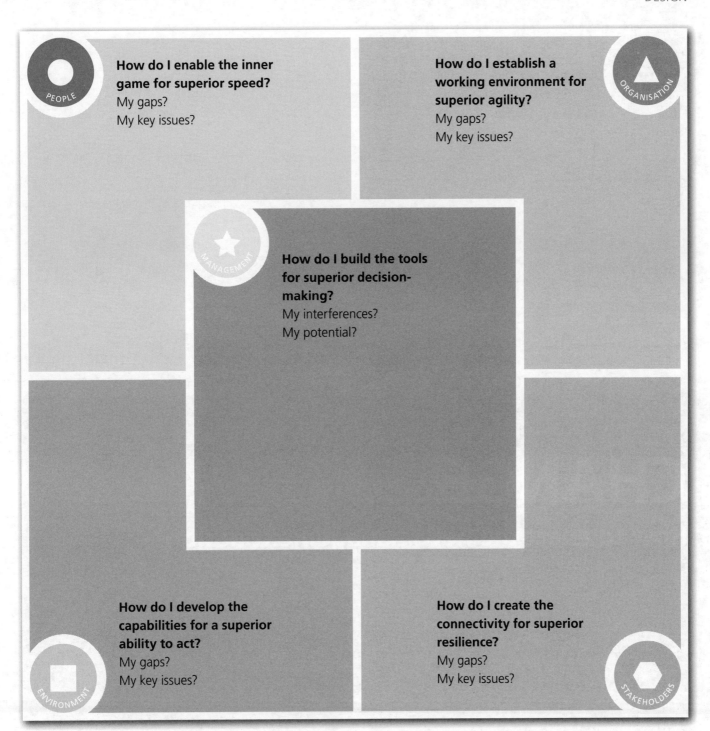

**How do I enable the inner game for superior speed?**
My gaps?
My key issues?

**How do I establish a working environment for superior agility?**
My gaps?
My key issues?

**How do I build the tools for superior decision-making?**
My interferences?
My potential?

**How do I develop the capabilities for a superior ability to act?**
My gaps?
My key issues?

**How do I create the connectivity for superior resilience?**
My gaps?
My key issues?

PEOPLE

ORGANISATION

MANAGEMENT

ENVIRONMENT

STAKEHOLDERS

NATURE DEALS WITH CHANGE THROUGH MUTATION –BUILDING THE CAPABILITIES TO DEAL WITH CHANGE!

# CHANGE

## How to enact the new management design?

# The steps to develop the change roadmap

## Leverage points

Intervention points

Levers of change

Intervention depth

Change programme

Program sketching

Transformation or evolution?

Change asks the question: which initiatives will help leaders adapt their new management model, capabilities, and systems to the needs of the specific business context?

The result of this step is a development roadmap and action programme to develop the required capabilities.

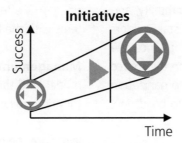

# Where do I start with the new design?

Change means 'work on the system'. It is all about the things one can change in an organization. This begs the question: what are the things that requires a new design?

**People**: exchanging people means change but, more often than not, people are the 'soft' factors and are difficult to change: doing this is expensive and time-consuming, one is probably not better off after the fact. People are one of the most important reasons why your management design may need the change.

**Stakeholders**: clients, owners, suppliers, community, and regulators often change. More often than not, stakeholders are not what you want change. But, they influence the resource base of an organization and are often the source for change. Changing the resource base of an organization is an important intervention through which to build new capabilities.

**Environment**: the increasing dynamics of the business environment is an important trigger for change but not the change itself. The task is to establish the capability to address ongoing change without recurring, disruptive change programmes.

**Organization**: the work environment, as represented by the performance triangle, is an important design element. However, success and culture cannot be changed directly. Both elements are strongly-influenced by leadership and systems. Culture represents the most effective intervention point. Any effective management design must address systems with the Leadership Toolbox™.

**Management**: the decision-making, the management model, and the capabilities are critical design elements as they determine the way in which we manage organizations.

What are the enablers and initiatives for the new design?

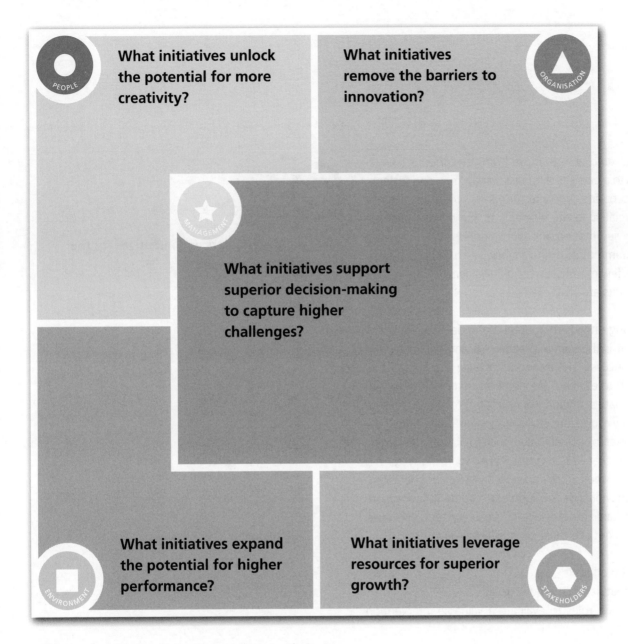

What are the initiatives to implement the new design?

What model, capabilities, tools, and behaviors support the new design?

# Where do I intervene in the system?

To fully understand how to move from the current management models to a new set of models, capabilities, and systems, we need to separate outcomes, triggers, symptoms, causes, and effects related to the elements of the performance triangle. I often see that organizations address symptoms with change programmes and find themselves back in the same mess within a few months. Exchanging leaders or cutting costs to change results are clear examples.

Profound change needs to address the underlying causes of interference: it is the systems, leadership and, indirectly, the culture, and success. The intervention table is a helpful tool through which to evaluate the elements that don't work and require immediate attention. For example, broken systems are often caused by exogenous challenges, for example, higher dynamics or a different internal setup, such as greater complexity. It is the triggers that cause systems to fail, so, fixing systems is needed. A lack of collaboration, individualism, poor decisions, erroneous behaviours, lack of purpose, and demotivation are signs of undesirable (side) effects of broken systems or flawed leadership. It is not the cause of interferences.

Here is how it works:
- Circle the features that require design
- Check on their roles to evaluate a valuable intervention points

**What are the enablers and initiatives for the new design?**

# Intervention Points

## Linking the leadership style with change culture

| Roles | and features |
| --- | --- |
| Outcomes | Value, growth, innovation, energy, flow, performance, and action |
| Triggers | Challenges ('the outer game'): dynamics, complexity, uncertainty, and ambiguities |
| Symptoms | Decisions on opportunities, resources, results, and people |
| Causes | Erroneous system, faulty leadership, infected culture, lack of success |
| Effects | Collaboration, purpose, relationships |
| Therapies | 'Inner game' with awareness, choice, trust, and focus of attention |

# What levers to I need to address?

**The search for high impact with ease to change**

System dynamics, and the work on leverage points, offer places for intervention within a system, helping us to find the right mix of size of impact and ability to address a specific lever. As leaders know from practical experience, people normally know where change is needed. Too often, these actions do not address the root causes of the issues. More often than not, they only represent the symptoms. They result in lots of action with little impact. This is why we need to pay attention to what is worthwhile, and possible, to change. The following table helps leaders identify the ideal intervention point.

The hierarchy of levers ranks intervention points with respect to their impact on the overall business system and the performance triangle elements. This means that a change in one area changes the nature of the overall system.

The change towards greater agility is a fundamental systems change for most organizations. It is a choice between two assumptions: either 'people are responsible by nature', or 'people need to be motivated'. But reality is never black and white. The distinction simply helps us make a deliberate choice and align the operating system with that choice.

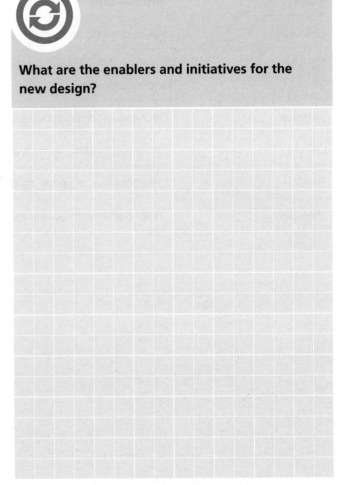

**What are the enablers and initiatives for the new design?**

# Levers of change

## Levers and their effect in systems

High and deep impact

| | | |
|---|---|---|
| **Work on the system** / **Hard to change** | **CEO** | 1 The power to change the paradigms |
| | **Culture** | 2 The mind-set deeply rooted ideas, and shared beliefs |
| | **Success / Business Model** | 3 The nature of the game, business model, success factors, and purpose |
| | **Management Model** | 4 The choice between self-initiative and outside-control |
| **+/- change** | **Rules** | 5 The choice of policies, constraints, and degrees of freedom |
| | **Routines** | 6 The use of diagnostic processes |
| | **Leadership** | 7 The generation of energy, relationships, and interactions |
| **Work in the system** / **Easy to change** | **Tools** | 8 The design of controls, measurement, and goals |
| | **Cycle** | 9 The availability and flow of information and timely feedback |
| | **Operations** | 10 The changes in use, levels, capacity, and stock of resources |

Small impact

# Hard to change – but highly effective

**CEO**: the leadership style sets the tone: The dominant leadership style shapes the way the organization thinks and what it does. A good fit between the leadership style and the organization's preferences supports change and prevents tensions, stress, or loss of control.

**Culture**: the shared mindset, intent, and values as the source of energy. Changes in the culture are critical, time- consuming, and potentially risky. Change within a culture that is not supportive of its purpose is unlikely to deliver the expected result.

**Success/business model**: the goals and expectations that determine the nature of the business model and the strategic direction. Change, in times of good results, is easier than when the organization does not deliver on expectations.

# Effective change – with impact

**Management model**: the principles that enable superior decisions. Models and capabilities create degrees of freedom for teams to organize themselves and create new structures. Change that is not supported by superior managerial systems requires an effort that is likely higher than the benefits.

**Rules**: the rules setting out how things are done: Managerial principles set the boundaries and scope of organizations. Principles work better than standard operating procedures in situations with ambiguities. Change without a base on solid principles will not last.

# Effective change – with impact

**Routines**: the information flows and feedback cycles. Managerial processes raise employees' awareness of what is critical. Processes are the tools that help leaders address increasing complexity in organizations. Change without supporting processes is likely to stall at an early stage.

**Leadership**: the interactions that maintain energy for growth. Interactions are the solution to dealing with uncertainty. Good interactions are enablers of successful change and growth. Positive feedback loops reinforce prevailing trends.

# Easy change – but little impact

**Tools**: the stable zones as source of trust. Controls enable people to focus the attention on important things. They work as stable zones, as negative feedback loops, controls stabilize situations. Changes in controls lead to different behaviours and actions by leaders and employees.

**Cycle**: the pacemaker for development. The leadership cycle of an organization determines the rhythm in an organization. Changes to the cycle are easy to make with a short time to impact. A stable leadership cycle supports change with a steady pace.

**Operations**: the buffers that stabilize organizations. The existence and the size of reserves have a stabilizing effect. Changes in these factors have little lasting impact. Parameters and standards: altering the distribution of resources, work goals, quality standards, instructions, or plans has comparably little impact.

# How deep should I dig?

*Management Design* follows: **Frameworks**; **Insights**, **Design**, and **Change**. Effective change is learning. Learning new management systems, models, and capabilities takes place at five levels with increasing leverage, complexity, and depth.

**Events** represent observable, specific examples that illustrate how management operates in reality: what do I notice?

**Patterns** of behaviour explain a series of events over time as the result of decisions and actions: how do we do?

**Systems** relate events and patterns into a systemic picture with structures, rules, routines, and tools: why do things happen the way they do?

**Models** symbolize the beliefs and assumptions on how we want to manage our organization: how do we lead our organization?

**Capabilities** include the potential and actual knowledge, skills, and competencies of people as espoused in organizations: how do we perform?

*Management Design* addresses various level of depth but always follows four steps guided by Diagnostic **Mentoring**.

The FRAMEWORK provides the overall concept.

INSIGHTS identifies the observation points.

DESIGN focuses the attention on critical areas.

CHANGE addresses the leverage points.

MENTORING guides the the development of new capabilities.

# Intervention depth

## Mapping desired depth with intervention steps

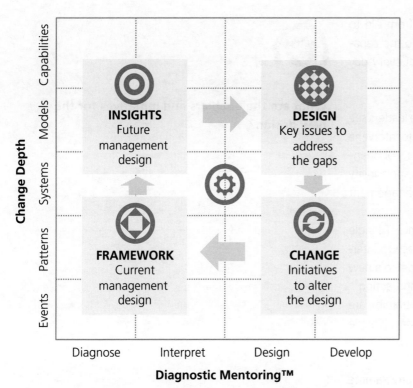

**Diagnostic Mentoring™** is a reflective process for executive teams to enhance their ability to act in four steps:

**Diagnose** management systems and models with the INsights Diagnostic Tools™.

**Interpret** results by using the performance triangle to define desired models and capabilities.

**Design** the Leadership Toolbox™ to meet the needs of a turbulent environment.

**Develop** the capabilities required to manage the organization in line with the selected model.

# What are my initiatives?

Changing the management model and systems from old to new is one thing, but, making it work, developing the capabilities to effectively 'work in the system' as part of every-day life in your organization, requires the following:

1. **Clarity about the intervention points**: where leaders see things going wrong might not be the best place to intervene with highest leverage. And, the shift from a control orientation to leading an organization built on self-responsibility is probably one of the most fundamental management transformations.
2. **Addressing the right levers**: The Performance Triangle explains that systems are the most effective place to intervene to enable change from an established model to a new way of thinking, behaving, making decisions, and acting.
3. **Work on the system**: design, mentoring, and training are required at the desired intervention depth in order to move from the old model to a new way of doing things.

As every organization is different, every change programme needs its individual design.

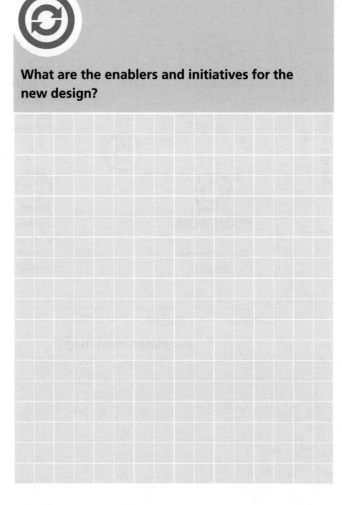

**What are the enablers and initiatives for the new design?**

# Change programme

Initiative to alter an organization's management model, system, and capabilities

### Intervention Points?
What needs to change?

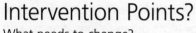

### Levers of Change?
Where to start the change?

### Intervention Depth?
How much change is needed?

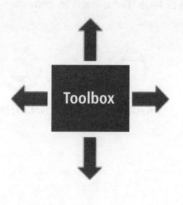

# What is your roadmap from diagnosis to implementation?

From an invisible, implicit model to a deliberate and shared model: the change from the current design to a new way of working seems more like an evolution or emergence than something entirely new. For most organizations, the existing management model is invisible and therefore hard to express. Making it explicit, to support your business model, is already a big step towards creating a competitive advantage that is hard to copy.

| |  FRAMEWORK |  INSIGHTS |  DESIGN |  CHANGE |
|---|---|---|---|---|
| **Time** | | | | |
| Conduct the diagnostic work | | | | |
| Articulate assumptions and competencies | | | | |
| Identify the potential and interferences | | | | |
| Develop key issues to close the gaps | | | | |
| Identify the initiatives to make the changes | | | | |

# Programme sketching

| **FRAMEWORK** Current management design | **INSIGHTS** Future management design | **DESIGN** Key issues to address the gaps | **CHANGE** Initiatives to alter the design |
|---|---|---|---|

**Measure**: use the INsights Diagnostik Tools to establish your starting point and base-line.

**Review** the diagnostic results. Use your experience and expertise to interpret the data.

**Create** a setting where ideas and creativity can prosper. Use the management model frame to sketch out your desired model.

**Define** the roadmap to change from your existing to the desire model.

**Walk and talk**: look for stories that support your case.

**Engage** your team in the review and make them establish their own solutions to the findings of the diagnostic work.

**Share** the model and test it with all your stakeholders.

**Experiment** with alternatives before you make it your new way of doing things.

# Do '2.0', 'new thinking', 'radical change', 'new paradigms', 'new codex' work?

Leadership advice is available in abundance as best practice, tips, or principles to follow. Most of these ideas are meant to replace old ways of doing things. Management is a practice that evolved through trial and error – not theory. Theory, after the fact, uses evidence of successful practices to distill principles that can be applied in general in the future. But the essence of management is how one puts these principles into action. This is where most advice fails. Facts are that advice does not always work. Here is why:

1. **Our minds cannot effectively translate "do this – do that" into practice**. Sport teaches us that only practice – not instruction - leads to peak performance. This is why management design is a learning process and essential practice for its success. Don't copy – create your own with the team: experiment!

2. **Planning and implementation cannot be separated**. If people are accountable for what they do, then planning and implementation belong together. This means the management design is part of its implementation. Don't delegate it – it is your own responsibility!

3. **Every context, every situation, and every organization is different**. 'General' does not apply. Often, management gurus present their insights as "from… to" choices. Management design is unique to every organization, context, and situation. Make it specific – this will be your individual roadmap!

4. **It is the action that matters over the thinking. Performance is real – not a concept**. While it is easy to think about a concept, its implementation requires potential and overcoming interferences. Thinking works with abstraction; action has to cope with reality. Management design provides a reality check and reference point. The doing delivers results – know where you are before you change!

5. **Context, situations, and organizations change**. As organizations grow by meeting and overcoming increasing challenges, they alter their ways of doing things, the context changes and specific decision-making situations differ. What worked in the past may not be useful for the future. This is why management design is a flexible process that caters to different situations.

# A transformation or an evolution?

## Initiative to alter an organization's management model, system, and capabilities

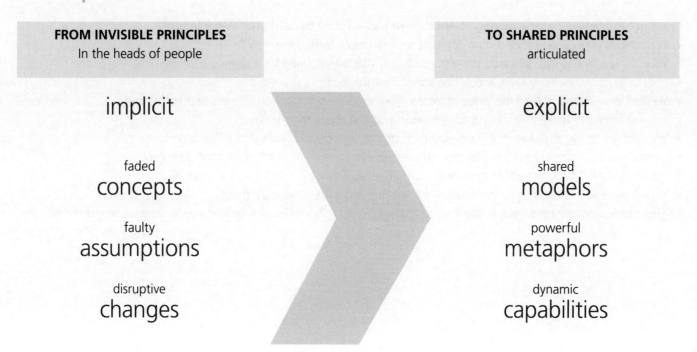

| FROM INVISIBLE PRINCIPLES | TO SHARED PRINCIPLES |
|---|---|
| In the heads of people | articulated |

implicit → explicit

faded **concepts** → shared **models**

faulty **assumptions** → powerful **metaphors**

disruptive **changes** → dynamic **capabilities**

# Why should you think about management design?

**Creating your own, unique management design has a set of benefits for every leader:**
- You look at your organization with a different filter to gain a fresh, new view.
- Your 'view of the world' becomes more granular and shaded, allowing for a refined management approach.
- Your ability to sense early signs and act on them are enhanced.
- You better understand how the hidden forces in your organization work to address them effectively.
- You are forced to make your assumptions explicit, test and revise them at times.
- Your stories become meaningful in the way they impact your people and other stakeholders.
- Your ability to address greater challenges increases as you have built your organization that way.
- Your organization has the ability to seize opportunities as they arise, quickly and effectively.
- Your people have the ability to make decisions sensibly and with good judgement.
- Your model connects the dots, puts meaning to the dots and their links, and enable you to address change holistically.

# Management design as a radical innovation

With the INsights Diagnostic Tools™ and the performance triangle model, management teams have the assessment, 'think', and design tools at hand that enable them to review management quality and performance. Some organizations call this 'fitness', others 'health'. The intent remains the same: providing insights into how management fits with the requirements of the environment, the organization, and people.

Insights provided the tools to decode management and organization as a system. Design outlined the logic for the fit of the work environment with the managerial challenges the organization faces. And change offered the roadmap to move from current state to the desired stage.

With this, we now can plot the performance of management design over time to recognize that its performance varies over time. Neither the design nor the environment are static. "It is as if they are made of rubber." (Waldrop, 1992)

The interrelatedness and dependences between management and the environment indicate that the management design from one organization cannot easily be translated to another (Arrow, 2000. The message here is clear. Any management design is different and context-specific, requiring its individual architecture as organizations co-evolve and the environment changes over time.

The question then becomes whether management design is an ongoing improvement task or whether it includes radical innovation? Most changes in the environment are non-linear which makes most improvement methods ineffective as they are built to cope with a stable environment. In a dynamic environment, organizations not only need incremental improvements but include radical innovations (Davila, 2006).

To close the loop, any radical innovation on management design starts with awareness of the current situation – using the diagnostic tools to decode the current design in view of a changed environment.

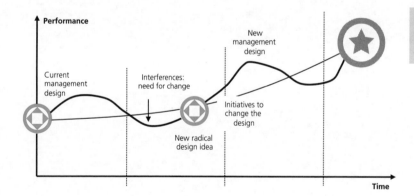

231

What are the initiatives to implement my new design?

Checklist: have you…

☐ Identified the initiatives to implement the new design?

☐ Determined the model, competencies and tools?

☐ Does the management style support the new design?

**What initiatives unlock the potential for more creativity?**
My behaviors?
My initiatives?

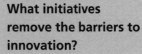

**What initiatives remove the barriers to innovation?**
My behaviors?
My initiatives?

**What initiative support superior decision-making to capture higher challenges?**
My behaviors?
My initiatives?

**What initiatives expand the potential for higher performance?**
My behaviors?
My initiatives?

**What initiatives leverage resources for superior growth?**
My behaviors?
My initiatives?

233

WHEN THE SUN GOES DOWN, WILL YOUR MODEL CONTINUE TO SHINE?

# MENTORING

## How do I manage with the new design?

# The process to facilitate the design of management

## Transformation

Diagnostic Mentoring

'Inner game' mentoring
Step 1: Diagnosis
Step 2: Interpretation
Step 3: Design
Step 4: Development and implementation

Diagnostic Mentors
The leadership cycle

Mentoring introduces the idea that management models are important but more than the models themselves, it is the capabilities that come with the model that truly make the difference. Hence, Diagnostic Mentoring introduces a four step process to build the systems and capabilities on how we manage our organizations for a superior ability to act.

Resources provide vfour practical tools for workshops in line with the mentoring.

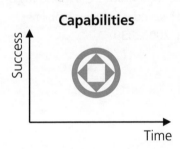

# Mentoring for management design

Diagnostic Mentoring helps executive teams to fix current issues and, at the same time, creates the capabilities needed to cope with the challenges of an ever-changing environment. Unlike traditional consulting, Diagnostic Mentoring leaves the energy with the executive team, enables insights, and guides the learning. It is not a quick fix, but rather an approach that strengthens an organization's overall competence.

As the monitoring approach for dynamic managerial competencies, the diagnosis provides a self-control mechanism with variety in observation points, processes, roles, and systems as second order observations (Clegg et al, 2006:.339)

Mentoring builds on the skills from the 'inner game' applied to individuals, teams, groups, and the organization as a whole. It includes:
- Observation, reflection, interpretation and learning for individuals.
- Interaction, differing points of view as a means to participate and shape the agenda for teams.
- A culture of constructive disagreement based on distributed power for groups and the organization.

What is my organization's approach to building the capabilities?

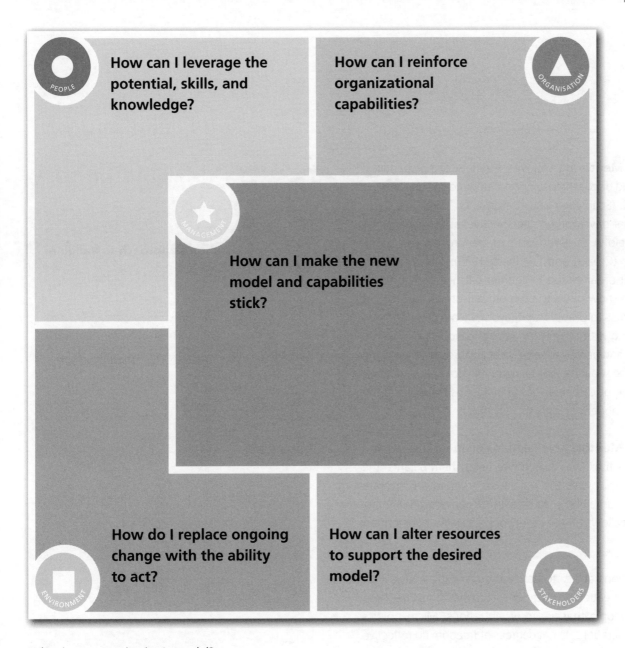

How can I leverage the potential, skills, and knowledge?

How can I reinforce organizational capabilities?

How can I make the new model and capabilities stick?

How do I replace ongoing change with the ability to act?

How can I alter resources to support the desired model?

PEOPLE

ORGANISATION

MANAGEMENT

ENVIRONMENT

STAKEHOLDERS

What is my organization's model?

What are my organization's capabilities?

How does my organization change from the current model to the desired model and capability?

# Reconnecting the thinking and doing

**Diagnostic Mentoring** requires a variety of perspectives, openness, and discovery to support authentic and challenging conversations (Schreyögg and Kliesch-Eberl, 2007). From an organizational development perspective, such 'uncertainty zones' are helpful as participants of the process can shape their agenda (Crozier and Friedberg 1979). The mentoring facilitates self-organization to counter-balance traditional hierarchies and show paths to promote self-organized work. It further activates, promotes, and involves team competencies such as dealing with complexity, self-reflection, combination, cooperation, and perceived self-efficacy. Moreover, mentoring reconnects the separation of thinking and doing as a result of the separation of competencies and systems by applying the dual process model.

**Diagnostic Mentors** combine facilitation techniques and business expertise. Their experience helps them balance the clarity of analysis with the politics of creating a corporate agenda. Their ambition is to establish a conversational environment that allows for the variety of perspectives (Habermas, 1981).

An organizations ability to act cannot be explained just by looking at bureaucratic categories (Crosier and Friedberg 1997). It is people that act in organizations. Micro-politics shape daily operations. What degrees of freedom do reflective observers have? Diagnostic Mentors ensure that "'double-loop learning' is the ideal frame for this discussion (Agyris, 1999)."

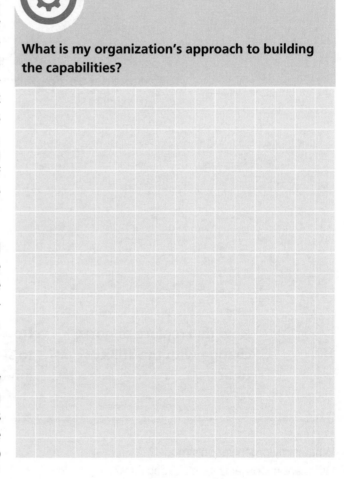

**What is my organization's approach to building the capabilities?**

# Diagnostic Mentoring

## Applied organizational learning

Organizational learning is the generic method for the adaptation of organizations to maintain competitive advantage. 'Strategic renewal' combines organizational learning with dynamic capabilities (Crossan et al, 1999). It connects the individual, team, and organization through a process including intuiting, interpreting, integrating, and institutionalizing. Moreover, organizational learning adds the actor's perspective to the economic view of dynamic capabilities, and it relates individual behaviours to organizational characteristic (Kim, 1993).

As such, Diagnostic Mentoring integrates the individual, team, group, and organizational perspectives into a holistic facilitation process. It combines the idea of strategic competence management with organizational learning techniques. Here is how it works. The following set of tools feature the following:

- **Management Design** combines speed, agility, resilience, and ability to act into a holistic concept.
- **The INsights Diagnostic Tools™** enable individual intuiting with a reflective review through experiences, images, and metaphors.
- **The Team Workshop** facilitates team interpretation through a shared language, cognitive maps, conversation and dialogue.
- **The Leadership Scorecard™** promotes group integration through a shared understanding, mutual adjustment, and interactive systems.
- **The Leadership Toolbox™** supports the organization, institutionalizing its routines, diagnostic systems, rules, and procedures.
- **The performance triangle** model operationalizes the capabilities: speed – creativity and implementation, agility –innovation and standardization, and resilience –balance, growth and stability.

# Integrating the Management Design Frames

Diagnostic Mentoring aims to build a solid bridge between people, organization, stakeholders, the environment, and management for the following outcomes:

**Creativity**. For higher speed, base leadership on a policy that enables people to apply their knowledge, skills, and creativity. Facilitate the' inner game' with awareness, choice, and trust.

**Innovation**. For superior agility, ensure there is minimal interference within your organization so people can meet bigger challenges and stimulate innovation. This may require a fundamental change from control to responsibility.

**Growth**. For greater resilience, derive your organization's goals from the needs and contributions of your stakeholders. Ensure your values follow your primary choice of stakeholders. Remind yourself that people-centric is the foundation for client-orientation and growth. It is your brand.

**Performance**. For peak performance, create an organization that caters to the needs of your people. Develop the capabilities of a superior ability to act. It trumps disruptive and ongoing change.

**Decisions & actions**. Superior implementation requires an environment where people make entrepreneurial decisions, collaborate to optimize resources, and are able to provide superior value to clients.

# Four steps: 'inner game' mentoring

## Applying the 'inner game' to management design

Diagnostic Mentoring follows the 'inner game' in four steps:

1. **Diagnose**: use your intuition with the Management Design Framework and the results of the INsights Diagnostic Tools™. The idea is to create awareness for the critical assumptions and principles as they determine your management design, the model, and the required capabilities.

2. **Interpret**: use the the Leadership Scorecard™ and the performance triangle model to interpret your results. Observation points help you focus the attention on the potential and interferences towards a superior ability to act.

3. **Design**: integrate your model and capabilities into the Leadership Toolbox™. The desired model is solely your choice. Once decided, the management design will guide your way to new capabilities and systems.

4. **Develop & implement**: institutionalize the new model, systems, and capabilities through your 'change roadmap'. Trust your organization's capability to address a changing environment, bigger challenges, and the new ways to work.

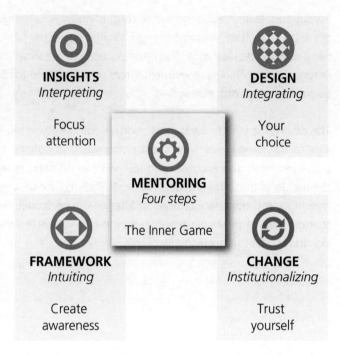

**INSIGHTS**
*Interpreting*

Focus
attention

**DESIGN**
*Integrating*

Your
choice

**MENTORING**
*Four steps*

The Inner Game

**FRAMEWORK**
*Intuiting*

Create
awareness

**CHANGE**
*Institutionalizing*

Trust
yourself

# Understand current state

For superior learning, it is more important to know how things are than how they should be. High awareness focuses our mind and initiates learning. This is the purpose of the INsights Diagnostic Tools™. The assessment forces participants to think about their own organization.

The diagnostic creates awareness, reduces complexity to relevant factors, and limits the influence of power and politics. It puts executives into an observing role with sense-making as the tool to understand and act (Weick, 1995:52f). The proven questions and the specific, unusual filter of the performance triangle model prevent responses being pre-formatted by dominant participants (Moldaschl, 2003).

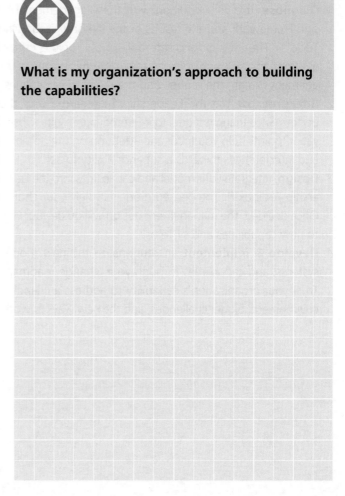

**What is my organization's approach to building the capabilities?**

# Step 1: Diagnosis

## The executive briefing

**INsights Diagnostic Tools™: offline and online**

**Offline**: First, answer the 30 question self-assessment from Insights for your own organization. Second, print the two assessment pages as a poster and perform the diagnostic with your team. Then use the Management Design workbook in line with The Performance Triangle (Michel, 2013a) to make sense of your responses.

**Online**: perform one of the six self-assessment options with your leadership team and selected executives. The diagnostic takes 10 - 30 minutes for every individual and taps into their intuition to enable them to answer an extended set of questions. Some organizations choose to include an additional question suite for their employees. After completion, a diagnostic mentor of your choice presents the results of the assessment to you for an initial interpretation of the data in the executive briefing.

**Result presentation**: Shortly after completion of the assessment, the Diagnostic Mentor shares the results and key findings to serve for an initial conversation on what the results mean and to initiate the next steps. A variety of reports present the results in line with the tools from Management Design.

**The executive briefing**: It is a brief meeting for a closed circle of executives that require first-hand information and control over the process, to filter the essence, in light of their specific context, and allow them to shape the direction of the project. Be aware that "to talk about interpretation without discussing a politics of interpretation is to ignore context."(Weick, 1995:53)

# Share and articulate the findings

The Team Workshop involves all members that have performed the diagnostic in a collaborative setting to understand and interpret the results. Its purpose is to use the collective knowledge, integrating the insights to generate a comprehensive 'laundry list' of issues that require executive attention. This integration is important as it shapes any group's sense for a shared action plan. Often, this is more than one workshop involving different groups of people.

The workshop establishes institutionalized rules through observation and conversation as an important part of dynamic capabilities (Schirmer and Ziesche, 2010). Context influences observation (Dutton et al, 1997). This is why the workshop design sets a context for all participants to share their observations and insights based on self-reflection, combination, and cooperation. Conversation styles enforce that statements can always be traced back to diagnostic data to ensure proper logic and resolve conflicts through appropriate rules (Weinreich, 2010).

For most participants, this is a 'first-time' conversation in a new field. Memory has the capacity to acquire fresh knowledge, to be recalled and applied. New knowledge is connected to existing structures. With more objects, patterns, and concepts anchored in our brains, it is easier to digest new information on an existing theme (Cohen and Levinthal 1990; Neisser 1967). Learning about new fields is more difficult than learning in a known setting. This is why the skills of a diagnostic mentor are required to facilitate learning in new fields.

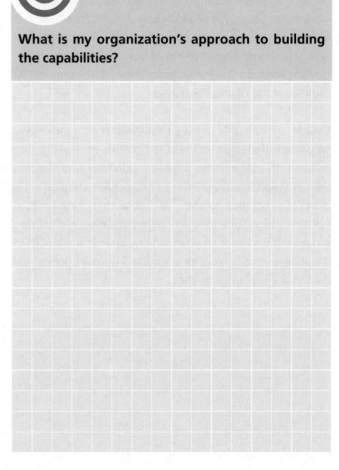

**What is my organization's approach to building the capabilities?**

# Step 2: Interpretation

## The Team Workshop

**The Team Workshop always follows the same agenda:**

| | | | |
|---|---|---|---|
| | | Pre workshop: perform the diagnostic | |
| 1 | 30' | **Introduction**: conversation on the context, nature of work, and challenges.<br>Purpose: intuition – gain insights by sharing experiences, images, metaphors. | Book: how do we deal with a dynamic environment in the knowledge economy? |
| 2 | 90' | **Results**: presentation and discussion on, ability to act, diagnostic, tools, and process.<br>Purpose: input, understand results, and expand options. | How do you enable an environment where people apply their full potential? |
| 3 | 30' | **Individual exercises**: interpretation of own results. Sharing with neighbour. Insights?<br>Purpose: apply own language, cognitive maps, conversation and dialogue style. | What is your organization's ability to act? |
| 4 | 60' | **Team exercises**: groups. Sharing of own story with the group and agreeing on five to seven shared themes. Ability to share and explain results.<br>Purpose: effective teamwork. | What does it take for organizations to reach a high ability to act? |
| 5 | 60' | **Organization exercise**: presentation of the team results. Discussion and summary.<br>Purpose: integration with insights –shape the thinking and acting of the group. | What so colleagues think of the solution? Things that one might add? |

# Perfection with the wrong design

**When staff departments have a life of their own**. The INsights Diagnostic Tools™ revealed two key issues that needed attention. First, people were unable to apply their creativity due to low trust , awareness 'on mute' and on-going distractions impeding focus. Second, when talking to the support staff about what they did, it became clear that all their efforts to introduce managerial support systems had one thing in common: the pursuit of perfection. For months, new managerial processes or tools were being developed in line with a text book model, then tested, revised, introduced to a pilot group, and modified to improve design, eventually being introduced to the overall organization, accompanied by global communications.

**Not following rules undermines reputation**. Staff were afraid to do something wrong and anecdotes showed their hesitation was justified. The consequences were huge: bureaucratic nightmares, demands to dilute the original design so that it catered to everyone, and slow reactions were common outcomes. Most of the managerial processes and tools were never developed with people ('clients') in mind. They had a life of their own and were even disliked by managers. As a result, managers circumvented formal procedures and distrusted all corporate things altogether.

**Learning rather perfection**. In complex systems, which large insurance firms certainly have, mutations, whether in-tended or not, are changes to the firm's 'Gestalt'. Eventually, it is the clients that determine whether systems 'errors' are a good thing or not. Hence, errors should be regarded as a means of learning rather than something that needs to be eliminated (Gell-Mann, 1994) The general management aim of this insurance firm was to be perfect and prevent errors at all cost. Errors and noise in complex systems irritate the system and force it out of a sub-optimal stage. A little randomness helps systems reconfigure at an optimal stage (Miller and Page, 2007; Lissack, 1999).

Through extensive **expert briefings**, diagnostic mentors worked with the staff from HR, organizational design, strategy, and control to revisit the design of every managerial tool in line with the principles of the 'inner game'. Within a few weeks, these refined approaches were introduced in line with the current management cycle in order to minimize the interferences in the organization.

**After-action review**. A second review with the INsights Diagnostic Tools™, after a full one-year cycle, clearly showed considerably higher scores on people and creativity. It improved overall performance as people felt responsible for what they did, rather than intimidated by the potential fall-out of making errors.

# Example: Insurance | Switzerland

## When staff departments take a life of their own.

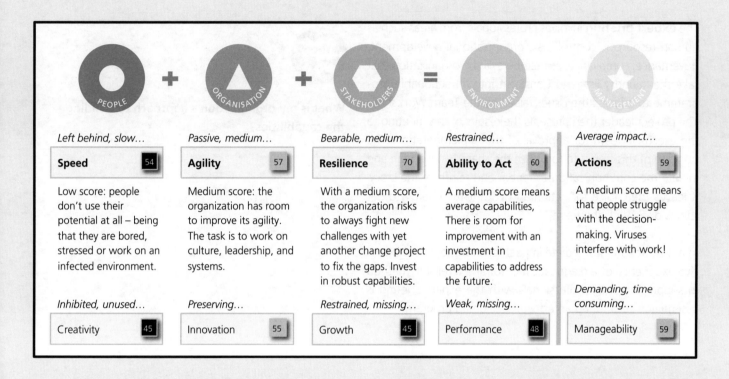

*Left behind, slow…*

**Speed**  54

Low score: people don't use their potential at all – being that they are bored, stressed or work on an infected environment.

*Inhibited, unused…*

Creativity  45

---

*Passive, medium…*

**Agility**  57

Medium score: the organization has room to improve its agility. The task is to work on culture, leadership, and systems.

*Preserving…*

Innovation  55

---

*Bearable, medium…*

**Resilience**  70

With a medium score, the organization risks to always fight new challenges with yet another change project to fix the gaps. Invest in robust capabilities.

*Restrained, missing…*

Growth  45

---

*Restrained…*

**Ability to Act**  60

A medium score means average capabilities, There is room for improvement with an investment in capabilities to address the future.

*Weak, missing…*

Performance  48

---

*Average impact…*

**Actions**  59

A medium score means that people struggle with the decision-making. Viruses interfere with work!

*Demanding, time consuming…*

Manageability  59

---

**H**  High scores: above average

**M**  Medium scores: average

**L**  Low scores: below average

# Develop the roadmap to build the competencies

The **expert briefing** involves professionals from areas such as human resources, control, risk, organizational development, governance, compliance, as members of the organization that take the 'laundry list' and transfer it into an actionable programme to address the issues raised by the Team Workshop. The project leader then presents the results of this meeting to the executive team for approval of the implementation. The purpose of this step is to formalize the shared action plan and initiate the communication to repeat and reinforce the story. It leaves the choice for action and with it the energy to get things done with the team.

In a 'fast action - immediate impact' environment, the extensive experience of a diagnostic mentor and a reliable method in supporting staff professionals with the expert briefing is essential in structuring an effective roadmap program.

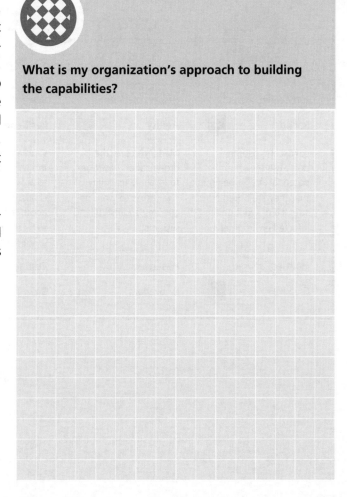

**What is my organization's approach to building the capabilities?**

# Step 3: Design

## The expert briefing

**DEVELOP & IMPLEMENT**

| Time |
| --- |
| Articulate the altered/new model |
| Redesign & implement the altered/new toolbox |
| Train leaders and employees in the new way of work |
| Review progress after one year |

# Make the changes – transform management

As the scope of the roadmap depends on the results of the previous steps, there is no standardized approach for this. Rather than another disruptive change programme, implementation follows within the normal conduct of business, using, and reinforcing, existing capabilities and intervention mechanisms.

The purpose of this step is to institutionalize a new way of working. The Diagnostic Mentoring approach is to trust the client to do this with their own resources. The mentoring task is to guide the development and support the implementation. Implementing the development roadmap means design work on an organization's management infrastructure and training managers in a new way of using the infrastructure. Such projects are specific to any organization and the issues at hand. Diagnostic Mentors have the experience and expertise to support executives in the design and management of such projects. The Development Lab is a workshop setting that expedites the development, and the leadership seminar is a ready-to-go programme that includes some diagnostic information for managers to help them understand why and what needs to change.

The Performance Triangle book (Michel, 2013a) serves as the source for the 'why of change' and provides tips and best practices for the 'what of change'. As these projects vary in scope and size with every client, the Diagnostic Mentor offers these services with a separate service agreement to the client. The Diagnostic Mentors facilitate the leadership seminar to complement the design work and train managers in their new approach to leading their organization and people.

**What is my organization's approach?**

# Step 4: Development and implementation

## Projects

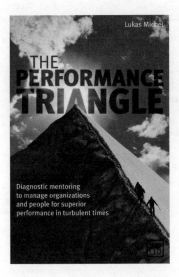

*The Performance Triangle* (Michel, 2013a) complements Management Design with a framework and guide to interpreting the results from the INsights Diagnostic Tools™ with the following:

A variety of tools: the performance triangle model, the Leadership Scorecard ™ and Toolbox
- 38 capabilities with questions for managers
- Nine examples that illustrate the mentoring
- 10 analogies with sports
- 63 insights from 10 years of research
- 138 worst-practices
- 164 best-practices
- 180 literature references on tools

Diagnostic Mentors use the book as a reference for all Management Design projects.

# Be aware of the paradox of the 'central tendency'!

*Management Design* may fundamentally change the way in which organizations operate. Diagnostic Mentoring guides the thinking about the 'espoused' theory through four steps. Economic theory is a positive theory. It explains the world as it functions. But this does not mean that every theory should be used as a blueprint for action. "All descriptive concepts, once they are used to organize reality and guide behavior become normative." (Agyris 1973) Such checklists or rules reinforce central tendencies with mediocrity as a result. Copying someone else is the attempt of becoming the same.

For example, economic theory states that (x% of) people reduce their effort in the absence of monitoring and sanctions. As Robert Simons (1995) reinforces: "We cannot ignore the 'central tendency'. In the absence of management action, self-interested behaviours at the expense of organizational goals are inevitable." But "effective managers do not work to achieve average outcomes." Why do we base a blueprint for action on mediocrity? We "need to reconcile self-interest with the desire to contribute." And Chris Agyris et al (1985) add: "many of the 'central tendencies' are caused by nonproductive forces."

Once per year, most management teams take time to rethink their design and alter the model, the capabilities, and systems as needed.

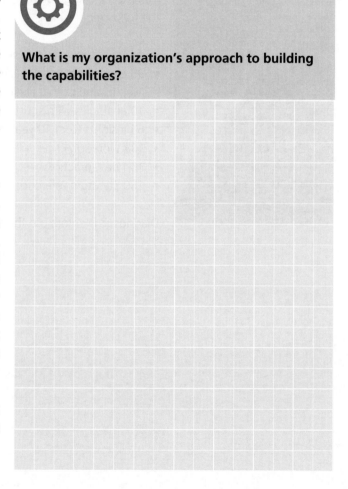

**What is my organization's approach to building the capabilities?**

# Diagnostic Mentors

## Entrepreneurs as trusted guides

Diagnostic Mentors act as impartial guides and facilitators without an agenda, using their skills, experience, and expertise as a reference point. They offer coaching or training in a specific capability, as appropriate, but may encourage leaders to seek help from other experts.

Diagnostic Mentors use the insights from their client's assessments to create awareness and to provide tools for reflection. They leave the choice to the leader but insist on translating insights into action. They:
1. Create observation points for insights
2. Help assess what is needed
3. Use experience and expertise for what works best
4. Know how to get around the hurdles to install new approaches

# Leadership think tank for 250 leaders worldwide

**Large-scale transformation**. A newly appointed CEO took charge of one of the worlds' largest mining firms with operations in most countries. One of the strategic decisions was to decentralize radically a traditionally-UK-focused approach to managing a diverse group of over 100 businesses worldwide.

**Corporate development**. The insights from various strategy sessions clearly indicated that the operating environment for the firm would change dramatically over the coming years, with increased volatility and uncertainty. In the past, the organization 'collected' local business across the globe without deliberate considerations on how to manage such a diverse group. Moreover, the ability to plan ahead and clarify strategy in longs cycles would become impossible in times of large mergers and a highly competitive environment.

**Executive education**. To follow on from a successful history, the CEO decided, among many other things, to hire an executive education firm to support the transformation effort. The task was to enable executive teams in more than 100 businesses worldwide to manage their operations strategically, rather than just the operations side – in the mining business, this seems like an impossible task

**Insights and foresight**. To facilitate the transformation, the INsights Diagnostic Tools supported the executive education firm with its three one-week education programme with 250 leaders worldwide. The management diagnostic exercise provided the necessary insights for every executive on the task at hand. These workshops turned into Diagnostic Mentoring sessions where every participant developed his own development path for the own organization.

**Changing mindsets**. It became clear that traditional rationalizing approaches to managing such diverse businesses did not work anymore. The CEO's foresight, with the insights from the diagnostic work, helped the organization change from analytical rigour as a dominant principle, to learning approach where best practices were shared and transferred from one successful business to other businesses.

Executive education served as a think tank for 250 leaders with Diagnostic Mentoring at its core: insights rather than recipes.

# Example: Mining I UK

## Large scale management transformation: from rationalizing to learning

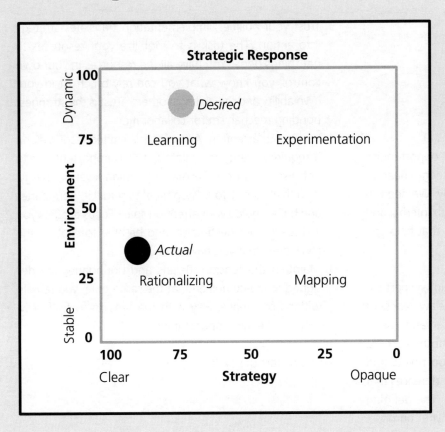

**Strategic Response**

- Dynamic — 100
- 75 — Learning | Experimentation
- Environment — 50
- *Actual*
- 25 — Rationalizing | Mapping
- Stable — 0

*Desired*

100 — Clear | 75 | 50 | **Strategy** | 25 | 0 — Opaque

# Translate the model and capability into a cycle

This is your self-mentoring cycle:
- How do I know with clarity?
- How do I move in one direction?
- How I mobilize my resources?
- How to I maintain my focus?
- How do I search for new opportunities?

The purpose of work is to capture relevant opportunities and add value. To perform at the peak, challenges need to match our ability to address them effectively. We need to be able to use our full potential and deal with internal and external interferences. Here are five phases that help you find your responses to these questions.

1. Create awareness: Feedback and information, in particular from critical performance variables, raise awareness of what is important. Non-judgemental observation helps you to translate data into meaningful information. Be relaxed. Simply focus on your observation points and learning takes place. This eliminates all interferences that keep you from using your full potential. The defining moment will let you know with clarity on your purpose.
2. It's your choice: Strategy clarifies the long-term goals and direction of the organization. As there are always alternative opportunities and temptations, it is important to be clear about your own contribution. Make a deliberate choice to move in your direction. But be aware that, as you always work with others, you need to share and agree on one direction to build reliable relationships.

3. Trust your abilities: Implementation translates strategy into action. The task is to mobilize your resources to get things done. You have all the resources in your own control; you know what you can rely on. Trust in your own ability and the ability of others. Trust is the strongest bonding mechanism for collaboration.
4. Focus your attention: Attention is a limited resource and it requires energy to maintain it. It is important not to get distracted from maintaining a high level of energy. Also think about your 'stop time' to refuel it. Boundaries and beliefs guide your attention span. Focus ensures you will reach your destination and be able to capture the challenges that you have set out.
5. Maintain the tension. Beliefs and boundaries are designed to create pull and, at the same time, you remain within your space. Play with the tension to find new, more challenging opportunities.

Simply restart the cycle.

# Leadership cycle

## From a static model to a dynamic cycle

It's the people who deliver performance. Awareness, choice, and trust enable people to focus on relevant things. To support this, leaders coach people to find purpose, to rely on relationships, and to collaborate across organizational boundaries. This leverages knowledge, focuses scarce attention, and drives performance. The leadership cycle supports the conversation on how to lead towards a superior ability to act.

How do we manage with the new model?

Checklist: have you…

☐ Clarified the new model?

☐ Outlined your approach to develop the capabilities?

☐ Clarified how to change from your current to the desired model and capability?

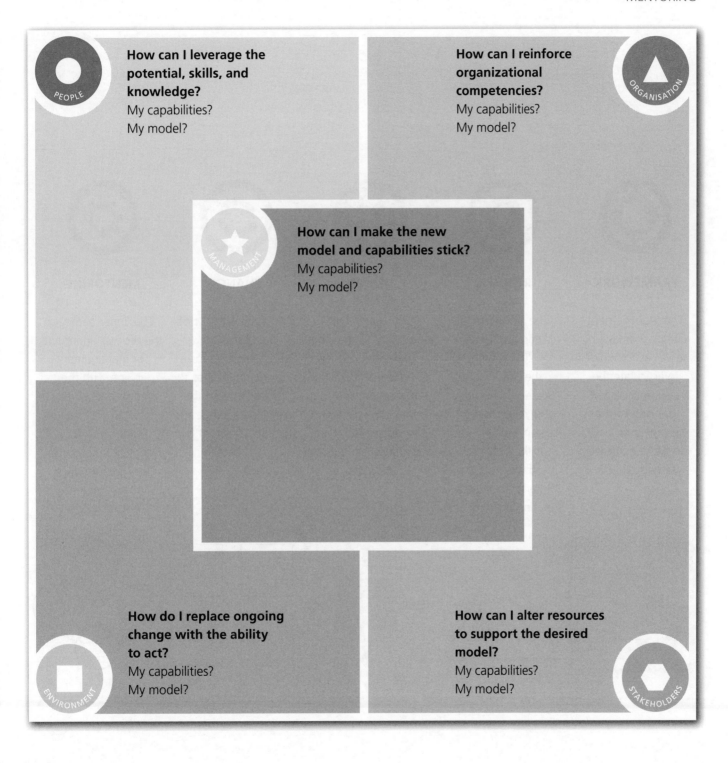

How can I leverage the potential, skills, and knowledge?
My capabilities?
My model?

How can I reinforce organizational competencies?
My capabilities?
My model?

How can I make the new model and capabilities stick?
My capabilities?
My model?

How do I replace ongoing change with the ability to act?
My capabilities?
My model?

How can I alter resources to support the desired model?
My capabilities?
My model?

PEOPLE
ORGANISATION
MANAGEMENT
ENVIRONMENT
STAKEHOLDERS

| **FRAMEWORK** | **INSIGHTS** | **DESIGN** | **CHANGE** | **MENTORING** |
|---|---|---|---|---|
| The Management Design Framework serves as the guide to articulate the assumptions and principles for a response to: how do we manage our organization? | The Performance Triangle (Michel, 2013a) with the Leadership Scorecard ™ guide the review of the current model: what is the potential and what are the interferences to a superior ability to act? | The Leadership Toolbox™ frames the capabilities needed to address a dynamic environment with an enabling mode or operations: what are the key issues to close the gaps? | Diagnostic Mentoring facilitates the transformation from current capabilities to managing with the new model: what are the initiatives that get us there? | The 'inner game, is the process and guide for management in line with the new capabilities: how do we enable higher creativity, innovation, growth, and performance in a turbulent environment? |

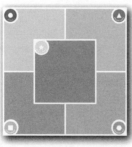  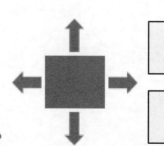 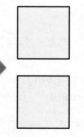 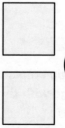 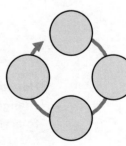

What is your talents' ability to apply its creativity?

How do we enable the inner game for superior speed?

What initiatives unlock the potential for more creativity?

How can we leverage the potential, skills, and knowledge?

What is your ability to innovate?

How do we establish a working environment for superior agility?

What initiatives remove the barriers to innovation?

How can we reinforce organizational competencies?

What is your ability to unlock the organization's potential?

How do we build the tools for superior decision-making?

What initiative support superior decision-making to capture higher challenges?

How can we make the new model and capabilities stick?

What is your ability to perform?

How do we develop the capabilities for a superior ability to act?

How do we replace ongoing change with the ability to act?

What initiatives expand the potential for higher performance?

What is your ability to grow?

How do we create the connectivity for superior resilience?

How can we alter resources to support the desired model?

What initiatives leverage resources for superior growth?

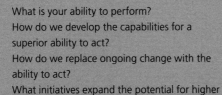

# Diagnostic Mentoring tools

Diagnostic Mentoring supports leadership teams on their way to design and implement their management model, capabilities, and systems for the specifics of their context.

**As a manager** use the tools to conduct the conversation with your team in line with the book.
- How do we manage our organization?
- What capabilities help us deal with a turbulent environment?
- What tools support our mode of operations?

**As an employee** use the Leadership Scorecard™ questions to make sense of the organization:
- How do I know with clarity?
- How do I move in one direction?
- How I mobilize my resources?
- How to I maintain my focus?
- How do I search for new opportunities?

**As a diagnostic mentor** use the tools to prepare and facilitate the team meeting, the expert briefing, and other workshops on the design of management.

# RESOURCES

 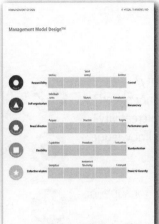  

### Context

The Management Design Frame captures insights, thoughts, choices, decisions, and development actions on one poster.

### Model

The Management Model Design poster facilitates the conversation on the desired management model.

### Capabilities

The Leadership Scorecard™ serves both, leaders on their way to work in the systems, e.g. the use of the organization's rules, routines, and practices in line with the design, and employees in their search for meaning and purpose.

The Leadership Scorecard ™ with the diagnostic results also serves as development for superior management practices.

### Systems

The Leadership Toolbox™ identifies the leverage points for superior leadership. It initiates work on the system with initiatives to adapt the toolbox to the needs of the environment and the chosen mode of operations.

# Management Design Framework: questions

- What is our talents' ability to apply its creativity?
- How do we enable the 'inner game' for superior speed?
- What initiatives unlock the potential for more creativity?
- How can we leverage the potential, skills, and knowledge?

- What is our ability to innovate?
- How do we establish a working environment for superior agility?
- What initiatives remove the barriers to innovation?
- How can we reinforce organizational competencies?

- What is our ability to grow?
- How do we create the connectivity for superior resilience?
- How can we alter resources to support the desired model?
- What initiatives leverage resources for superior growth?

- What is our ability to perform?
- How do we develop the capabilities for a superior ability to act?
- How do we replace ongoing change with the ability to act?
- What initiatives expand the potential for superior performance?

- What is our ability to unlock the organization's potential?
- How do we build the tools for superior decision-making?
- What initiative support superior decision-making to capture higher challenges?
- How can we make the new model and capabilities stick?

 Assumptions and principles?

 Potential and interferences?

 Gaps and key issues?

 Initiatives?

 Model, systems, and capabilities?

**Instruction**: print the Management Design Frame as a poster and use it as your mentoring guide to develop answers to the questions!

**Download** your copy from www.managementdesignbook.com

## Management Design Frame

# Management model

What are your choices on the management model?
- People: how do we engage people?
- Organization: how do we coordinate work?
- Stakeholders: how do we set goals?
- Environment: how do we manage change?
- Management: how do we make decisions?

**Instruction**: print Management Model Design™ as a poster and use it as your mentoring guide to develop answers to the questions!

**Download** your copy from www.managementdesignbook.com

# Management Model Design™

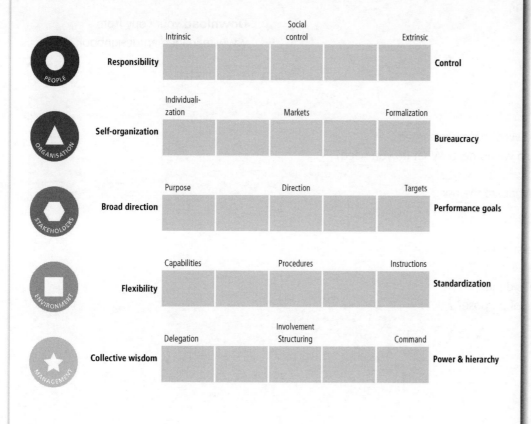

| | Intrinsic | | Social control | | Extrinsic | |
|---|---|---|---|---|---|---|
| **Responsibility** | | | | | | **Control** |

| | Individuali-zation | | Markets | | Formalization | |
|---|---|---|---|---|---|---|
| **Self-organization** | | | | | | **Bureaucracy** |

| | Purpose | | Direction | | Targets | |
|---|---|---|---|---|---|---|
| **Broad direction** | | | | | | **Performance goals** |

| | Capabilities | | Procedures | | Instructions | |
|---|---|---|---|---|---|---|
| **Flexibility** | | | | | | **Standardization** |

| | Delegation | | Involvement Structuring | | Command | |
|---|---|---|---|---|---|---|
| **Collective wisdom** | | | | | | **Power & hierarchy** |

PEOPLE

ORGANISATION

STAKEHOLDERS

ENVIRONMENT

MANAGEMENT

# Work in the System: capabilities

**What are your organization's managerial capabilities?**

**Systems**
- What is going on?
- What game are we playing?
- How do we succeed?
- What are our ambitions?
- Where are the limits?

**Leadership**
- What does that mean?
- Why are we going there? What have we learned?
- Are we on track? What do we do next? What do you need?
- How can we contribute?
- What can we tolerate? What are the risks?

**Culture**
- What is our shared understanding?
- What is our shared intent?
- Do we get the right things done?
- What is our shared sense of purpose?
- What gets you ahead?

**Instruction**: print the Leadership Scorecard™ as a poster and use it as your mentoring guide to develop answers to the questions!

**Download** your copy from www.managementdesignbook.com

# The Leadership Scorecard™

|  | The ability to understand? | The ability to think? | The ability to contribute? | The ability to engage? | The ability to adhere? | The ability to act? |
|---|---|---|---|---|---|---|
| The ability to diagnose? | Information + | Strategy + | Implementation + | Beliefs + | Boundaries = | Systems |
| The ability to interact? | Sense Making + | Strategy Conversation + | Performance Conversation + | Contribution Dialogue + | Risk Dialogue = | **Leadership** |
| The shared mind set? | Understanding + | Intent + | Agenda + | Aspirations + | Norms = | **Culture** |
| The shared goal? | **Responsiveness** + | **Alignment** + | **Capabilities** + | **Motivation** + | **Cleverness** = | **Success** |

# Work on the system: rules, routines, and tools

**What are your organization's managerial systems?**

**Rules** **How do we cope with higher ambiguity?**
- How do we tune our sensors?
- How do we think about the future?
- How do we model our business?
- How do we get the mileage?
- How do we set the rules?

**Routines** **How do we address complexity?**
- How do we make meaning?
- How do we create the future?
- How do we implement?
- How do we engage people to contribute?
- How do we safeguard our assets?

**Tools** **How do we deal with volatility?**
- What is our performance?
- What is our direction?
- What are our steps to get there?
- What are our expectations?
- What are our rules?

**Interactions** **How do we manage uncertainty?**
- How do we convey meaning?
- How do we learn?
- How do we talk about performance?
- How do we engage people?
- How de we guide risk-taking?

**Instruction**: print the Leadership Toolbox™ as a poster and use it as your mentoring guide to develop answers to the questions!

**Download** your copy from www.managementdesignbook.com

# The Leadership Toolbox™

| | The systems to understand? | The systems to think? | The systems to contribute? | The systems to engage? | The systems to adhere? | The systems to act? |
|---|---|---|---|---|---|---|
| The rules to provide choice? | | + | + | + | + = **Rules** |
| The routines to create awareness? | | + | + | + | + = **Routines** |
| The tools to focus attention? | | + | + | + | + = **Tools** |
| The interactions for trust? | | + | + | + | + = **Leadership** |

# AFTERWORD

Management Design has evolved over the past 12 years as a combination of diagnostic work with more than 100 clients all over the world, mentors that have contributed their insights on what works, and the research in preparation of The Performance Triangle (Michel, 2013a). Parallel to writing this book, the author has advanced the online INsights Diagnostic Tools™ with software and reports that match Management Design.

In combination, Management Design turns into a Diagnostic Mentoring workbook for leaders, advisors, and coaches in the fields of management, organization design, and culture. It complements The Performance Triangle which as a manual provides the logic and scientific foundation for The performance triangle model with definitions, illustrations, insights from research, and useful 300 practices. Both, Management Design and The Performance Triangle translate Diagnostic Mentoring in to a fresh, new, and transparent approach to helping leaders cope with the challenges of a dynamic business environment.

Management Design would not have been possible without the help from a global network of experienced Diagnostic Mentors and their interest in both, advancing the practice and science simultaneously. A special thank you goes to the colleagues that have been instrumental in the creation of Management Design.

To continue the note, it is needless to say, that creating a book with a 'big' title does not go without the support from many people ranging from sharing ideas, providing pilot sites, or promoting the idea through their network. In particular, my big thanks go to Dr. Richard Straub, the founder and president of the European Drucker Society and organizer of the Global Drucker Forum in Vienna, supporting me, The Performance Triangle, and Management Design in many ways.

Thomas Kupferschmied, the designer of this book, has committed to making this project happen with the challenges of an ongoing balance of time between working for client projects and devoting time to an exciting project. Thank you Thomas, your dedication to Management Design shines through!

Management Design is the beginning of a journey for many leaders that transform their management and organizations to cope better with the challenges of a turbulent environment. Let me know how it works in your organization. I believe we are the beginning of a new era with organizations that use the full potential of their people, in businesses that are fun places to work in and that are successful in what they do.

Lukas Michel
michel@AgilityINsights.com

Thomas Kupferschmied
thomas@kupferschmied.ch

# Bibliography

Ackoff, R. (1973). Science in the Systems Age: beyond IE, OR and MS. Operations Research. 21(3), p. 661–671.

Agyris, C. (1973). On Organizations of the Future. Beverly Hills, CA: Sage.

Agyris, C., Putnam, R., and Smith, D. (1985). Action Science: Concepts, Methods and Skills for Research and Intervention. San Francisco: Jossey-Bass.

Alpaslan, M., and Mitroff, I. (2004). Bounded Morality: the Relationship Between Ethical Orientation and Crisis Management, Before and After 9/11. In Rahim, M., Mackenzie, K., and Golembiewski, R. (eds.). Current Topics in Management. Stanford CT: JAI Press, 6:13-43.

Anderson, D. (2004). Agile Management for Software Engineering. Upper Saddle River, NJ: Prentice Hall Technical Reference.

Anzengruber, J. (2013). SKM, die Strategie des Erfolgs - das Kompetenzmanagement bei der Siemens AG. In Erpenbeck, J., von Rosenstiel, L., and Grote S. (eds.)Kompetenzmodelle von Unternehmen: Mit praktischen Hinweisen für ein erfolgreiches Management von Kompetenzen. Stuttgart: Schäffer-Poeschel,p. 315-327.

Arrow, H. (2000). Small Groups as Complex Systems. Thousand Oaks, CA: Sage.

Augier, M., and Teece, D. (2007). Dynamic Capabilities and Multinational enterprise. Pentrosean Insights and Omissions. Management Internal Review. 47 (2), p175-192.

Barney, J. (1991). Organizational Economics. San Francisco: Jossey-Bass.

Barreto, I. (2009). Dynamic Capabilities: a Review of Past Research and an Agenda for the Future. Journal of Management. 36 (1), p. 256-280.

Bassi, L., and McMurrer, D. (2007, March). Maximizing Your Return on People. Harvard Business Review. 85 (3), p. 115.

Beck, U. (2002). The Terrorist Threat: World Risk Society Revisited. Theory, Culture and Society. 19 (4), p.39-55.

Beer, M., & Nohira, N. (2000). Cracking the Code of Change. Harvard Business Review. 78 (3), p.133-143.

Beinhocker, E. (1999). Robust Adaptive Strategies. Sloan Management Review. 40 (3), p.95-106.

Bennet, A., and Bennet, D. (2004). Organizational Survival in the New World. Amsterdam: Elsevier.

Birkinshaw, J. (2010). Reinventing Management: Smarter Choices for Getting Work Done Chichester: Wiley.

Brown, S., and Eisenhardt, K. (1997). The Art of Continuous Change: Linking Complexity Theory and Time-paced Evolution in Relentlessly Shifting Organizations. Administrative Science Quarterly. 42, p.1-34.

Brown, S., and Eisenhardt, K. (1998). Competing on the Edge: Strategy as Structured Chaos. Boston, MA: Harvard Business School Press.

Camillius, J. (2008, May). Strategy as a Wicked Problem. Harvard Business Review. 86(5): p. 98.

Castrogiovanni, G. (2002). Organization Task Environments: Have They Changed Fundamentally Over Time? Journal of Management. 28 (2), p129-150.

Christensen, C., and Overdorf, M. (2000). Meeting the Challenge of Disruptive Change. Harvard Business Review. 78(2): 66-77.

Clegg S., Courpasson, D., and Phillips, N. (2006). Power and Organizations. London: Sage.

Cohen, W., and Levinthal, D. (1990). Absorptive Capacity: A New Perspective on Learning and Innovation. Administrative Science Quarterly. 35, p.128-153.

Conrad, P. (2004). Organizational Citizenship Behavior. In

Schreyögg, G., and Werder, A. (eds.). Handwörterbuch Unternehmensführung und Organisation. Stuttgart: Schäffer-Poeschel, p. 1101-1108.

Courtney, J. (2008). Decision Making and Knowledge Management in Inquiring Organizations. Decision Support Systems, p. 31, 17-38.

Coutu, D. (2002). How Resilience Works. Harvard Business Review. 80(2), p 46-55.

Covey, S. (1989). The Seven Habits of Highly Successful People. New York, NY: Simon & Schuster.

Crossan, M., Lane, H., and White, R. (1999). An Organizational Learning Framework: From Intuition to Institution. Academy of Management Review. 24 (3), p.522-537.

Crozier, M., and Friedberg, E. (1979). Macht und Organisation. Königstein: Athenäum-Verlag.

Csikszentmihalyi, M. (1990). The Psychology of the Optimal Experience. New York NY: Harper & Row.

D'Aveni, R. (1999). Strategic supremacy through disruption and dominance. Sloan Management Review. 40, p.127-135.

Davila, T. (2006). Making Innovation Work. Upper Saddle River, NJ: Wharton Business School Publishing.

Dawkins, R. (1989). The Selfish Gene. Oxford,: Oxford University Press.

Deloitte 22013; Deloitte study on Culture of Purpose: A Business Imperative http://www.deloitte.com/view/en_US/us/About/Leadership/3b7a33d2eacae310VgnVCM-1000003256f70aRCRD.htm

Deming, Edwards W. (1994). The New Economics for Industry, Government, Education. Ch. 2 -The Heavy Losses-, page 33

Deevy, D. (1995). Creating the Resilient Organization. Englewood Cliffs, NJ: Prentice Hall.

Doz, Y., and Baburoglu, O. (2000). From Competition to Collaboration: the Emergence and Evolution of R&D Cooperatives. In Faulkner, D., and de Rond, M. Cooperative Strategy: Economics, Business and Organisational Issues, New York, NY: Oxford University Press, p. 173-192.

Drucker, P. (1954). The Practice of Management. New York: Harper & Row.

Drucker, P. F. (1967). The Effective Executive: The Definitive Guide to Getting the Right Things Done. Harper Business Essentials.

Drucker, P. (1980). Managing in Turbulent Times. Harper Paperbacks, New York, NY.

Drucker, P. (1988, Jan/Feb). The coming of the new organization. Harvard business review, p. 45-53.

Drucker, P. (1996, April). Leaders Are Doers. Executive Excellence.

Drucker Forum blog: Article: People-centric Neural Networks: The Key to Managing Organizational Complexity http://www.druckerforum.org/blog/?p=612

Dutton, J., Ashford, S., O'Neill, R., Hayes, R., and Wierba, E. (1997). Reading the wind: how middle managers assess the context for selling issues to top management. Strategic Management Journal. 18, p.407-425.

Dyer, J., and Singh, H. (1998). The relational view: cooperative strategies and sources of interorganizational competitive advantage. Academy of Management Review. 23 (4), p.660-679 .

Eccles, R., and Nohira, N. (1992). Beyond the hype. Boston, MA: Harvard Business School Press.

Eisenhardt, K., and Martin, J. (2000). Dynamic Capabilities: Why Are They? Strategic Management Journal. 21, p.1105-1121.

Emery, F., and Trist, E. (1965). The casual texture of organizational environments. Human Relations. 18, p21,32.

Eoyang, G., and Conway, D. (1999). Conditions that suport self-organization in complex adaptive systems. Available from IFA: http://amauta-international.com/iaf99/Thread1/conway.html (Accessed: January 2014, 14-17)

Erpenbeck, J., and Rosenstil, I. (2007, 2nd ed.). Handbuch Kompetenzmessung: Erkennen, verstehen und bewerten von Kompetenzen in der betrieblichen, pädagogischen und psychologischen Praxis. Stuttgart: Schäffer-Poeschel

Foerster, H. (1984). Principles of Self-Organization in a Socio-Managerial Context. In Ulrich H., and Probst, G. (eds.). Self-organization and management of social systems .New York, NY. p. 2-25.

Forrester, J. (1996). Industrial Dynamics. Waltham, MA: Pegasus Communications.

Friedman, A. (1977). Industry and Labour. London: Macmillan.

Galbraith, J. (1995). Designing Organizations: An Executive Briefing on Strategy, Structure, and Process. San Francisco: Jossey-Bass.

Gallup. (2013). State of the Global Workplace: Employee Engagement Insights for Business Leaders Worldwide. Available from: http://www.gallup.com/strategicconsulting/164735/state-global-workplace.aspx (Accessed: 7th August 2014)

Gallwey, W. (2000). The Inner Game of Work. New York, NY: Random House.

Gell-Mann, M. (1994). The Quark and the Jaguar. Clearwater: Owl Books.

Ghoshal, S., and Gratton, L. (2002). Integrating the Enterprise. MIT Sloan Management Review. 44 (1), p.31-38.

Gilmore, T., Shea, G., and Useem, M. (1997). Side Effects of Corporate Culture Transformations. Journal of Applied Behavioral Science. 33 (2), p.174-189.

Gladwell, M. (2002). The Tipping Point. Boston, MA: Back Bay Books.

Habermas, J. (1981). Theorie kommunikativen Handelns. Frankfurt am Main: Suhrkamp.

Habermas, J. (1988). Moralbewusstsein und kommunikatives Handeln, 3. Aufl. Frankfurt am Main: Suhrkamp.

Haken, H. (1982). Synergetik. Berlin: Springer Verlag.

Hales, C. (2001). Does it matter what managers do? Business Strategy Review. 12 (2), p.50-58.

Hamel, G. (2007). The Future of Management. Boston, MA: Harvard Business School Press.

Hamel G (2011). First Let's Fire all the Managers. Harvard Business Review. http://hbr.org/2011/12/first-lets-fire-all-the-managers/ar/1

Hamel, G., and Valikangas, L. (2003). The Quest for Resilience. Harvard Business Review. 81(9).

Handy, C. (1989). The Age of Unreason. London: Hutchinson.

Handy, C. (2013). Speech at the Global Drucker Forum 2013 in Vienna. http://www.druckerforum.org/2013/the-event/video-library/

Haneberg, L. (2011). Training for Agility. T&D. 65 (9), p50-55.

Hax, A., and Wilde II, D. (2001). The Delta Model, Discovering New Sources of Profitability in a Networked Economy. New York, NY: Palgrave.

Hedlund, G. (1986). The Hypermodern MNC: a Heterarchy. Human Resource Management. 25, p.9-35.

Hedlund, G. (1993). Assumptions of Hierarchy and Hetrarchy, with Applications to the Management of the Multinational Corporation. In Ghoshal, S., and Westney D. (eds.). Organization Theory and the Multinational Corporation . London: St. Martin's Press, p. 211-236.

Hendry, C. (1992). Balancing corporate power. A federalist paper. Harvard Business Review. 11/12, p.59-72.

Highsmith, J. (2009, 2nd ed.). Agile Project Management. Boston, MA: Addison-Wesley.

Hill, A. (2013). The Management Revolution. Financial Times. [Online]. June. Available from: http://www.ft.com/cms/s/0/25def0a6-d352-11e2-b3ff-00144feab7de.html#axzz2olZrUIOx [Accessed: 7th August 2014]

Homkes, R. (2011). Enhancing Management Quality: the Potential for Productivity Growth after the Recession. Available from: CentrePiece Winter 2010/11: http://cep.lse.ac.uk/pubs/download/cp328.pdf [Accessed: 7th August 2014]

Hope, J., and Player, S. (2012). Beyond Performance Management: Why, When, and How to Use 40 Tools and Best Practices for Superior Business Performance. Boston, MA: HBS Publishing.

Huy, Q., and Mintzberg, H. (2003). The rhythm of Change. MIT Sloan Management Review. 44 (4), p.79-84.

Iansiti, M., and Levien, R. (2004). Strategy as Ecology. Harvard Business Review. 82, p.69-78.

Jackson, M., and Johansson, C. (2003). An Agility Analysis From a Production System Perspective. Integrated Manufacturing Systems. 14 (6): p.482-488.

Kanter, R. (1989, Nov/Dec). The New Managerial Work. Harvard Business Review. 11/12, p.85-92.

Kao, J. (2007). Innovation Nation. New York, NY: Free Press.

Kaplan, R., and Norton, D. (2006). Alignment; Using the Balanced Scorecard to Create Corporate Synergies. Boston, MA: Harvard Business School Press.

Kappelhoff, P. (2006). Kompetenzentwicklung in Netzwerken: Die Sicht der Komplexitäts und allgemeinen Evolutionstheorie. In Windeler A., and Sydow J. (eds.). Kompetenz. Wiesbaden: Gabler.

Katz, D., and Kahn, R. (1978, 2nd ed.). The Social Psychology of Organizations. New York, NY: Wiley.

Kay, J. (2010). Obliquity: Why Our Goals are Best Achieved Indirectly. London: Profile Books.

Kerber, K., and Buono, A. (2005). Rethinking Organizational Change: Reframing the Challenge of Change Management. Organizational Development Journal. 23(3), p.23-38.

Killmann, R., Saxton, M., Serpa, R., and Associates (Eds). (1985). Gaining Control of Corporate Culture. San Francisco: Jossey-Bass.

Kim , D. (1993, Fall). The Link Between Individual and Organizational Learning. Sloan Management Review, p.37-50.

Labovitz, G., and Rosansky, V. (1977). The Power Of Alignment: How Great Companies Stay Centered and Accomplish Extraordinary Things. New York, NY: Wiley.

Leavitt, H. (2005). Top Down. Boston, MA: Harvard Business School Press, p.49.

Lissack, M. (1999,). Complexity: the Science, its Vocabulary, and its Relation to Organizations. Emergence. 1 (1).

Luhmann, N. (2008). Social Systems. Palo Alto, CA: Stanford University.

Maitland, E., and Sammartino, A. (2012). Flexible Footprints: Reconfiguring MNCs for New Value Opportunities. California Management Review. 2,p.92-77.

Malik, F. (2008). Unternehmenspolitik und Corporate Governance: Wie sich Organisationen von selbst organisieren. Frankfurt; Campus Verlag.

March, J. (1991). Exporation and Exploitation in Organisational Learning. Organization Science. Special Issue, p.71-87.

Marion, R., and Uhl-Bien, M. (2007). Paradigmic Influence and Leadership: the Perspectives of Complexity Theory and Bureaucratic Theory. In Hazy, K. (ed). Complex Systems Leadership Theory. Goodyear: ISCE Pub.

Martin, R. (2005, August). Why Decisions Need Design, part 1. Business Week Online.

Martin, R. (2005, 30 August and 1 September). Why Decisions Need Design, part 2. Business Week Online.

McCann, J. (2004). Organizational Effectiveness: Changing Concepts for Changing Environments. Human Resource Planning Journal, p.42-50.

McCann, J., and Selsky, J. (1984). Hyperturbulence and the Emergence of Type S environments. Academy of Management Review. 9 (3), p.460-470.

McCann, J., and Selsky, J. (2003). Boundary Formation, Defense and Destruction: Strategically Managing Environmental Turbulence. Presented at Academy of Management national meetings, August.

McGregor, D. (1969). Human side of enterprise. New York, NY: McGraw-Hill.

McGregor, D., & Cutcher-Gershenfeld, J. (2006). The human side of enterprise. New York, NY: McGraw-Hill.

Meadows, D. (2009). Thinking in Systems - A Primer. London: Earthscan.

Michel, L. (2007). Understanding Decision Making in Organizations to Focus Its Practices Where it Matters. Measuring Business Excellence. 11 (1),p. 33-45.

Michel, L. (2008, January). Enable Tomorrow's Decisions. Perspectives on Performance. p.14-16.

Michel, L. (2013a). The Performance Triangle: Diagnostic Mentoring to Manage Organizations and People for Superior Performance in Turbulent Times. London: LID Publishing.

Michel, L. (2013b). The Performance Triangle: A Diagnostic Tool to Help Leaders Translate Knowledge into Action for Higher Agility. Organizational Cultures: An International Journal. 12 (2), p.13-28.

Michel, L., and Seemann, P. (2005, July/August). Organizing the CEO's Sphere of Power. Critical Eye.

Michel, L., and Nold, H. (2013). People-centric Neural Networks: The Key to Managing Organizational Complexity. Global Drucker Forum Blog: http://www.druckerforum.org/

blog/?p=612

Miller, J., and Page, S. (2007). Complex Adaptive Systems. Princeton, NJ: Princeton University Press.

Mintzberg, H. (1994). The Rise and Fall of Strategic Planning. New York, NY: Free Press.

Mintzberg, H. (1998). Covert Leadership: Notes on Managing Professionals. Harvard Business Review, p.140-147.

Mintzberg, H. (2009). Managing. Canada: McGill University.

Mitroff, I., and Alpaslan, M. (2003). Preparing for evil. Harvard Business Review. 81(4), p.109.

Mohrman, S., Cohen, S., and Mohrman, A. (1995). Designing Team Based Organisations. Jossey-Bass.

Moldaschl, M. (2003, 2nd ed.). Foucaults Brille. In Moldaschl M. (ed.). Subjektivierung von Arbeit . München: Hampp, p. 135-177.

Molinsky, A. (1999). Sanding down the edges: Paradoxical Impediments to Organizational Change. Journal of Applied Behavioral Science. 35(1), p.8-24.

Moorman, R. (1991). The Relationship Between Organizational Justice and Organizational Citizenship Behaviors: do Fairness Perceptions Influence Employees' Citizenship? Journal of Applied Psychology. 76, p.845-855.

Nadler, D., and Tushman, M. (1988). Strategic Organization Design. Glenview, IL: Scott, Foresman.

Nathan, Nathan, M., and Kovoor-Misra, S. (2002). No Pain, Yet Gain: Various Organization Learning From Crisis in an Interorganizational Field. Journal of Applied Behavioral Science. 38 (2), p.245-266.

Neisser, U. (1967). Cognitive Psychology. New York, NY: Appelton-Century-Crofts.

Nelson, R., and Winter, S. (1991). The Schumpetrian tradeoff revisited. The American Economic Review. 72 (1), 114-132.

Nold, H. (2011). Merging Knowledge Creation Theory with the Six-Sigma Model for Improving Organizations: The Continuous Loop Model. International Journal of Management. 28 (3), p.469-477.

Nold, H. (2012). Linking Knowledge Processes with Firm Performance: Organizational Culture. Journal of Intellectual Capital. 13(1), p.16-38.

Norman, R., and Ramirez, R. (1993). From Value Chain to Value Constellation: Designing Interactive Strategy. Harvard Business Review, p.65-77.

North, K., & Reinhard, K. (2005). Kompetenzmanagement in der Praxis. Mitarbeiterkompetenzen systematisch identifizieren, nutzen und entwickeln. Wiesbaden: Gabler.

Penrose, E. (1959; 2nd. Ed. 1980). The Theory of the Growth of a Firm. Oxford: Oxford University Press.

Penrose, E. (1969). The Growth of the Firm - a Case Study: the Hercules Powder Company. The Business History Review. 34 (1), p.1-23.

Peters, T. (1987). Driving on Chaos. New York, NY: Knopf.

Porter, M. (1980). Competitive Strategy: Techniques for Analyzing Industries and Competitors. Boston: Harvard Business School Press.

Porter, M. (1985). Competitive Advantage: Creating and Sustaining Superior Performance. New York, NY: Free Press.

Porter, M. (March/April 1997). How Competitive Forces Shape Strategy. Harvard Business Review, p.203-212.

Prahalad, C., and Hamel, G. (1990). The Core Competence of the Corporation. Harvard Business Review. 68 (3), p.79-91.

Rittel, H., and Webber, M. (1973). Dilemmas in a General Theory of Planning. Policy Sciences, p.155-169.

Rosenstiel, L., Pieler, D., and Glas, P. (2004). Kompetenzmanagement in der Praxis: Mitarbeiterkompetenzen systematisch identifizieren, nutzen und entwickeln. Wiesbaden: Gabler.

Schilling, D. (2013, April 19). Knowledge doubling every 12 month, soon to be every 12 hours. Retrieved from Industry TAP News: www.industrytap.com/knowledge-doubling-every-12-months-soon-to-be-every-12-hours/3950

Schirmer, F., and Ziesche, K. (2010). Dynamic Capabilities: Das Dilemma von Stabilität und Dynamik aus organisationspolitischer Perspektive. In Barthel, E., Hanft, A., and Hasebrook, J. (Eds.). Intergriertes Kompetenzmanagement im Spannungsfeld von Innovation und Routine. Münster: Waxman, p15-43.

Schreyögg, G., and Kliesch-Eberl, M. (2007). How Dynamic

Can Organizational Capabilities Be? Towards a Dual-Process Model of Capability Dynamization. Strategic Management Journal. 28, p.913-933.

Selsky, J., Goes, J., and Baburoglu, O. (2006). Contrasting Perspectives of Strategy Making: Applications in 'Hyper' Environments. Organizational Studies. 28(1): 71-94.

Senge, P. (1990). The Fifth Discipline: The Art and Practice of Learning Organizations. New York, NY: Doubleday.

Sharma. D., and Blomstermo, A. (2008). The internalization process of born globals; a network view. International Business Review, p. 139-158.

Simons, R. (1995). Levers of Control: How Managers Use Innovative Control Systems to Drive Strategic Renewal. Boston, MA: Harvard Business School Press.

Sprenger, R. (2007). Vertrauen führt. Worauf es in Unternehmen ankommt. Frankfurt am Main: Campus.

Sprenger, R. K. (2010). Mythos Motivation, Wege aus der Sackgasse, 19. Ed. Frankfurt am Main: Campus.

Stacey, R. (1999). Strategic Management and Organizational Dynamics: the challenge of complexity. New York, NY: Financial Times.

Stacey, R. (2000). Complexity in Management. New York, NY: Routledge.

Starck, R. (2012). Realising the Value of People Management: BCG Perspectives. Available from https://www.bcgperspectives.com/content/articles/people_management_human_resources_leadership_from_capability_to_profitability/ (Accessed: 7th August 2014)

Tapscott, D., and Williams, A. (2008). Wikinomics. City: Portfolio Hardcover.

Teece, D. (2007). Exlicating Dynamic Capabilities: the Nature of Microfoundations of (Sustainable) Enterprise Performance. Strategic Management Journal. 53 (4), p.287-294.

Teece, D., Pisano, G., and Shuen, A. (1997). Dynamic Capabilities and Strategic Management. Strategic Management Journal. 18 (7), p.509-533.

Tolmann, C. (1996). Problems of Theoretical Psychology. Canada: ISTP, Captus University Publications

Waldrop, M. (1992). Complexity. New York, NY: Simon & Schuster.

Watson, Thomas J Jr, A Business and its Beliefs (1963)

Towers Watson Global Workforce Study. Towers Watson. Available from: http://towerswatson.com/assets/pdf/2012-Towers-Watson-Global-Workforce-Study.pdf (Accessed: 7th August 2014)

Weber, M. (1947). The Theory of Social and Economic Organizations. Translated by A. M. Henderson and Talcott Parsons. Edited with an introduction by Talcott Parsons. New York, NY: Oxford University Press.

Weber, M. (1969). Gesammelte Aufsätze zur Wissenschaftslehre. Tübingen: J.C.B Mohr, p.427–452.

Weerawardena, J. et al (2007). Conceptualizing Accelerated Internalization on the Born Global Firm: a dynamic capabilities perspective. Journal of World Business. 42(3), p. 287-294.

Weick, K. (1995). Sensemaking in Organizations. Thousand Oaks, CA: Sage.

Weick, K., and Quinn, R. (1999). Organizational Change and Development. Annual Review of Psychology. 50, p.361-386.

Weinberg, G. (2001). An Introduction to General Systems Thinking: Silver Aniversary Edition. New York, NY: Dorset House.

Weinreich, H. (2010). Der Einsatz von Spielregeln als Autorisierende Interventionsplattform in Innovativen Arbeitsgruppen. In Lichtberg Immer eine Idee voraus: wie innovative Unternehmen Kreativität systematisch nutzen. Hartland Media, p. 249-258.

Wernerfelt, B. (1984). A resource-based view of the firm. Strategic Management Journal. 5, p.272-280.

Zahra, S., and George, G. (2002). Absorptive capacity: a review, reconceptualization, and extension. The Academy of Management Review. 27, p 185-203

Zollo, M., and Winter, S. (2002). Deliberate learning and the evolution of dynamic capabilities. Organization Science. 13 (3), p.339-351.

# Resources

Global Drucker Forum: http://www.druckeforum.org

Manz book shop, Drucker Forum 2013 book list: http://www.manz.at/service/kunden/praxisliteratur/drucker/d.html (Accessed: 7.8.2014), www.druckerforum.org

Towers Watson Global Workforce Study. Available from: http://towerswatson.com/assets/pdf/2012-Towers-Watson-Global-Workforce-Study.pdf (Accessed: 7.8.2014)